P
B

tial Ros

Firmly grounded in today's most recent incisive research from around
the world, this book is a timely review and analysis of student behaviour in
schools today. The authors of this comprehensive text discuss the possible
causes of disruptive behaviour, tackle assessment issues and outline effective intervention strategies that will be of practical use to teachers and
other educators. While theorising behaviour management from a range
of perspectives: psychodynamic, behavioural and socio-cultural, the authors
remain firmly focused on practical issues of policy-making, assessment and
intervention, and address a wide range of related issues, such as:

- policy in relation to behaviour in schools at local authority, national
  and international level;
- cultural concerns, particularly race, ethnicity, school discipline and
  exclusion;
- medical perspectives of topical interest such as AD/HD, autism and
  diet;
- assessment at district, community, classroom and individual level, and
  how these underpin theory.

This book will appeal to those for whom behaviour in schools is a key concern,
including student teachers, teacher educators, senior school managers and
practising teachers undertaking further study in the field.

Janice Wearmouth is a senior lecturer in the Faculty of Education and
Language Studies, at the Open University, UK.

Ted Glynn is Foundation Professor of Teacher Education at the University
of Waikato, New Zealand.

Mere Berryman is Manager of the Ministry of Education Poutama Pounamu
Education Research and Development Centre, New Zealand.

Perspectives on Student Behaviour in Schools

Exploring theory and developing practice

Janice Wearmouth, Ted Glynn
and Mere Berryman

Routledge
Taylor & Francis Group

LONDON AND NEW YORK

The Open
University

The
University
of Waikato
Te Whare Wānanga
o Waikato

First published 2005
by Routledge
2 Park Square, Milton Park, Abingdon, Oxon OX14 4RN

Simultaneously published in the USA and Canada
by Routledge
270 Madison Ave, New York, NY 10016

RoutledgeFalmer is an imprint of the Taylor & Francis Group

© 2005 The Open University and The University of Waikato

Typeset in Sabon
by Keystroke, Jacaranda Lodge, Wolverhampton
Printed and bound in Great Britain
by TJ International Ltd, Padstow, Cornwall

British Library Cataloguing in Publication Data
A catalogue record for this book is available from the British Library

Library of Congress Cataloging in Publication Data
A catalog record for this book has been requested

ISBN 0–415–35401–3 (hbk)
ISBN 0–415–35402–1 (pbk)

Contents

Preface

There are many ways of understanding how students behave in schools. We might look at student behaviour from any one of a number of positions: psychological, medical, biological, sociological, cultural, or, indeed, a combination of these. In recent years there has been a universal shift from locating the problem behaviour within the person ('It's his/her fault', or 'It's in the genes', for example) to locating that behaviour within the interaction that occurs between the person and the context (that is, everything and everyone within that context).

This book adopts a position that states:

- All students' behaviours are understandable on the same bases, that is that they result from interactions between people and their environments or social events.
- All students, including those with physical disabilities, challenging behaviours and difficulties in learning, have a fundamental need to be responded to positively and made to feel that they belong and are respected.
- Schools, school systems, classes and teachers at all levels in the system are capable of responding and adapting to meet the needs of an increasingly diverse student population by creating learning environments where all students are valued, respected and belong.
- With appropriate support, an increasingly diverse range of students can adapt and respond positively within learning environments where they are valued, respected and feel that they belong.

The book focuses on ways in which teachers, schools and communities have worked to establish responsive learning environments and pedagogies that value all students, respect all students and assist them to construct a positive view of themselves and their capacity to succeed in the classroom, school and in the community.

The book draws on international practice, with particular reference to the UK and New Zealand, in order to show how these countries are developing policy and practice that respond to the needs of students from diverse cultural backgrounds. Through international comparisons, readers will gain a deeper appreciation of how policy and practice are developed and advanced in the context of different societal norms.

Chapter 1

Understanding inclusion and behaviour management

Introduction

Education systems across the world are facing the common challenge of finding ways to provide for the diversity of their student populations. Over the years in many countries there has been a variety of provision for students who display 'difficult', 'disturbed' or 'disruptive' behaviour. Since the beginning of formal schooling, historically, the response to behaviour judged as challenging to the social order in schools has been to assume that the problem lies with the individual young person and to resort to medical and/or psychological approaches to assessment and 'treatment' outside the mainstream educational context.

As noted by Cole (2004), in the past, the experience of students identified as difficult to manage within the mainstream system has varied considerably depending on:

- the beliefs of particular professionals;
- the kind of provision that happens to be available;
- whether the behaviour itself is understood as a 'personality disturbance' that should be treated like a disease or as a rational reaction to environmental circumstances.

Interventions for these students might be punitive and harsh, rehabilitative or therapeutic. Some of the tensions between notions of good practice stem from differences in theoretical orientation. For example, there are applied behavioural practices associated with understanding of behaviour as being controlled by external events. There are also educational or therapeutic practices related to holistic or humanistic approaches associated with understandings of students as having agency or exercising control over their own behaviour.

In the latter part of the twentieth century, however, understandings of difficulties in learning and behaviour began to veer towards a view that the source of students' difficulties in behaviour and learning is not always intrinsic to the learner. Hargreaves (1975), exploring the relationship between the student and the learning environment, noted that any disruption or disturbance is representative of a discordance within the system to which the student belongs. This discordance is indicated by the lack of correspondence between the student and the system where the student–system interaction causes disruption (Bronfenbrenner, 1979). If a student belongs to a specific social system, both the responses of that student to the surroundings and the responses of significant adults and peers to that student have to be taken into account when assessing the significance of individual acts. Fulcher (1989), for example, has noted that disaffection in the form of disruptive behaviour can be provoked by the demand for compliance from unwilling students by those in authority seeking to establish control in the classroom:

> Classroom order requires docile bodies . . . Herein lies some of the resistance to integrating those with less docile bodies: . . . larking about . . . absence, verbal abuse, etc., all instance the failure to subordinate bodies to the requirements of classroom docility. The control responses to these forms of disruption include . . . suspension and other sanctioning practices . . . It may therefore be argued that it is the educational apparatus's failure to provide an inclusive curriculum . . . rather than the problems specific disabilities pose, which constructs the 'problems' and politics of integration.
>
> (1989, pp. 53–4)

In the latter half of the twentieth century also, there was a growing international concern for equality of opportunity in the education system and social cohesion in society at large. The practice in recent years of requiring mainstream schools to accept and respond to a wider range of educational needs (particularly from a human rights perspective) and the needs of society, required those schools to become more 'inclusive'. This requirement is not straightforward, however. Inclusion is a problematic term about which there is a considerable amount of confusing, and confused, rhetoric. The term has lacked clear definition or consensus about what the concept entails. In addition, it is easy to assume that policy-making related to inclusion is a 'top-down' process, for example, in the case of education policy, that a national government decides the strategy or plan of action and tells the local education authorities and schools to put it into operation. The practice, however, may have only a tenuous link with what was originally proposed.

In this chapter we look first of all at the notion of inclusion and discuss this concept as it relates to the education system as well as to society generally. We interpret 'inclusion' in the field of education as needing to take account of the processes of engaging with learning and the social representation of individuals and groups in society as well as issues of human rights. We go on to discuss the national policy context, issues related to policy-making in the area of problematic behaviour in schools and the tensions and contradictions in policy implementation.

Inclusion

'Inclusion' is a term which lacks adequate theorising or consensus about what it means in practice. Commonly it is described as a process, a set of practices or an issue of human rights. One factor that is often missing from much of the debate on inclusion is the situated nature of difficulties in learning and behaviour in schools. Curricular experiences offer students ways of knowing the world. Within an institution, educators and students are defined by that institution's social practices. The understanding of the individual whose behaviour is seen as challenging is part of that social practice.

Current definitions

Booth *et al.* (2000, p. 12) describe 'inclusion' as a process, one that involves 'increasing the participation of students' in local schools. The Centre for Studies on Inclusive Education (CSIE) also adopts a position on inclusion from its implications in practice:

Inclusion in education involves:

- Valuing all students and staff equally.
- Increasing the participation of students in, and reducing their exclusion from, the cultures, curricula and communities of local schools.
- Restructuring the cultures, policies and practices in schools so that they respond to the diversity of students in the locality.
- Reducing barriers to learning and participation for all students, not only those with impairments or those who are categorised as 'having special educational needs'.
- Learning from attempts to overcome barriers to the access and participation of particular students to make changes for the benefit of students more widely.
- Viewing the difference between students as resources to support learning, rather than as problems to be overcome.
- Acknowledging the right of students to an education in their locality.
- Improving schools for staff as well as for students.
- Emphasising the role of schools in building community and developing values, as well as in increasing achievement.
- Fostering mutually [respectful and] sustaining relationships between schools and communities.
- Recognising that inclusion in education is one aspect of inclusion in society.

(http://inclusion.uwe.ac.uk/csie/csiefaqs.htm#
RighttoBelong)

Many teachers might well feel that a number of these points are rarely seen in operation in schools (Open University, 2004). Although there has been a clear move towards mainstreaming generally across the world, there has been an uneven degree of integration of students perceived as experiencing difficulties of different kinds. Education in mainstream schools is still generally organised on the basis of group instruction and not on the basis of meeting the diversity of students' learning needs. The accommodation of individual differences within mainstream schools challenges the very basis of both the social and political purposes of mainstream public schooling and hence the implied notion of social justice. The notion of average, normal or typical ability and hence learning potential or capacity determines the traditional system, organisation and resourcing of mainstream public schools.

CSIE goes on to justify inclusion on three grounds: human rights, good education and social sense.

Regarding human rights, CSIE claims that:

1   All children have the right to learn together.
2   Children should not be devalued or discriminated against by being excluded or sent away because of their disability or learning difficulty.
3   Disabled adults, describing themselves as special school survivors, are demanding an end to segregation.
4   There are no legitimate reasons to separate children for their education. Children belong together – with advantages and benefits for everyone. They do not need to be protected from each other.

Regarding good education, CSIE claims that:

5   Research shows children do better, academically and socially, in integrated settings.
6   There is no teaching or care in a segregated school which cannot take place in an ordinary school.
7   Given commitment and support, inclusive education is a more efficient use of educational resources.

Regarding social sense, CSIE also claims that:

8   Segregation teaches children to be fearful, ignorant and breeds prejudice.
9   All children need an education that will help them develop relationships and prepare them for life in the mainstream.
10 Only inclusion has the potential to reduce fear and to build friendship, respect and understanding.

(http://inclusion.uwe.ac.uk/csie/10rsns.htm)

Mittler (2000, p. 10) also assumes a human rights view in describing 'inclusion' as 'based on a value system that welcomes and celebrates diversity arising from gender, nationality, race, language of origin, social background, level of achievement or disability'. We discuss the issue of human rights further below.

Critical views

In England, as in many other countries, education for all in mainstream schools is the government's stated intention, and moves in this direction have existed for some 30 years. Not all researchers are totally supportive of this policy, however. Inherent in the argument for inclusion is a social, ecological or environmental model for understanding and responding to behavioural difficulties which emphasises the factors in the environment, for example, the home, the school and the community, including other people's stereotypes and preconceptions; that is, factors outside the student.

Lindsay (2004) claims that the increasing influence of the social model has been a welcome development from a previously predominant emphasis on a 'medical' or functional deficit model in which 'within child factors', learners' individual and unique capacities, interests and learning needs were over-emphasised. Lindsay argues that the 'social model' of learning difficulties has been increasingly influential in the past 30 years but may now have diverted too much attention away from 'within child' factors and in particular the interaction between 'within child' factors and environmental factors which themselves can change over time. He further argues that the learning needs of children and their educational progress, once placed in mainstream settings, tend to be overlooked by researchers because inclusion itself has become a matter of rights and not evidence.

However, Lindsay recognises that inclusion is the current policy framework (Lloyd, 2000) in which responses to learning needs have to be made. Hence his distinction between rights and efficacy: producing the desired effects. In his view, prevailing notions of inclusion and associated research do not take sufficient account of the interpretation and implementation of inclusion in practice. Research should take account of the strengths of effects and their relevant impact on different children within inclusive settings:

> it is simply not good enough to ignore the question of within-child factors or the research evidence pertaining to all aspects of inclusion, including classroom practice, school organisation, LEA systems and government policies.
>
> (Lindsay, 2004, p. 278)

Lloyd (2000) argues that inclusion has been seen as the means to equality of educational opportunity:

> Since the Warnock report (DES 1978), education policy in the UK for children identified as having special educational needs (SEN) has been

> based on the assumption that the means to ensuring equality of educational opportunity is the mainstream school.
>
> (Lloyd, 2000, p. 133)

Inclusion, *per se*, tends to be perceived as increasing educational opportunity and removing barriers to progress. However, inclusion of itself does not ensure equity. Social and economic disadvantage, cultural diversity, and so on are factors known to be associated with access, or lack of access, to educational entitlement. Similarly, Lindsay, while recognising that inclusion is the policy context, claims that the human rights argument for inclusion ignores concern for the quality of the education provided for individual needs and the progress learners make in 'inclusive' settings.

In the context of the education system in the United States, Gerber (2004) notes an early period in American public education when compulsory schooling for all children was perceived as educational opportunity. Failure for individual students was seen as their unwillingness to make the most of that opportunity. Early reform, recognising individual differences, encouraged schools to accept responsibility for the success or otherwise of students' learning but threatened existing school systems, organisation and distribution of resources based on the notion of the average student. Gerber argues that substantive 'educational opportunity' is not guaranteed for children with disabilities either by access to similar educational resources or by participation in a common and universal curriculum, the very conditions which created special education. Educational equity requires an educational strategy which responds to individual differences to promote at least satisfactory levels of development and achievement.

Gerber claims that special education has always been concerned with individual differences and with changing institutions to accommodate these differences. Hence special education always imposes a demand for additional resources and institutional change from educational administration and school management. For administrators and for the institutions, the concern is how these differences might be accommodated without substantial cost and structural change. At one time, Gerber argues, segregated special classes met these requirements.

Schools attempting to accommodate to a vague inclusion policy find themselves recreating the pressures from which they are always trying to escape: redistribution of resources and the increased demands on teachers of included students. Gerber's claim is for a different curriculum, responsive to individual differences and needs, with different intentions or outcomes. Differential deployment of resources including training and support for teachers is inevitable. Equity that accepts the need for differential resources to reach similar outcomes for students requires the acceptance of differential resources for different but equally valid outcomes.

Gerber points out that the challenge by special education to mainstream schools to respond to real individual differences, threatens existing measures of school effectiveness which are based on average attainment and take no account of the fact that schools produce a range of individual students. Instead, these measures encourage schools to treat diverse students as alike in learning characteristics and alike in response to given curriculum or teaching strategy. He claims that if schools changed to respond to individual differences, then they would be effective when their poorest performing students demonstrate significant achievement gains.

Conceptualisation of learning and behaviour

Current moves towards inclusive approaches for all students of statutory school age require a re-conceptualisation of both learning and behaviour as situated, dynamic and interactive between students and the learning environment. If this is to occur, teachers need to be able to reflect critically on notions of 'behaviour difficulties', inclusion and the values associated with them. Consequently, emphasis in teacher education and professional development should be given to reflective practice (Schön, 1983, 1987) no less than to training in competencies and the 'tools' of the trade. As we discuss later in Chapter 6, learning occurs through engagement in society. Pedagogy therefore needs to be interactive and 'intersubjective' to take account of individual meaning-making. Schools play a critical part in shaping students' beliefs in their sense of self-efficacy that is their ability, responsibility and skill in initiating and completing actions and tasks. The way schools mediate success and failure is crucial to the development of a sense of personal agency (Bruner, 1996). Teachers should therefore reflect continuously on the impact of school processes and practices on young people's sense of agency and ability. Student learning in schools takes place within an educational community. The sense of belonging to, or marginalisation from, that community affects every aspect of participation and, therefore, learning within it, and necessarily affects a student's behaviour and self-perception. 'Inclusion', therefore, can be interpreted as the extent to which students are able to participate in the school community. Failing to support the development of students' understanding and ability to act in a social context risks marginalising and alienating young people and limiting their autonomy. It is not an easy task to engage with students whose behaviour in schools is experienced as challenging or otherwise worrying. Nevertheless these students have the same basic needs as any other students.

The current national policy context

In many countries, current government policies in relation to young people whose behaviour is seen as challenging in schools, need to take into account that:

- research that continues to demonstrate the relationship between exclusion or non-attendance at school and diminished future life chances, including later imprisonment;
- pressure at government level towards inclusion in mainstream schools as a matter of 'human rights';
- a sense that the behaviour of the young is deteriorating, as exemplified by a number of stories occurring in the media.

Research evidence

Research from a number of countries has repeatedly shown the detrimental effects of school exclusion to the welfare and future life chances of young people. In the 1990s exclusions from mainstream schools in the UK were showing an upward trend. The Welsh document on Student Support and Social Inclusion (NAW, 2001) directly links low attendance with under-performance against SATS and GCSE exams:

> In schools with 0.5% or fewer sessions missed, some 54% of students achieved five or more GCSEs at grades A* to C in 1997–8. For schools in the highest band of absence (over 3% of sessions missed) the proportion of students achieving these grades fell to%.
>
> (National Assembly for Wales Education Department, 2001)

In New Zealand, school exclusions have also been showing an upward trend especially for Māori and Pacific Island students. Despite making up approximately 20 per cent of the student population, the rate of suspension from school for Māori is three times higher. Some 38 per cent of Māori leave school with fewer formal qualifications as opposed to 19 per cent non-Māori (Ministry of Education, 2001a).

In Scotland, Munn *et al.* (2004) feel that the consequences of school exclusion lie in the curtailment of opportunities for educational achievement and qualification and, thus, entry into further education and/or employment. These further adversely affect a sense of belongingness and socialisation into socially acceptable forms of behaviour. Research in the Republic of Ireland has also established a close connection between early school-leaving, school absenteeism and academic failure (Rudd, 1972; Swan, 1978) and such social problems as delinquency (Fahy Bates, 1996), long-term unemployment (Breen, 1991) and adult illiteracy (Morgan, 2000), as well as indications of the alienation of some pupils within post-primary schools (McDonnell, 1995).

Research such as this has highlighted the need to address the issue of school attendance, student disaffection and overall levels of school achievement at national policy level. Besides being mutually reinforcing, these issues, together with the general problem of educational disadvantage require programmes of intervention if they are to be dealt with preventatively and effectively.

Human rights

Human rights, as we have implied above, are associated with social justice, removing barriers to learning, access, fairness and choice. Visser and Stokes point out that:

> Human rights, sometimes called natural rights, are rights agreed inter-nationally, usually in Treaties or Conventions, which lay down a code by which all humans should be treated, such as the right not to be tortured. Human rights are not usually directly enforceable in national courts. Yet, human, civil and legal rights often coincide, in these circumstances human rights are enforceable by the courts. For example, the United Nations Declaration of Human Rights gives a child a human right to education, in the UK this right is a civil right under The Human Rights Act 1998, and the legal right to education for all children was established in the Education Act 1972.
>
> There is no automatic guarantee of any right, be it legal, civil or human, being successfully enforceable in every situation. A major problem with any rights argument is that individual rights conflict.
>
> (2003, p. 67)

Interest in the human rights of children within education policy was supported by the Salamanca Statement (UNESCO, 1994). In June 1994, representatives of 92 governments and 25 international organisations formed the World Conference on Special Needs Education, held in Salamanca, Spain. They agreed a statement (UNESCO, 1994) on the education of all disabled children and adopted a new Framework for Action, the guiding principle of which is that ordinary schools should accommodate all children, regardless of their physical, intellectual, social, emotional, linguistic or other conditions:

> The guiding principle that informs this Framework is that schools should accommodate all children regardless of their physical, intellectual, social, emotional, linguistic or other conditions. . . . Many children experience learning difficulties and thus have special educational needs at some time during their schooling. Schools have to find ways of successfully educating all children, including those who have serious disadvantages and disabilities. There is an emerging consensus that children and youth

with special educational needs should be included in the educational arrangements made for the majority of children. This has led to the concept of the inclusive school.

(UNESCO, 1994, p. 6)

This framework outlines a number of principles for action:

- Every child has a fundamental right to education, and must be given the opportunity to achieve and maintain an acceptable level of learning.
- Those with special educational needs must have access to regular schools which should accommodate them within a child-centred pedagogy capable of meeting these needs.
- Regular schools with this inclusive orientation are the most effective measures of combating discriminatory attitudes, creating welcoming communities, building an inclusive society and achieving education for all.

(ibid., p. viii)

Often the rights for children are given to parents, as in the European Convention on Human Rights. Under this convention, there is a qualified right, a right which can be adapted by a legal process, to education.

No person shall be denied the right to education. In the exercise of any functions which it assumes in relation to education and to teaching, the State shall respect the right of parents to ensure such education and teaching in conformity with their own religions and philosophical convictions.

(Council of Europe, 1996, Protocol 1, Article 2, p. 16)

Under Article 6 (Convention, p. 4) 'everyone is entitled to a fair and public hearing . . . by an independent and impartial tribunal', but the 'everyone' is the parents. Under Article 5 (p. 4), 'everyone has the right to liberty and security of person' except in a number of defined circumstances which may include disciplinary exclusion from school. This issue of disciplinary exclusion raises an important issue of whose rights should be paramount: the individual's right to education or a student community's right to schooling without disruption by individuals.

Individual versus school community rights

There are occasions in schools where the rights of individual students may conflict with the rights and entitlements of the majority. This issue may be particularly serious where individual behaviour is seen to be having an adverse effect on the learning of the peer group. Where students' behaviour is perceived to have a seriously detrimental effect on their peers, in many countries the law may support the removal of those students from the mainstream. Students whose behaviour is seen as impinging adversely on the education of their peers may still, by law, be denied access to mainstream education in the UK in consideration of what is in the best interests of the majority, despite developments towards inclusion generally.

In England and Wales, for example, the 1996 Education Act places a duty on governors of schools to ensure that a student with special educational needs joins in the activities of the school together with students who do not have special needs, so far as this is compatible with the student receiving the necessary special education provision, the efficient education of other children in the school and the efficient use of resources (Education Act 1996, section 317(1)–317(5)). The emphasis is therefore on the rights to their education of all the other children who attend the school.

The Special Educational Needs and Disability Act 2001 amended this section of the Education Act 1996 (and the Disability Rights Act 1995) for children with Statements of Special Educational Needs to remove 'the efficient use of resources' as grounds for excluding a child. Two grounds for exclusion remain. The act requires such children to be educated in a mainstream school unless this would be incompatible with the wishes of the parent or the provision of efficient education of the other children. Any course of action must be judged to be 'reasonable'. The Special Educational Needs and Disability Act 2001 through the associated Code of Practice (DfES, 2001a) also requires that all students have the same right of access to participate in the social and extra-curricular activities as well as the educational opportunities in the school.

In England, guidance from the DfES (DfES, 2001b), while advising that all reasonable steps be taken to enable the inclusion of students with statements for emotional and behavioural difficulties in mainstream schools without compromising the rights of other children in the school to an efficient education, provides instances when it is inappropriate to include specific children: 'pupils whose behaviour systematically, persistently and significantly threatens the safety of and impedes the learning of others' (ibid., p. 13). However, the guidance goes on to warn that the 'efficient education' caveat must not be abused and that:

> It is also unacceptable for a school to refuse to admit a child thought to be potentially disruptive or to exhibit challenging behaviour, on the grounds that the child ought first to be assessed for special educational needs.
>
> (ibid., p. 20)

However, for schools, students whose behaviour is viewed as very threatening or disruptive can present problems to which exclusion seems the only recourse. DfES guidance suggests that students can be excluded:

(a) in response to serious breaches of the school's behaviour policy; and
(b) if allowing the student to remain in school would seriously harm the education or welfare of the pupil and others in the school.

(DfES, 2003, p. 3)

It suggests that permanent exclusion is appropriate for:

(a) serious actual or threatened violence against another pupil or a member of staff;
(b) sexual abuse or assault;
(c) supplying an illegal drug;
(d) carrying an offensive weapon.

(ibid., p. 3)

or for:

(e) persistent and defiant misbehaviour including bullying (which would include racist or homophobic bullying) or repeated possession and/or use of an illegal drug on school premises, the Secretary of State would not normally expect the governor's Discipline Committee (see DfEE, 1999b) or an Independent Appeal Panel (see DfEE, 1999b) to reinstate the pupil.

(ibid., p. 4)

As Parsons (1999) notes, the law in England and Wales is not representative of that in all countries, however. Unlike England and Wales, in Northern Ireland, Scotland and in many other countries in Western Europe, the child's right to continue full-time education is enshrined in law. Schools that want to move students must find another school and do this with the consent of the parents. In Scotland the local education authority (LEA) decides on exclusions. In Northern Ireland exclusion figures are one-tenth of those in England and Wales.

In England the Social Exclusion Unit has taken a first step in reducing exclusions in its report (SEU, 1998a), in that 'there is a recognition of the longer term damage to social cohesion where exclusion and truancy occur and that criminality too often follows on from students' non-inclusion in schooling' (Parsons, 1999, p. 180).

Further positive developments by the government in England (ibid.) are:

• emphasis on early intervention and prevention through multi-agency working partnership with parents;
• a range of suggestions to respond to a child's educational needs;
• requirements on schools, through the Pastoral Support Plans to liaise widely, planning over an extended period and monitoring carefully before resorting to exclusion;
• the involvement of LEAs.

However, as Parsons comments, there remain substantial weaknesses:

- the role of parents is not exploited to the full when working through the family can be effective;
- the role of LEAs is weak in that they have lost the power to direct children back to school;
- the promotion of learning support units, on-site special classes, for specific groups of children, which have a history and can be seen, although not always, as stigmatising and punitive.

Anti-social behaviour

In many countries, current government policy in relation to children and young people with emotional and behavioural difficulties is to be understood against the background at the turn of the twenty-first century of a number of stories occurring in the media which tended to imply the 'deteriorating behaviour of the young'. In the UK, for example, incidents which involved a tiny minority of children and young people preying on other children were given major prominence in the media because of the grave consequences of their behaviour.

The following headline story comes from the *Guardian* newspaper of 29 November 2000:

> On Monday, 10-year-old Damilola Taylor was stabbed to death in Peckham, south London. His death is just the latest tragedy for a community blighted by teenage gangs and violence, says Sarah Helm.

Stories also occurred in the media relating to individual young children perceived to be out of control and creating mayhem in the communities where they live. The English HMI report *Exclusions from Secondary Schools* (1996) noted that the way that specific cases are sensationalised in the media gives rise to a mistaken belief that, in English schools, there has been a rapid deterioration in the standard of students' behaviour.

At the same time there were claims that significant numbers of children and young people were truanting from school, sometimes with their parents' or carers' complicity, often hanging about in shopping centres during school hours, harassing shoppers and sometimes stealing from shops. One of the features common to these stories was the claimed complicity of parents and carers or the alleged inability of parents to control or manage their children's behaviour.

The New Labour government from 1997 onwards in the UK, aware of the political effect on the electorate of stories of extremely challenging behaviour, responded with punitive, exclusionary measures: so-called child curfews, parenting orders and anti-social behaviour contracts (ABCs), an informal procedure and anti-social behaviour orders (ASBOs), a statutory procedure, (Crime and Disorder Act 1998 and the Police Reform Act 2002). ABCs are voluntary agreements between people involved in anti-social behaviour and the local police, the Housing Department, the registered social landlord or the perpetrator's school. ASBOs can be placed on children as young as 10 years. The 1998 Crime and Disorder Act also allows courts to impose detention and training orders on 10- and 11-year-olds.

This report from *The Daily Telegraph* of 17 April 2002 illustrates government reaction to the pressure of public opinion in its decision to encourage the reporting of children who receive anti-social behaviour orders:

Child criminals are targeted

By Philip Johnston, Home Affairs Editor

DAVID BLUNKETT called yesterday for tougher measures to deal with child criminals as young as 10 even though he has yet to implement powers he already has.

The Home Secretary said he wanted to strengthen the law to tackle 'persistent offenders' aged 10 and 11 who were increasingly involved in criminal activity.

He cited recent cases involving a girl of 11 photographed smashing a shop window in Bristol and a boy of the same age who was charged with 70 offences in Cardiff before being bailed to roam the streets.

'I am now looking seriously at how we can strengthen the law in respect of those 10- and 11-year-olds who commit persistent but low level crime and who, due to their young age, fall outside the range of powers available to magistrates and judges.'

He added: 'One of the biggest challenges we face is how to deal with young offenders who believe that their age makes them untouchable, who flout the law, laugh at the police and leave court on bail free to offend again.'

One reason they are 'untouchable' is that the Government has not yet triggered a clause in its own 1998 Crime and Disorder Act allowing courts to impose detention and training orders on youngsters of 10 and 11 for persistent offending.

Mr Blunkett, addressing a youth crime conference in London, said he wanted to expand care orders and to consider 'protective custody' where the family had broken down and misbehaviour had continued unchecked.

He announced that he had decided to implement powers contained in last year's Criminal Justice and Police Act whereby 'medium level' persistent offenders aged 12–16 could be detained on remand while awaiting trial. As a result, magistrates in 10 high crime areas will have stronger powers to remand this age group into secure accommodation.

(© *The Daily Telegraph*)

LEAs in England and Wales have Truancy Watch schemes removing truants found in public areas to school or other settings.

'Social inclusion'

Exclusion from school can deny students the right of access to a suitable education, although Wright *et al.* (2000) note that the government's Social Exclusion Unit (SEU) in the UK has increasingly recognised the effects of exclusion on children and the rights of all children to an adequate education (SEU, 1998a). It has also acknowledged that denying an equal right to education can result in young people no longer having the ability to participate fully in social life. It is in this way that school exclusion is a contributory factor in social exclusion.

There is an association between juvenile crime and being out of school. The Audit Commission (1996) found that 42 per cent of young offenders had been excluded from school and a further 23 per cent were regular truants. Almost half of most offences of theft and handling committed by juveniles in the Metropolitan Police force area are committed during school hours.

The governments of some countries have been proactive in policy-making to ensure that, as far as possible, all school students, including those whose behaviour is seen as challenging, threatening or otherwise worrying to teachers, have access to the mainstream curriculum. At national level, in the UK, the advent of a New Labour government in 1997 brought with it an agenda of 'social inclusion' intended to enhance the life chances of groups previously marginalised in society. Included in these groups were students with limited, or no, access to educational provision, for example, individuals not attending school as a result of behavioural issues.

In England, the 'Programme for Action' (DfEE, 1998c) gives a sense of the direction of government policies at the start of the twenty-first century in relation to children and young people 'with emotional and behavioural difficulties'. In it, specific initiatives were proposed in the area of student behaviour in schools: local education authority (LEA) behaviour support plans which detail advice and local resources available to schools, primary stage nurture groups, government-sponsored research into effective mainstream schools for meeting behavioural needs and mentoring projects for older students. Changes to the National Curriculum requirements for 14- to 16-year-olds apply to all students but might have particular relevance to a more flexible response to the needs of young people with emotional and behavioural difficulties. Other initiatives included guidance on exclusion from school, provision otherwise than at school, and funding sources for student inclusion.

In England, the 'social inclusion' strategy has developed a number of measures and schemes to promote effective schools for youngsters with behaviour difficulties particularly for schools serving disadvantaged populations. The emphasis has moved from the individual student and their behaviour to the role of the school in preventing exclusions. The Excellence in Cities initiative, which grew out of a subsequent report *Bringing Britain Together: A National Strategy for Urban Renewal* (SEU, 1998b), recognised that some schools serving similar disadvantaged communities are more successful than others in reducing exclusions and improving attendance and the attitudes and behaviour of students. An Office for Standards in Education (OFSTED) (2000) report as a response to the Social Exclusion agenda on improving city schools had among its aims to evaluate how effective schools serving disadvantaged urban areas engage potentially disaffected students and found the key features to be:

- attention to improving behaviour is aligned with efforts to improve commitment to learning;
- a definite policy on behaviour, embodying clear expectations, is understood and supported by all, implemented consistently and supported by good systems and training;
- a short list of rules is backed up by forthright procedures for dealing with poor behaviour, especially bullying and harassment;
- deliberate steps are taken to develop pupils' belief in themselves, their respect for others, their sense of responsibility and their stake in the school;
- teachers actively support non-teaching staff, especially breaktime supervisors;
- clear lines of communication link teachers with education welfare officers, community workers and parents in efforts to improve attendance and attitudes.

(OFSTED, 2000, p. 23)

In some respects the general trends in addressing issues related to behavioural concerns in schools in Scotland have reflected those elsewhere in the UK, although there are differences in the details. Since the inception of the UK Labour government in 1997 there has been 'a huge expansion in the whole social inclusion agenda' (McLean, 2004) in Scotland as well as in other areas of the UK. In 1999, for example, the Scottish Executive of the new Scottish Parliament introduced its own social strategy in the document *A Scotland Where Everyone Matters* (Scottish Executive, 1999). In 2000, the Standards in Schools (Scotland) Act had a 'key presumption that the education of all pupils will normally be provided in a mainstream school unless exceptional circumstances apply' (McLean, 2004) and its main focus was on all children having a right to an education that aimed at developing their personality, talents, mental and physical abilities to their fullest potential. A range of strategies have been conceptualised to achieve this aim. McLean comments that, prior to the 1980s, there was a 'very punitive culture where discipline dominated the landscape'. Following this trend towards punishment as the primary, reactive response to students' behaviour came 'a more reward culture'. Many current developments in Scotland continue to reflect this interpretation. However, in McLean's view, the current situation is in a state of transition, 'moving towards the third and hopefully final phase, which is self-regulation, self-discipline and so on'. This change is,

> epitomised by one of the national priorities articulating self-discipline and pupils as a key national priority and underpinned by 'the main government document 'Better Behaviour – Better Learning' (Scottish Executive, 2001) which looks at effective teaching and learning as a context in which to develop self disciplined children.
>
> (McLean, 2004, audio interview, track 4)

Policy conflict

The reality of how a policy translates into practice can have tenuous links to the original intentions of those who created the policy (Wedell, 2000). There are bound to be implementation problems arising when one policy initiative impacts on the implementation of another, as is clear from an examination of tensions within the national policy context.

In order to achieve coherent practice in the area of behaviour management in schools, policy frameworks need to stem from a shared set of beliefs and values (Palmer et al., 1994). This is the case at national as well as local and school levels. In New Zealand, while the Ministry of Education (MoE) has taken a leadership role in policy development generally, with the disestablishment of the Specialist Education Services in 2001, it has recently had more direct input into special education policy that will ensure closer links between policy and its implementation. The MoE, Group Special Education (GSE) now takes responsibility for the following:

- strengthening linkages across education in areas of suspension, truancy, literacy, teaching practices and early intervention;
- developing different and more effective ways of working with educators, providers and family that build capability, enhance service delivery and take better advantage of existing policies.

(Ministry of Education, 2003a, p. 23)

However, sometimes government policies in the area of education conflict with each other in ways that militate against the inclusion of particular student groups in mainstream schools. For example, in the UK, 'social inclusion' has been closely linked to the school improvement movement in the government's rhetoric. However, sometimes ways in which school improvement can be interpreted in practice militate against the inclusion in mainstream schools of particular student groups. Further, market orientation is increasingly common in education policy-making in some countries. Additionally, the continued existence of two paradigms, the functional deficit (within-person) model of behaviour difficulties and the ecological/contextual model evident in many places, reduces the pressure for the change and development that is needed in the mainstream in the direction of greater inclusivity. At the level of society, government reaction to newspaper stories in the UK reporting gross acts of anti-social behaviour has been punitive and exclusionary rather than rehabilitative, despite the rhetoric of social inclusion.

School improvement

In varying degrees across the UK, targets have been central to government school improvement strategies since 1998 when all schools were required to set targets for student performance with timescales using the results from national testing. The emphasis is on testing, target setting and performance (DfEE, 1998d). Assessment for school improvement purposes is normative in that one school is compared with another. In England, a rise in exclusions in the 1990s has been associated with the advent of the National Curriculum and national testing. Parsons (1999) argues that the acceptance and involvement of all children within school conflicts with school improvement as measured by National Curriculum tests and GCSE results. Rouse and Florian point out that:

> Many of the market oriented education policies since 1988 implemented by national government in recent years for example the publication of 'league tables' of examination results, have resulted in schools being less willing to accept some students. Those who might lower the mean examination or standard assessment task (SAT) scores through their own low attainment or through their effects on others and those who are perceived as difficult to manage may be particularly unpopular.
>
> (1997, pp. 323–6)

The effect of all this is, according to Parsons, likely to increase the pressure on schools with an associated rise in exclusions.

> With open enrolment, money following pupil numbers and parents supposedly informed by league tables, schools are encouraged to 'sell'

themselves and are tempted to remove anything which might diminish their reputation – such as problem children.

(1999, p. 183)

Although compulsory tests for 7-year-olds in Wales have been abandoned, education culture and government policy in England and Wales continue to emphasise raising achievement as measured by external examination results and national testing at the end of the year in which children are 7, 11 and 14 years of age. Schools are required to demonstrate performance against normative criteria. The Office for Standards in Education (OFSTED) is required to judge the effectiveness of a school using 'the educational attainment of students in relation to some clear (national) benchmark' (OFSTED, 1999c, p. 23). The comparative attainment of students in a particular school in the subjects of the National Curriculum, particularly in the core subjects of English, mathematics and science, against national averages is the bench-mark.

The effect of market-orientation

Creating an inclusive environment is not compatible with the competitive climate currently encouraged by central governments intent on target setting and narrowly conceived achievement:

> In my view, it seems clear that creating competitive markets in education based on parental 'choice' of schools and fuelled by league tables and competition for resources, is totally incompatible with developing an inclusive education system. In England there is now a divided and divisive school system, with middle-class and aspirant parents avoiding schools catering for children with special educational needs, and some schools finding ways of rejecting socially and educationally vulnerable children.
>
> (Tomlinson, 2001, p. 192)

The rise in permanent exclusions from 3,000 in 1990 to over 12,000 in 1997–8 (DfES, 2002a) coincided with the implementation of the National Curriculum, the publication of league tables of school examination and test results and the local management of schools in which individual school budgets were largely determined by the number of children on the roll.

Parsons notes that, in England, policy is directed at enabling opportunities for participation in schools through providing additional resources for access while in some countries the concern is with equality of outcome. The experience that some groups are clearly unsuccessful at taking advantage of opportunities suggests that policies based on equality of opportunity are unlikely to result in equality of outcome:

In Esping-Anderson's (1990) analysis, England is distinctly in the 'liberal' camp with regard to social welfare, which means that individuals must bear responsibility and the motivation for state support is limited (lest it encourage others to be feckless). The social democratic approach to welfare, at the other end of the spectrum, is where a society takes upon itself the responsibility to make sure that individual citizens' suffering is limited. . . . [in some countries] intervention is about enabling citizens to function in specific ways, to participate in different levels and institutions of society, and to experience belonging rather than alienation – economic, social, political or criminal.

(1999, p. 182)

Where education policies implemented by national governments have become increasingly market-oriented, for example, in England since the 1988 Education Act and the publication of 'league tables' of examination results, the result has been that, despite the rhetoric of inclusion' some schools are less willing to accept some students. In England, those who might lower mean exam or standard assessment task (SAT) scores through their effects on others (Rouse and Florian, 1997) and those who are perceived as 'difficult to manage' may be particularly unpopular. The significant increase in exclusions in England during the 1990s (see OFSTED, 1996) testifies to this.

The effect of two conflicting paradigms

In the education system operating in England, Wales and Northern Ireland, all students of school age have a legal entitlement to access to the National Curriculum. There is a duty for local education authorities to make special provision at the level of the school for those students identified as needing it because students have the statutory right to have their 'special educational needs' assessed and met. Identification labels the student as different with the possibility that s/he may feel stigmatised. Lack of identification, however, means that s/he may be denied access to additional support. A similar dilemma accompanies the choice of appropriate curricula. Young people sharing identical learning aims may be deprived of the opportunity to develop competencies appropriate to their needs, yet may be made to feel inferior if their curriculum is different.

The law in many countries supports a deficit notion of students with behavioural problems. Young people 'with special educational needs' that result from difficult behaviour are entitled, in law, to have those needs identified, assessed and then met with appropriate provision guaranteed by their LEA.

Those thought to have 'emotional and behavioural difficulties', a term first introduced by Warnock (DES, 1978) to apply to students whose behaviour is seen as difficult to manage, have been identified as one group whose problems prevent them from learning in the same way as other students, and who therefore might need special provision. There is considerable confusion surrounding this term which Garner and Gains feel is hardly surprising:

> given that the terms 'emotion' and behaviour' are amongst the most difficult concepts in the educational lexicon. Moreover, further difficulties arise because definitions of what comprise EBD are closely bound up with the personality and professional experiences of the person who is assessing the student.
>
> (1996, p. 141)

The notion of 'emotional and behavioural difficulties' employed by the 1993, now the 1996, Education Act clearly adopts a within-person, deficit model. Circular 9/94, *The Education of Children with Emotional and Behavioural Difficulties*, which is associated with the 1996 Education Act, asserts that:

> Prevalence [of EBD] varies according to:
> - sex – boys rather than girls;
> - age – adolescents, rather than younger children;
> - health and learning difficulties – rates are higher among children with other difficulties;
> - background – rates are higher in inner city areas and socially deprived families.
>
> (DfE, 1994b, Para 5)

Circular 8/94 continues with the theme of the deficit model of difficulty, implying that 'having EBD' is a fixed state, that the causes may be family background or sensory impairments and that schools may alleviate or worsen the student's 'condition' by their mode of operation and organisation and by individual teachers' behaviour.

Causes:

There may be one or many causes:

- Associated factors may be family environments or sensory impairments.
- EBD children always have special educational needs because they are facing barriers which cause them to have significantly greater difficulty in learning than most of their peers.
- EBD is often worsened by the environment, including schools'/ teachers' responses.
- Schools vary widely in the extent to which they help children overcome their difficulties.

> (ibid., Paras 1–9)

The current approach therefore continues to predispose to a reification of the concept 'special educational needs' and, therefore, to a reification of categories of need on which funding ultimately depends. Without an objectified category of need, quantifying how a student is special enough to warrant additional or alternative provision is highly problematic.

The Special Education 2000 (SE2000) policy in New Zealand contains similar internal contradictions. It introduced professional development for around 800 Resource Teachers of Learning and Behaviour (RTLB), who were to work within an inclusive paradigm, supporting classroom teachers whose classrooms included students with behaviour and learning difficulties. The RTLB works with teachers within an ecological paradigm to support students with learning and behavioural needs. The role and status of RTLB developed from the Mangere Guidance and Learning Unit positions of 1975 (Thomas and Glynn, 1976). Later Guidance and Learning Units in New Zealand began to provide learning and behavioural support for students using an in-class ecological model of assessment and intervention, and teacher support rather than a separate student withdrawal model. This ecological model focused on assessment within the students' educational setting that included assessment of teacher and peer behaviour as well as the students' current performance in the context of the academic programme that was being provided.

Trained teachers, supported by educational psychologists and management committees of professionals from contributing schools, were the pioneers of this approach that led to a more inclusive ecological model. This ecological model draws on the theory of applied behaviour analysis that locates the behaviours within the environment in which they are occurring and understands behaviour as being shaped and maintained by antecedents and consequences within that environment.

One of the core roles of the RTLB is the provision of professional development in the use of effective inclusive teaching strategies. However, under an earlier policy that promoted autonomous (self-managing) schools (Lange, 1988) some principals required the RTLB to work in a 'hands-on' fashion with a small class of students in a withdrawal context. This individualised view of the location of behavioural problems is in opposition to an inclusive approach which shifts the focus onto the school rather than the student. With the focus of the ecological model on the school, it follows that mainstream class teachers should see themselves not only as part of the problem but also as part of the solution.

The notion of inclusion therefore appears to be concerned, above all, with human rights issues. Inclusion is a question of rights and concerns a philosophy of acceptance and requires a framework within which both schools and their students are able to adapt and change so that individuals can be valued, respected and enabled to learn. This position is also consonant with inclusivity in society as a whole (Centre for the Studies of Inclusive Education, 2004).

Conclusion

In countries which have adopted a principle of universal education for all their young people, the national policy context has to reconcile principles of individuality, distinctiveness and diversity with inclusion and equal opportunities, and is therefore bound to be characterised by tensions and contradictions (Norwich, 1996). Ultimately, the dilemmas created in schools by what often appear to be somewhat fragmented and contradictory government policies may be insoluble without a reconceptualisation of current policies at national level. Creating an inclusive environment is not compatible with maintaining the competitive climate currently encouraged by governments intent on target setting and narrowly conceived achievement. This conflict has been made sharper in the UK since the advent of the Labour Government in 1997 and official recognition of the need to take seriously the issue of social inclusion of those groups seen to be marginalised in society. Between 1990/1 and 1997/8 the number of pupils recorded as 'permanently excluded' from schools rose from 2,900 in 1990/1 to 12,298 in 1997/8 (Harris, Eden with Blair, 2000). This high number of exclusions under a Labour government committed to inclusion was seen by some, for example, Parsons, (1999), as a consequence of the continued operation of elements of the neo-liberal market in education established under the previous administration (Booth *et al.*, 1998).

In England and Wales, the government's 'social inclusion' agenda has led to the issuing of further guidance to schools about ways to reduce student disaffection and, consequently, challenging behaviour, in order to keep students in school and in touch with mainstream education. The real dilemma for schools is how to *act* in a situation which is beset by often irreconcilable tensions. School improvement, for example, is a problematic term. It is difficult to identify on whose and on what terms a school is said to be improving, that is, whose interests the basis of the improvement serves. Margerison and Rayner (1999, p. 87) refer to the 'new performance teaching culture' and point to the potential for conflict between the needs of students with behavioural difficulties and school needs. Nevertheless, as they go on to argue, assessing students with behavioural difficulties can contribute to school improvement if they relate to meeting the special educational needs of individual students and if students' existing knowledge, understanding and skills are the basis for successful future teaching and learning.

What is required is a view of learning and behaviour, both of students and those who teach them, as situated, dynamic and interactive between learner and context and, therefore, a view of difficulties in learning and behaviour also as situated, dynamic and interactive. From this point of view, conceptualisation of an inclusive environment in schools is often complex and challenging. However, a dynamic interactive view of behaviour difficulties together with a view of teachers as needing to be reflective practitioners is crucial for the successful development of policy and practice in the area of inclusion of students whose behaviour is seen as problematic in schools.

Within such a situative perspective, issues of ownership and belonging are highly significant in contributing to a positive orientation towards activities of learning and construction of knowledge (Belencky *et al.*, 1997). In pluralist societies policy-making at national level is complex and has to take account of a whole range of different, often conflicting, viewpoints and interests. Often the law is enabling rather than prescriptive in that it does not always impose legal duties. A particular course of action or practice may be based on agreed or individual personal motives, the result of a belief or set of beliefs about how things should be. Often a course of action is advantageous, prudent or expedient for someone or some group. As the policy is being created, some of those involved have more power than others. This power may be professional, relate to higher status, greater political influence, control over resources, and so on. Those most affected by the policy, for example, children, parents, young people and minority community groups, are rarely consulted (Gersch, 2001). Even if they are, they are likely to have very limited power relative to politicians, civil servants, education professionals and others (Gewirtz *et al.*, 1995). However, cooperating and working with a group of people with similar interests or concerns, for example, a voluntary society, can make parents and those likely to be affected by a policy more powerful (Simmons, 1996). On the other hand, a poorly thought out or incomplete policy can lead to polarisation of parents, communities and schools.

Teachers need to be able to reflect critically on their understandings of students' 'behaviour difficulties' and on their understandings of what might need to change if these students are to be 'included' rather than excluded. In any event, the notions of 'behaviour difficulties' and 'inclusion' need to be understood as social constructs. As Eraut comments:

> New knowledge is created . . . in each professional community . . . The particularistic nature of knowledge gained by practising professionals presents yet another barrier to knowledge creation: both its exchange with other professionals and its incorporation into theory are limited by its specificity, and often by its implicitness.
>
> (1994, pp. 20–1)

Chapter 2

Everyday explanations
Student or environment?

Introduction

Conceptualising approaches to ensure that all students are included in schools depends on ways of understanding human behaviour and learning, particularly of those children experiencing emotional and/or behavioural difficulties. In schools teachers are surrounded by different kinds of explanations for student behaviour (Watkins and Wagner, 2000). It is important to consider this carefully because some ways of explaining behaviour are much more productive than others in designing effective ways to address issues of behaviour and to raise overall levels of achievement in a school.

In this book we repeatedly distinguish between behaviour seen as the attribute of individuals and behaviour seen as influenced by the context and by the group norms in which it occurs. We make this distinction because we believe that the perspective taken on the root causes of problem behaviour strongly influences how that behaviour is addressed. There is considerable research evidence to suggest that how teachers conceptualise the causes of behaviour they see as worrying or disturbing, bears a strong relation to their own emotional and cognitive responses. These, in turn, relate to their 'intentional behaviour' and their 'actual behaviour' (Poulou and Norwich, 2002, p. 111). Poulou and Norwich comment that the 'link between teachers' thoughts and actions' cannot be viewed as neutral and 'devoid of emotions and feelings' (ibid., pp. 111–12). They also note that teachers' feelings can be difficult to hide and students can be 'very sensitive receivers of teachers' messages . . . and send their own personal messages back to them. Thus teaching becomes a circular and continuously interactive process, with complex causal relationships among the events taking place within it.'

In this chapter we first outline a number of everyday explanations for problematic student behaviour and consider how useful these are for adopting a positive approach to including students in mainstream schools. We go on to examine different ways in which bullying as an example of problematic behaviour, can be interpreted and understood and their implications for practice.

Everyday explanations of behaviour

Watkins and Wagner note a number of common explanations that many will have encountered in schools:

- 'They're that sort of person.'
- 'They're not very bright.'
- 'It's just a tiny minority.'
- 'It's their age.'
- 'This is a difficult neighbourhood.'

(2000, p. 3)

Attributing particular behaviour to 'that sort of person' is invoking a classic deficit model of the person. The problem is seen to be within that individual. However, as Watkins and Wagner (ibid., p. 4) comment, the use of 'prevalent stereotypes' is inadequate to explain the behaviour of the individual student. In addition, stereotypes can be used to justify the school abnegating its responsibility for the welfare and progress of the individual student and referring him or her to an external agency trained to deal with 'that sort of person'.

The explanation 'they're not very bright' implies an innate lack of ability by certain students and therefore may operate as justification for a school's reluctance to modify its curriculum tasks and its teaching in ways that will engage all students in learning.

Where the cause of difficult behaviour is located in 'a tiny minority', the implication is that 'they' are very different from 'we' (that is, the majority) and therefore are difficult to understand. There is little incentive to examine the classroom or school context as a possible source of provocation to students, but more incentive to remove the miscreants before they contaminate the majority. One serious drawback of this reaction is that, where the 'tiny minority' has been removed, 'new members have emerged to fill the deviant roles' (ibid., p. 7).

Watkins and Wagner go on to note that 'it's their age' is used largely to apply to students of secondary-school age. They relate from their experience how they have heard biological determinism in the form of 'it's their hormones', or adolescent moodiness and unpredictability used to explain the higher incidence of disaffection among students at secondary level compared with those at primary level.

The stereotypical explanation of difficult students who come from a difficult neighbourhood, like the other explanations above, does little to illuminate individual students' patterns of behaviour. Of course, one cannot deny that socio-economic factors do have a great deal of influence on school populations. Gewirtz et al. (1995), among others, note the increase in inequality and the differential distribution of educational success along lines of social class. This appears to be especially the case where, as in the current context, education is viewed as a 'commodity'. The market system ensures the flow of resources from children with greatest need to those with the least. However, research outcomes do not support the application of a simple cause and effect model to explain student disaffection from, and disruptive behaviour in, schools in economically impoverished neighbourhoods. The structure and organisation of schools can make a difference to student behaviour even in disadvantaged areas (Rutter *et al.*, 1979; Lauder and Thrupp, 2004; Thrupp *et al.*, 2002).

Behavioural descriptors applied to students often have no absolute meaning and may be understood only within the context in which the behavioural act took place. A number of researchers have noted that student behaviour perceived by others as unacceptable is influenced at a number of levels, including the level of the individual student, the teacher in the classroom and the whole school. At the level of the student in the classroom, the effects of classroom peer groups, individual teachers (Hargreaves, 1982), teacher expectation (Rosenthal and Jacobsen, 1968) and lack of self-esteem of the individual student (Coopersmith, 1967) have been seen to influence students' attitudes and behaviour. From their eight-school study of school improvement carried out over three years, Gottfredson *et al.* (1993), among others, concluded that the most effective interventions intended to reduce the risk of unacceptable behaviour are those that operate at all three levels, given that:

(a) Some individuals are more likely than others to misbehave.
(b) Some teachers are more likely than others to produce higher levels of misconduct in their classroom by their management and organization practices.
(c) Some schools more often than others fail to control student behaviour.
(Gottfredson et al., 1993, cited in Watkins and Wagner,
2000, p. 17)

One of the authors wrote a personal account of the turning point in her understanding of student behaviour and ways in which assigning students to particular categories which imply within-student deficits is highly problematic:

> Fairly early in my teaching career in the 1970s a specific incident had served as the catalyst for a turning point in my conceptualisation of what constitute 'remedial' and 'behaviour difficulties'. 'Jamie' was categorised as both having behaviour and learning difficulties. I was told that he was disruptive and lazy. He was placed in the bottom band of three, the 'remedial' band, in the comprehensive school in which I was teaching. With his class group, I taught Classical Studies and shared stories from Greek mythology which Jamie loved. He was always the first with the answer to everything and was verbally very articulate.

At the end of one year, a particular incident with him in class led to my consciously reflecting on the fact that the category 'remedial' as it related to Jamie certainly did not mean slow-learning, and that 'behaviour difficulties' were not always attributable to the student alone. I was telling the tale of Minos, King of Crete, and his pursuit of the escaping inventor, Daedalus. I had reached the point of describing Minos's undignified demise when Jamie suddenly corrected me. He reminded me that I had given a different version of Minos's death nearly three terms previously. He was correct. I had forgotten. He then related, in detail, the whole of my previous account.

I reflected on this piece of empirical evidence for a very long time after the event. I was fairly new to teaching and not in a position at that particular school to influence his categorisation as 'remedial' or his placement in the bottom, 'remedial' band. However, the disjunction between the label 'remedial' and my perception of him as articulate, interested and engaged in his learning forced me to re-think my conceptualisation of him as both slow learner, termed a student 'with moderate learning difficulties' at that time, and as 'disruptive' as he had been described to me. I reconceptualised the challenges that he presented to teachers from a slowness in his thinking and from pathological resistance to anything teachers said or wanted him to do to literacy difficulties of a dyslexic nature which had gone unrecognised by teachers and had led to profound frustration in his inability to cope with written text or to express himself in writing. Hence it was unsurprising if he loudly resisted writing tasks. Jamie's disaffection seemed to me to be the product of a social context. To be disaffected a person must be feeling alienated from something. In some lessons Jamie was expressing this feeling in obviously hostile behaviour. In my lessons I was relying largely on narrative so his hostility to having pressure placed on him to cope with text did not apply. In school students are in a very different position from professionals in the hierarchy of power and influence. Those with a professional responsibility for sustaining existing organisational structures may well experience the rejection of school provision by students such as Jamie as challenging to the existing order as well as to themselves. They may then go on to interpret the behaviour of these students, and the students themselves, as deviant.

(Wearmouth, 2002, pp. 51–3)

The educational system has arguably failed to provide an effective inclusive curriculum. It has failed to provide a pedagogy to address the learning needs of a diversity of students:

The terms 'children with special educational needs', or even 'SENs', is used in common parlance in schools. This terminology is reinforced in a multiplicity of government documentation as if the term 'special educational need' itself is a given. Lessons I had learnt from reflecting on my experiences with 'Jamie' and others had made me aware of the contradiction between official rhetoric and my own understanding that any conceptualisation of the behaviour of students is constructed by individuals within particular contexts . . . 'it is culture . . . that shapes the human mind' (Bruner, 1990, p. 34).

(ibid., p. 53)

Stress is an example of student behaviour in schools, which can be understood as an attribute of the student or resulting from pressures within the environment. Individuals may be said to suffer from stress and their symptoms may be treated, using a so-called 'medical model'. Alternatively, pressure and stress in the learning environment may be seen to set the occasion for, or to provoke particular kinds of student behaviour.

As Cornwall (2004) notes, too few demands and too little pressure on students may result in boredom. Too much pressure may negatively affect students' attentional skills, emotions, health and general behaviour. Different students have different tolerance levels of stress and pressure. Treading the line between too little challenge and too much pressure requires an understanding of the learning process as well as an awareness of individual differences between students.

Explanations of bullying

An example of student behaviour which is the focus of teachers' concerns in many schools and which can be explained from a variety of viewpoints is that of bullying. As Rigby (2002, p. 13) notes, the last decade of the twentieth century witnessed an 'extraordinary rise in interest' in the topic of bullying. This has been reflected in the way in which many schools have felt obliged to develop anti-bullying policies and procedures.

One might choose to trace a history of the term 'bully' through sources cited in a dictionary, for example, the *Oxford English Dictionary*. Here we find that, in the sixteenth century when it was first used it described a man who is admired by many for his forceful personality. By the seventeenth century it had come to mean more of an empty, swaggering but cowardly kind of person. By the nineteenth century, as used by the novelist Charles Dickens, for example, the link between cowardice and intimidation in the person of the bully had been firmly established. Rigby (2002) has carried out an analysis of previously published work on what constitutes bullying behaviour (for example, French and Raven, 1959; Besag, 1989; Randall, 1991; Farrington, 1993; Olweus, 1993, 1999; Smith and Sharp, 1994). He concluded that it is a combination of the wish to hurt somebody together with hurtful action, an imbalance and unjust use of power, enjoyment on the part of the bully, the victim's feeling of oppression and, often, repetition of the bullying behaviour.

Bullying behaviour in the natural world

Apart from Olweus's (1973, 1978) work in Scandinavia, until recently there had been little work carried out on bullying *per se*. Investigation into bullying may be of recent origin, but bullying itself is not. Rigby (2002) references Lorenz's (1969) work in noting that bullying of outsiders in nature may be intended to preserve the purity of the species by driving away other animals. Lorenz summarises three advantages to survival in nature of aggressive behaviour towards others in the same species: (1) the fittest of the species and those who can best dominate others have the best chance of mating and passing on their genes to future generations; (2) the result of bullying may be a stable, hierarchical social structure that contributes to the viability of the group; and (3) aggression within the group results in the creation of space from which each member of the group benefits.

In schools the incidence of bullying appears to rise at the transfer (transition) stage between primary and secondary school, and at other transition points. This may result from the jockeying for position in the new pecking order and the drive to establish oneself in the student hierarchy. Although there are clear parallels between animal and human behaviour, one certainly cannot conclude that bullying within human society evolved from a notion of what is 'good' for the group. A common perception is to see it as the epitome of evil, for example, as in the portrayal of the bullying that led to the murder of the infant Jamie Bulger in England in 1993.

The influence of situational factors on bullying behaviour

The Second World War and then, later, the Vietnam War, stimulated interest in social psychology research projects into the issues of obedience to malign authority, and the influence of group pressure to conform to a group norm where the actions of one person or a group acting under the orders of an authoritative other were clearly to the detriment of another. For example, Milgram's (1963, 1974) 'electric shock' experiments were designed to investigate the extent to which individuals were prepared to obey authoritative instructions from others to deliver electric shocks to adult learners.

Studies on conformity and obedience typically indicate a 'fundamental attribution error' (Nisbett *et al.*, 1973); that is, that people generally over-estimate the role of the characteristics of individual people and under-estimate the role of contextual factors in regulating human behaviour (Atkinson *et al.*, 1993). Zimbardo's (1970) 'prison experiment' where volunteers acting the part of prison guards were prepared to humiliate and victimise other volunteers acting as 'prisoners' is an example of the kind of experiment designed to test the hypothesis that, under certain conditions, members of a group can lose their personal identities and experience a sense of mob aggression and much greater impulsive behaviour against other individuals. In literature, William Golding's (1954) *Lord of the Flies* is a very well-known example of a novel which traces the development and ultimate tragic consequences of bullying behaviour among a group of young boys living on a desert island, isolated from adults. It is noteworthy that, in schools, there is a negative relationship between the presence of teachers at breaktimes and lunchtimes and bullying (Olweus, 1993).

There are examples of whole societies which train their citizens in violent, aggressive acts from birth. For example, ancient Sparta was a military society which rejected babies seen as physically weak and left them to die of exposure, and subjected its children to a regime of toughness, discipline, pain and violence in an attempt to train them into fighting machines. Sparta was in a permanent state of readiness for war. Contemporary studies of bullying in schools in various countries indicate that the incidence of bullying by peers appears to be more common in some countries than others (Rigby, 2002). Within countries Rigby (1997) has shown that differences between schools in the incidence of bullying can also be considerable.

The cycle of bullying

Bullying is often associated with an imbalance of power between victim and perpetrator. Once the victim begins to react to the bullying by showing signs of stress, the bully or bullies may experience great pleasure and enjoyment from their feelings of power and dominance. The cycle of bullying may continue and/or grow more intense and continue for a long time. Sometimes the victim may fight back (literally), sometimes she or he may find ways to avoid the bullying by hovering around teachers or staying at home.

Some schools have attempted to combat bullying by encouraging students to inform on bullies. This may lead to an improvement in the victim's situation, or, alternatively, it may lead to the reverse. Research in Australia has indicated that 6 per cent of boys and 9 per cent of girls have truanted from school to avoid being bullied. It has also indicated that the outcome of 'telling' on the bully depends on the status and position of who is told and what actions she or he takes (Rigby, 2002). A 'No blame' approach, developed in the UK by Maines and Robinson (1991) to address bullying behaviour in schools has been developed, premised on the victim being prepared to come forward and 'tell' on the bully. Once the bullying behaviour has been identified, a particular process is initiated to bring victim and bully together to enable a reconciliation. We discuss this issue later in Chapter 10.

One of the crucial factors in accounting for the degree of severity of bullying in schools is the behaviour of bystanders. Research on bystander behaviour gained popularity after the murder of a New Yorker, Kitty Genovese in 1964, which became notorious as a result of the non-intervention of 38 neighbours who heard her screams for help for over 30 minutes but failed to assist her (Atkinson *et al.*, 1993). Social psychologists researching what they termed 'bystander apathy' found that the presence of others seems to deter individuals from intervening in difficult or dangerous situations where they could be of assistance to the person in danger or trouble. However, a training programme focusing on raising awareness of bystander apathy can be shown to make a significant difference to the preparedness of bystanders to help others in trouble (Beaman *et al.*, 1978). The abduction in England of a young boy, James Bulger, was also witnessed by many bystanders who did nothing to intervene with the two 10-year-olds who marched him around Liverpool before murdering him. Another factor which appears to be of consequence in inhibiting intervention is the perceived relationship between these boys. They were assumed to be brothers (Levine, 1999).

Group pressure to conform to a majority view can also be shown to influence individuals to act against their own judgements. In a classic series of studies, Asch (1952, 1955, 1958) showed that individuals confronted with the unanimous views of a group about an issue were unlikely to disagree openly with the group's judgement even where this was clearly wrong. In Asch's experiments individuals were asked to judge the length of a line that was clearly estimated incorrectly by the group. Many subjects preferred to accede to the group's view rather than risk challenging the group's apparent competence and thus the fear of 'What will they think of me?' (Atkinson *et al.*, 1993).

Rigby (2002) warns against any assumption that the descriptors 'bully' and 'victim' should suggest a stable personality trait. Many of those who bully in their younger years do not repeat this behaviour later on. Some of those who bully in one situation would never do so in another. The author Roald Dahl recounts, for example, in his autobiography *Boy: Tales of Childhood* (Dahl, 1984) how the head teacher of the residential public school he attended bullied students through his use of corporal punishment but later became an eminent figure in a Christian church community in England.

It is tempting to think of bullies as being socially inadequate (Field, 1999). However, this may be a gross over-simplification. To take advantage of, and manipulate, other less powerful individuals, bullies may need to be very skilful in the social situation (Sutton *et al.*, 1999). On measures of self-esteem, school bullies are average (Rigby, 1997). However, bullies tend to be less able to imagine another's point of view (Rigby, 2002) and to experience stronger feelings of depression (Slee, 1995). They also appear to be more positively disposed towards violence (Olweus, 1993).

Despite the risk of supporting the use of stereotypes, there does seem to be some consensus among researchers about the correlates of victimisation:

- having low self-worth and self-esteem;
- being non-assertive;
- having poor social skills;
- being psychologically introverted;
- being physically less strong than others;
- being relatively uncooperative;
- not being group oriented;
- not being competitive;
- being shorter than average;
- being less stable than others;
- lacking poise, not being relaxed;
- having a bad stammer;
- being lonely, isolated;
- prone to anxiety, depression and suicide.

(Rigby, 2002, pp. 139–40)

As Rigby notes, in order to assess the relative importance of any one particular explanation of bullying behaviour, it would be necessary to tease out each one separately. In a school situation, this is not always possible. In judging which explanation is the most likely for a particular behaviour, we are likely to be influenced by our own experiences. Herein lies a problem. As noted above, the fundamental attribution error means that many of us may over-estimate the extent to which behaviour is driven by personality characteristics and under-estimate the influence of the particular situation in which the behaviour occurs. However, we cannot affect a student's biological inheritance or even the influence of the supernatural, but we can manipulate or re-organise aspects of the school environment to make bullying behaviour among students in schools less likely.

Given a situational view of the causes of bullying, many schools have adopted a whole-school approach to addressing the problem. Approaches often employed include (Rigby, 2002):

- negotiating and developing anti-bullying policies in discussion with both students and parents;
- training students in the skills of conflict resolution and mediation;
- systematic, consistent responses to incidents of bullying.

Conclusion

The kind of understanding that schools have of problematic behaviour among their students is important because it has an influence on the strategies that are adopted to address it. Among the explanations for difficult or challenging behaviour it is common to find a within-person (medical or deficit) cause for other people's anti-social behaviour, but an environmental cause when it comes to our own. This is the 'fundamental attribution error' (Nisbett *et al.*, 1973). One of the difficulties for schools in adopting a position that the problem lies entirely within the student is that this tends to remove either the incentive, or a sense of the agency, for addressing such behaviour in ways that will allow the student to remain within the mainstream classroom and school.

Watkins and Wagner (2000) summarised the following list of the characteristics of practice in more than 1,000 well-disciplined schools from a study by Wayson *et al.* (1982). It is clear from this list that these schools tend strongly to the view that they have the major responsibility for creating learning environments conducive to positive learning and good behaviour rather than assuming that problematic behaviour is the fault of their students:

1 These schools did many things that have been done by good schools and good educators for a long time (i.e. no new tricks, no quick fixes).
2 These schools create a wholeschool environment that is conducive to good discipline rather than adopting isolated practices to deal with discipline problems.
3 Most teachers viewed the school as a place where staff and students come to work and to experience the success of doing something well.
4 These schools are student-oriented.
5 These schools focused on causes of discipline problems rather than symptoms.
6 Programmes in these schools emphasised positive behaviours and used preventive measures rather than punitive actions to improve discipline.
7 These schools adapted practices to meet their own identified needs and to reflect their own styles of operation.
8 The headteacher plays a key role in making these schools what they are.
9 The programmes in these schools often result, either through happy coincidence or through deliberate design, from the teamwork of a capable head and some other staff member who has the personal leadership qualities that complement those of the head.
10 The staff of these schools believe in their school and in what its students can do; and they expend unusual amounts of energy to make that belief come true.
11 Teachers in these schools handle all or most of the routine discipline problems themselves.
12 The majority of these schools have developed stronger-than-average ties with parents and with community agencies.
13 These schools were open to critical review and evaluation from a wide variety of schools and community sources.

(Watkins and Wagner, 2000, p. 25)

One further area to be addressed in order for schools to reduce the level of problematic behaviour in students would be to move from a totally teacher-controlled learning environment to one in which students are able to contribute their own ideas and cultural experiences to their learning.

Chapter 3

Societal understandings

Introduction

The issue of disruptive, challenging behaviour by students in schools and what kind of measures might address it is long-standing. Indeed, challenging behaviour has a history 'as long as mass education itself' (Furlong, 1985). The Roman poet, Horace, for example, recounts how the early morning air in Rome often resounded to the cries of schoolboys being beaten for some form of misbehaviour or failure to complete the required work to the requisite standard. In the seventeenth century in Britain students were often armed and occasionally took part in violent mutiny (ibid.). There appear to be recorded instances of students destroying all of the most famous public schools at least once (Ogilvie, 1957). Galloway *et al.* (1994) have noted how, during the early nineteenth century, prior to compulsory education, delinquent children whose parents were poor or dispossessed and considered socially undesirable were sent to workhouse schools or 'ragged' schools with their focus on the 'depraved' and 'vicious' poor in the inner cities. There is a record from the late nineteenth century of the schoolteacher in a primary school on the Isle of Wight requesting money from the school managers for shin pads for himself. His students, the children of poor farm workers, hated school so much that every time they came into the classroom they kicked him (Wearmouth, personal communication). They would rather have been earning money working on the land.

In many countries, once education becomes compulsory for all children and the whole educational apparatus comes under state control, the issue of the social control of potentially difficult students, expected to come mostly from the poorer groups in society, assumes a particular significance (Ford *et al.*, 1982). The question of how to manage students whose behaviour is seen as challenging the social order within schools is of paramount importance to those who control a nation's education system.

In this chapter we look first at the historical context, particularly in the UK and New Zealand, once universal education became mandatory. In the light of this context, we can better understand current interpretations of the behaviour of students seen as threatening the smooth running of the educational apparatus. We discuss a range of educational provisions that have been made at different times and in different places for students whose behaviour is judged problematic in some way, and a number of interpretations of the interests that are served by these kinds of provision.

Historical context

Following the introduction of compulsory state education for all young people, policy-makers are necessarily faced with the fundamental dilemma of how to make educational provision for all students, including those whose presence in the classroom is seen as holding others back. This dilemma had to be addressed in England and Wales, for example, after the Elementary Education Act of 1870. According to Galloway et al. (1994), the need for social control of these children resulted in politicians looking to the medical profession and later to educational psychologists to 'identify, assess and treat the symptoms, if not the causes, of deviant and disruptive behaviour' (1994, p. 111). One solution was the kind of categorisation and segregation of students that resulted from a largely medical and, subsequently, psychological, response to the problem. Across the world many other countries followed the same kind of pattern. In the UK in the late nineteenth and early twentieth centuries, students might be assessed and labelled as 'idiots', 'feebleminded' and 'imbeciles' through the expertise of doctors and/or the growing profession of psychologists, and separated off from the rest for the good of the majority in society. Admission to asylums was considered suitable for those categorised as 'imbeciles'. The 'feeble-minded' were educated in special schools or classes while the group labelled 'idiots' was not thought to be educable (DES, 1978).

In the early twentieth century the eugenics movement assumed that children who displayed disruptive behaviour were the product of the lower classes. The category of moral imbeciles or defectives included children who displayed emotionally disturbed or disruptive behaviour, and was introduced by the 1913 Mental Deficiency Act. The maladjusted category emerged as an official category in 1945, although reports from the Board of Education in the 1920s recommended that the maladjusted child was in need of child guidance. Galloway et al. suggest that the category implied personal deficiencies and inadequacies, moral depravity and a variety of social evils:

> the social identity of any child assessed post-1944 as maladjusted, and later as emotionally and behaviourally disturbed, is one which has a powerful history of stigma, being associated with undesirable personal and social characteristics.
>
> (1994, p. 112)

Moore *et al.* note how, internationally, two characteristics of the development of special education policy and practice have been its rapid expansion
and its 'piecemeal nature' (1999, p. 7). These characteristics suggest that,
historically, special education practices have been driven more by localised
responses to emerging pressures and crises rather than by coherent government policies. In England and Wales, for example, students might receive
education and/or care through a range of services other than the special
school run by a local education authority:

> Types of provision included juvenile prisons (post-1840), large poor law
> residential schools (1860–1970s), day and residential industrial schools
> (from 1857, transmuting into approved schools in 1933, and community
> homes with education [CHEs] after the 1969 Children and Young
> Persons Act), fostering and attending local day schools (mid to late
> 1800s), National Children Homes or Barnardo's 'cottage' and 'village'
> homes (after about 1880), residential schools for the maladjusted/EBD
> (from c.1920), special day schools (rare before the 1970s), mental or
> psychiatric hostels, residential hostels from which the maladjusted
> would attend mainstream schools (post-1945), special classes attached
> to mainstream schools (mainly post-1970), off-site special units (seen in
> London in 1950s but mainly post-1970), educational units attached
> to Child Guidance Clinics, sometimes based in hospitals (mainly post-
> 1945), classrooms in children's homes/observation and assessment
> centres (mainly post-1969 Children and Young People Act). In fact some
> forms of provision, seen in the 1980s and 1990s as progressive alter-
> natives to 'segregated', often residential special schools, which furthered
> the movement towards greater school and community inclusion, already
> had a long history.
>
> (Cole, 2004, p. 19)

Within the system that operated in England and Wales, particular types of
intervention were developed, some of which had an ephemeral existence,
others more permanent:

> There were short-term industrial schools where persistent truants were
> initially locked in solitary confinement, 'feeding schools' providing meals
> and baths for 'at risk' working class poor (pre-1900), nautical schools
> to train the crew for the empire's navy (pre-1900 to post-1945).
>
> (ibid.)

Not all regimes were harsh:

> In deliberate contrast to the often harsh, militaristic regimes of many
> reformatory and industrial schools, some of the pioneer schools for the

'maladjusted' opted for democratic and permissive regimes (Bridgeland, 1971) from Homer Lane's 'Little Commonwealth' (1914–1918), through A.S. Neill's early Summerhill to therapeutic regimes after 1945 (Cole, 1989). Here the views of children were sought, for example through daily school meetings and pupils sometimes allowed to dictate schools' policy in a way that could frighten orthodox school inspectors (Bridgeland, 1971; DES, 1974a; Cole, 1989).

(ibid.)

Where a choice of placement outside the mainstream existed, it might relate to a whole range of factors, for example, local views or personal beliefs of individual professionals on whether the approach to students seen as aberrant should be disciplinarian and punitive or clearly rehabilitative or therapeutic:

> A local psychologist or education officer might be sympathetic to a particular therapeutic community. The local LEA might have particular historical experience of placing children in specific residential or day special settings. More widely, the behaviour of the young person might be seen as a personality disturbance that could be 'treated' (the medical model) or a rational reaction to an adverse environment that might be changing the environment through choice of a different home or school (Min. of Ed., 1955; Laslett, 1983).

(ibid., pp. 19–20)

Within such regimes, perhaps, can be seen the beginnings of an understanding of behaviour as influenced by the contexts in which it occurs, and therefore amenable to change by altering those contexts.

Trends towards integration

In the latter part of the twentieth century there was a growing concern for equality of opportunity and social cohesion in society at large (Clark *et al.*, 1997). Internationally, in relation to special education, the result was the integration of some children from special to mainstream schools. In the UK, for example, the 1978 Warnock Report reviewed educational provision in Great Britain for children and young people who, up to that time, were considered 'handicapped by disabilities of body or mind'. It introduced the concept of 'special educational needs', recommending that this should replace categorisation of handicap. Under the terms of the 1981 Education Act in England and Wales, a child 'has special educational needs if he or she has a learning difficulty which calls for special educational provision to be made for him or her' (DfE, 1994c, 2:1). 'Learning difficulty' itself is a relativist notion in this Act. If the pedagogy, including resources and curriculum, that suits the student is already available in a school as a regular part of a school's provision, in theory that student has no 'special' learning need.

The 1981 Education Act attempted to translate the Warnock Report into action, underpinned by legislation, and reaffirmed the principle of integration. All children should be educated in mainstream schools but with certain provisos: that their needs could be met there, and that it was compatible with the education of other children and with the 'efficient use of resources' (1981 Education Act, Schedule 10, paras 3–5 (1), Regulations 12 to 14). In principle, however, the law continued to be based on individually defined need. An arbitrary figure of 2 per cent of students (drawn from a count of students in special schools in 1944) was seen by policy-makers as the number likely to have difficulties requiring additional or extra resources to be provided for them (DfE, 1994c, 2:2). The move away from 'remedial' education to a 'whole-school' approach constituted the first attempt at a coherent structural merger of special and mainstream education (Clark *et al.*, 1997). Nevertheless the criticism began to be voiced that, on the whole, this provision still amounted to 'a bolt-on extension of what was planned for the majority, rather than an integrated whole designed to address the entire diverse body of pupils' (Wearmouth, 2000, p. 18).

In New Zealand there was a similar move towards inclusion in mainstream schools. By the mid-1980s, the ecological model of understanding problems of learning and behaviour as associated with context was becoming more evident and accepted around the country. However, the functional limitations paradigm of 'test and tell' (test the student and tell what is wrong with him/her and remove him/her to a 'specialist' setting where those identified deficits could be remedied) was still very firmly in place. Also alive and well was the accompanying strong reliance on psychometric assessment by educational psychologists and others, to identify profiles of deficits with individual students. By 1985, the Director of Special Education had issued a memorandum removing the requirement for standardised intelligence testing as the means for accessing special education resources (Brown, 2002). This move recognised that 'differential diagnosis and categorisation through psychometric assessment were inadequate methods of identifying and addressing educational need' (Brown, 2002, p. 38). This action encouraged a more ecological approach to assessment and located at least part of the problem of the lack of achievement of many students in terms of pedagogical practices within schools. This was a bold step towards legitimising an inclusive and ecological approach to special education. However, in practice two different paradigms were still in existence, resulting in the continuation of special classes and schools, much more so in some regions of the country than others.

The late 1980s saw the return of many special education resources and personnel to the mainstream (Brown and Thomson, 1988). In Wellington a group of special school principals, school inspectors and members of the Department of Education Psychological Service were particularly strong drivers in this move towards establishing a more inclusive education for all.

Although this move reflected growing support for human rights initiatives in the Western world, it was not until 19 August 1993 that the rights of individuals were recognised by law in New Zealand with the passing of the Human Rights Act (Brown, 2002). The movement towards inclusion, however, was well underway and has continued to gather momentum around the country albeit in rather an *ad hoc* manner.

In the mid-1980s, the closing of a large South Island residential school for boys with behavioural and learning difficulties was one of the turning points within special education in New Zealand. Special residential schools such as this had been a long-standing feature of segregated special education in New Zealand and they had previously withstood many challenges to change. Many students were young Māori who had presented challenging behaviour and had been removed from their families in the North Island in order to attend the facility. Finally some educators and policy-makers were saying what the families of these students already knew: 'It was no longer appropriate to uproot these youngsters from their culture and community and segregate them from the rest of society' (ibid., p. 39). The closure of this school and the movement to close other similar schools were further signs of the growing influence of the inclusive paradigm and an indication of the future directions in New Zealand special education. Money saved from the closure of schools such as these was used to fund initiatives within the mainstream schools that accepted these students. One such initiative involved seventeen school-based Support Teacher teams in three different areas (Moore *et al.*, 1993). Educational psychologists provided further training and support for those effective teachers with proven skills and knowledge in teaching special needs within their regular classes. Those effective teachers had been identified within each school as the best people to fill the Support Teacher role.

Although there were sixty-nine New Zealand schools with support teams by 1990, it was unclear how many were working within an inclusive paradigm. The role and function of the support teacher were defined and modified to suit the needs of individual schools. Interestingly, wherever selection, training and management committee support for the inclusive role of the support teacher was weak, a drift back to segregation and functional limitations paradigm was evident particularly at secondary (year 9 to year 13) schools (Brown, 2002). Local operation and control allowed principals considerable flexibility in the interpretation of policy requirements.

The curriculum Review (Department of Education, 1987a) and the Draft Review of Special Education (Department of Education, 1987b) further influenced the development of the support team model (Moore and Sheldon, 1989). The Draft Review of Special Education stated: 'To achieve the ultimate aim of normalization through mainstreaming it will be necessary to move to a single stream of education with special education acting as a support service' (Department of Education, 1987b, p. 93, quoted in Brown, 2002,

p. 41). While the intentions of this review document would undoubtedly have moved the inclusive education initiatives forward, it was over-ridden by the effects of 'Tomorrow's Schools' (Department of Education, 1987a, 1987b), a policy that emerged in a period of massive nation-wide reform of education curriculum and administration. This was a major political reform that saw administration of schools devolved from central control to individual school control (Lange, 1988). These changes took their inspiration from the concept of locally driven education, and were based on the assumption that communities knew best what was appropriate in the education of their children. One outcome of these reforms was the establishment of the stand-alone, that is independent of the newly established Ministry of Education, New Zealand Special Education Services (SES). Another outcome of the 'Tomorrow's Schools' reform and the subsequent curriculum reforms was that inclusion in special education was seen by some to be put on hold as inclusion was not necessarily accepted or approved by all of the nation's newly autonomous schools. Butterworth and Butterworth (1998, p. 189, quoted in Brown, 2002, p. 42) noted that only the following three recommendations survived this process:

1   to ensure that educational provisions for students with special need were as normal as possible;
2   to establish a process involving parents, the community, the students, and educators to decide the best way to assist any student;
3   to emphasise individual assessment and programme development.

However, in 1996, SE2000 (Special Education 2000), a new special education policy, was announced (Ministry of Education, 1997, 1998a). This policy was, arguably, New Zealand's first attempt to break away from piecemeal provision for students with special needs and to establish a coherent overall policy attempt at an inclusive education for all. Ryba and Annan note that SE2000 was seen to encompass the following recommendations from the Draft Review of Special Education:

> the removal of administrative categories of disability, national guidelines for schools to set priorities for the allocation of resources for special needs, a new emphasis on teacher training to meet special needs in regular schools and classes, support systems for mainstream settings, in-service training for regular class teachers, and specialist training for resource personnel including an urgent need 'in establishing support for students and teachers'.
> (Ryba and Annan, 2000, p. 91, quoted in Brown, 2002, pp. 42–3)

The SE2000 policy specified that the New Zealand National Curriculum was to be delivered to all students and called for a further move away from the functional limitations paradigm, and also went further than simply main-streaming by requiring schools to adapt their practices. The policy clearly called for a more inclusive method of responding to children with learning and behavioural difficulties through changes at both classroom and school levels. It also clearly signalled that families and *whānau* (extended families) were definitely expected to be consulted and to contribute to the shaping of special education provision for their children. Part of the Special Education Policy Guidelines of 1995 required that information relating to barriers to learning and the provision of resources should be shared between families/*whānau* and the providers of education (Mitchell, 1999).

Individual education programmes (IEPs) were to be developed for each child within this policy context. In line with models of inclusion, schools and other organisations were now required to adapt educational environments so that the needs of students with a diverse range of needs would be better met (Thomson *et al.*, 2001).

Patterns of provision in the late 1990s/ early 2000s

As Cole comments, there are continuing debates about 'the control, therapy, welfare and education functions of provision/programmes, for young people whose behaviour is seen as troublesome in schools. This is the case in many countries across the world:

> Cooper (1993), reporting his research in the late-1980s, stressed the need for staff to use democratic, collaborative approaches, listening and responding to the views of the individual pupils. This is now a common message but *how far* sites of practice should proceed down this road has been a topic of sometimes intense debate and subject to the current values and beliefs of government departments and individuals. The history of provision for troubled youth indicates the apparently effective work of many of a highly paternalist attitude. In some schools staff were open about claiming to know what was best for the immature and uncertain children in their care (see, for example, Bridgeland, 1971 for pioneer mal-adjusted schools; Millham *et al.*, 1975 in relation to 'approved schools'). Where the adults were respected, the young people could be content to accept the safety and escape from the personal responsibility of decision making, offered by these paternalist 'significant others'. The flattened hierarchies and 'permissive' nature of therapeutic communities rarely won HMI approval (Cole, 1989) but could appeal more to some psychiatrists and social workers from health-service child guidance clinics. HMI in the past, as now, tended to favour an educational approach with expectations of 'normal' behaviour within clear boundaries set by staff.
>
> (Cole, 2004, pp. 21–2)

However, whatever the recurrent tensions, a consensus seems to have emerged on some aspects of effective practice. For example, Cole *et al.* (1998) like Wilson and Evans (1980) before them, found that many senior staff experienced in dealing with such students believed that the most significant aspects of effective approaches were:

- the importance of working through positive relationships;
- building self-esteem through successful basic skills, wider educational and social achievement;
- high educational expectations, linked to a 'normal' curriculum;
- the creation of caring communities, where the voice of the child was heard;
- clearly understood routines and behavioural boundaries.

According to Cole (2004):

> Government guidance [in the UK] contained in Circular 9/94 (DFE, 1994a) supported the above components of effective practice. Cooper (1993) and Cooper, Smith and Upton (1994) offered a similar message, distilling the essence of provision of good practice into the '3Rs' of *relationships*, *respite* from adverse experience and *re-signification* of self whether in special school or mainstream settings.
>
> (2004, p. 23)

However, delivering any provision for students that has of necessity to be labour-intensive, has always been expensive. As Hyland (1993) has noted in relation to community homes with education (CHEs) in the UK, cost has contributed to the demise of a number of institutions. Where there is tight constraint on resources, it is difficult to argue the case for spending money 'on a tiny minority of children when the prognosis for investment may be poor' or to argue for 'money spent on early intervention' when there is no guarantee of saving society greater sums in the future:

> Cost has posed recurrent worries for local government and practitioners over the last two centuries and increasingly since the 1944 Education Act and compulsory secondary education . . . An important element of 'good practice' is the physical environment. Here values (and consequently prioritisation of resource allocation) come into play and have affected the design and quality of the built environment. The provision of privacy, comfort and wide-ranging facilities is recognised as relevant to the achievement of effective intervention (DHSS, 1970; Cole *et al.*, 1998). Yet government inspectors have too often found it necessary to condemn the ill-kept mansions or temporary 'huts' in which troubled youth have so often been cared for and educated (e.g. DES, 1989b).

Improving physical facilities obviously related to the availability of – or at least choosing to make available – financial resources.

(Cole, 2004, p. 22)

Currently, as Cole (ibid., p. 17) notes in the context of the UK, the range of services is 'untidy and varied'. Cole *et al.* (2003a) estimated that in 1998 there were about 350 maintained, non-maintained and independent special EBD schools in England and Wales. However, a few of these schools had or were about to relocate most or all provision for pupils aged 14–16 to units based in their local further education (FE) colleges. Some mainstream secondary schools and/or their LEAs were actively developing links with FE colleges for pupils who were at risk of, or had been, excluded, including pupils deemed as 'having EBD'.

Cole (2002) also reported that the numbers of pupils sole-registered in pupil referral units (PRUs) increased from 5,043 in 1995 to nearly 10,000 in 2002, which more than offset reduction in places provided in EBD schools. Many PRUs had great difficulties in achieving the re-integration into mainstream schools of their students (Parsons and Howlett, 2000; Daniels *et al.*, 2003). Many, contrary to their official function of being short- to medium-stay placements for students, were accommodating for long periods, sometimes years, significant numbers of pupils whose behaviour was seen as problematic in mainstream schools (Cole, 2002).

Cole *et al.* (2003b) suggested that in 1998 the total population of pupils with EBD outside mainstream schools equated to 0.4 per cent of the total compulsory school-aged population, virtually the same proportion as that reported by the Elton Report (DES, 1989).

As we saw in Chapter 1, in the 1990s in the UK, a new government published a Programme of Action (DfEE, 1998a) for special educational needs following a Green Paper (DfEE, 1997) with a message of inclusion in mainstream schools, except for pupils whose behaviour is seen as problematic. Government responses to the problems of social exclusion as evidenced in Circular 1/98 (DfEE, 1998b) required LEAs to create comprehensive and coherent arrangements for pupils with behavioural difficulties at local education authority level in *behaviour support plans* (BSPs) by the end of 1998. As Cole (2004) comments, in the early BSPs it was commonly noted that behaviour support services ideally should devote their energies to preventive work in mainstream schools. However, often LEAs could not escape a 'fire-fighting' and maintenance role with individual long-term excluded students, or students on the verge of exclusion. Cole (2004, p. 27) reports that, in January 1998:

- 101 out of the 131 LEAs then existing (77 per cent) maintained one or more EBD schools;
- 110 out of 131 LEAs (84 per cent) had one or more PRUs;

- many LEAs possessed and hoped to expand their behaviour support services to reduce difficulties in mainstream schools and dependence on segregated provision.

In general terms, the early BSPs reported by Cole

> showed LEAs seeking to move towards more inter-agency working, early identification and preventive interventions that, arguably, might lessen the need for alternative provision . . . without giving a convincing picture of how this reduction of need would be achieved. Although a few LEAs claimed to be progressing towards locational inclusion (educating children with EBD on the same physical sites as mainstream schools – see, for example, Barrow, 1998), the vast majority . . . found it necessary to maintain or to access a spectrum of off-mainstream-site provision from residential schools and PRUs to 'alternative' and 'vocational' FE courses.
>
> (ibid., pp. 27–8)

Even in the most inclusive schools, intractable behaviour difficulties required placement outside the mainstream (Clark *et al.*, 1999).

Behind the rhetoric of inclusion in LEAs' BSPs and the government's Programme of Action (DfEE, 1998a) there is an underlying assumption of the need to make provision for some students outwith the mainstream. Special schools will 'continue to play a vital role' (DfEE, 1998a, Para. 3.5). *The Report of the Special Schools Working Group* (DfES, 2003) took a similar view, that there needed to be a range of provision. This included pupil referral units and special schools as well as appropriate approaches to curricula and links with further education colleges:

> In practice, beneath the inclusionist veneer, the government message remained similar to that of the Elton Committee, which had stressed in 1989
>
> > 'that ordinary schools should do all in their power to retain and educate all the pupils on their roll on-site. However, we recognise that in the case of a small number of pupils this may be difficult, and in some cases impossible' (DES, 1989, para. 6.39, p. 152).
>
> (Cole, 2004, p. 28)

In New Zealand, although inclusion became national policy with SE2000, there are still tensions over its implementation (Brown, 2002). It is interesting to note that the New Zealand government's Special Education 2000 policy provided for all schools to access the services of Resource Teachers Learning and Behaviour (RTLB), who were trained in just this type of preventative role. However, management of the RTLB as a school resource was under the control of individual schools or clusters of schools rather than local or regional authorities. Hence, many schools chose to utilise their RTLB resource in ways that are incompatible with the inclusionary strategy of SE2000. Furthermore, a number of schools actively seek alternative placements for students with severe behavioural needs. Failure to reach consensus on special education policy and practice, especially given the policy of autonomous schools, has resulted in agreements over policy decisions taking longer. As Fraser *et al.* (2000) note, in May 1997, a new approach was announced for the management of students 'with behaviour difficulties'. For those with 'severe' difficulties, this initiative consisted of two elements:

1   Behaviour Education Support Teams (BESTs) whose focus is 'upon increasing those students' positive participation in school and enhancing their learning outcomes', and 'to assist teachers and school boards to increase their skills in managing students with severe behaviour difficulties' (ibid., 2000, p. 38).
2   For students where intervention from BEST does not succeed, students 'may be referred to a Centre for Extra Support for short-term, intensive programmes . . . Students would remain in a Centre for a specified number of weeks or months' (ibid.).

Moore *et al.* (1999) discuss their interpretation of current special education provision in New Zealand as 'caught between stories'. Two paradigms, ecological and functional limitation, continue to exist side by side. The same can be said of other countries also. Brown (2002) provides evidence from Ritzer (1980, p. 12) that shows supporters of one paradigm in New Zealand constantly defending themselves against attacks from those who support the alternative paradigm. Such actions, he reasons, are behind why it has taken so long (25 years) for the concept of inclusion to be embedded in the professional development training of any group of national special educators (Resource Teachers Learning and Behaviour). The movement of the former Specialist Education Services (SES) back into the Ministry of Education in 2002 (known as 'Group Special Education') has seen initiatives at both the Ministry and school level continue to evolve. Specialist support and service delivery to students with learning and behavioural needs as well as teachers' interpretation of curriculum and administration continue to both challenge and stretch educators as they move to define and facilitate more inclusive education practices for all students in New Zealand. Also, from a humanitarian point of view, it might be argued that separate provision can absolve teachers and schools from any serious attempts to examine and modify their current curriculum tasks and pedagogies, by introducing inclusive teaching strategies that reduce the barriers to participation by students with challenging behaviours, or by students who are just 'different'. Challenging behaviour may at least in part arise from inappropriate pedagogies.

A moral position

Cole (2004) concludes that the evidence from his various research projects, for example, Cole (1986, 1989), Cole *et al.* (2003a), suggests the wisdom of maintaining a range of provision, within and without the mainstream, for students whose behaviour is problematic in schools. 'Professional pragmatism will continue to take precedence over politically preferred ideology' (Cole, 2004, p. 28). He asks whether this can be interpreted as 'a denial of children's rights or perpetuation of damaging social exclusion' (ibid.) and cites the value placed on education in separate special schools by both families and students as evidence to the contrary:

> Campaigners for total school inclusion might usefully reflect on DfEE's (1998a) belief that special schools for pupils with EBD were sometimes 'valued by parents and pupils' (para. 3.11, p. 13). This is not an unexpected statement given similar evidence offered by Wilson and Evans (1980), Cooper (1993), Sanders and Hendry (1997), Cole *et al.* (1998), and OFSTED, (1999a). Berridge *et al.*(2001) and Daniels *et al.*(2003) and some inspection reports (e.g. OFSTED, 1999b; Cole, 2002) also indicate that similar parental and pupil appreciation can be found for some PRUs [pupil referral units]. Special, unit or other 'alternative' provision, though in the past often flawed, can sometimes be more supportive and educationally appropriate than mainstream settings for pupils with behavioural difficulties.
>
> (ibid., p. 29)

However, whatever reason might be given for justifying provision for individual students, there remains a moral question to be addressed regarding the interests that are served by particular kinds of provision. Although the changing social and historical context of provision during the twentieth century meant that many labels once attached to pupils ('imbeciles', 'feeble-minded') became unacceptable as a result of the changing social and historical context of provision, the practice of constructing categories of, and thus reifying, difficulties in learning and behaviour for the purpose of organising and maintaining the education system has been maintained. We have already discussed in Chapter 1 how, in the UK, for example, of the total number of students, approximately 2 per cent are seen by policy-makers and resource-providers as likely to have difficulties which require additional or extra resources to be provided for them (DfE, 1994a, para. 2:2).

From a humanitarian point of view it might be argued that separate provision can offer a more protective, supportive and, where appropriate, therapeutic environment than is possible in the mainstream. However, segregation from mainstream peers may also be perceived as stigmatising, anti-inclusionary and morally unacceptable in relation to the human rights of the individual, excluded student.

The case of 'maladjustment'

One of the problems with categorical notions of student attributes is that labels become pervasive and fixed to suit the existing national context, as the history of the rise and demise of the term 'maladjusted' within special education illustrates. Until 1945 there was no formal category of 'maladjustment' enshrined in central government regulations. It had its origins both in early labels of mental deficiency:

> The 1913 Mental Deficiency Act created a category of moral imbeciles or defectives, and children who displayed emotionally disturbed or disruptive behaviour came to be associated with both mental defect and moral defect.
>
> (Galloway *et al.*, 1994, p. 110)

It was identified with the unstable, nervous child identified in Board of Education Reports in the 1920s, and also the: '"difficult and maladjusted" child recommended in the 1929 Board of Education report as in need of child guidance' (ibid., p. 112). After 1945 all local education authorities had a responsibility to establish special educational treatment in special or ordinary schools for students defined in this way. 'Maladjustment' is a vague term. Nevertheless, there is a major problem in that once a category has been 'invented', it creates its own discourse:

> Discourses are about what can be said and thought, but also about who can speak, when, and with what authority. Discourses embody meaning and social relationships, they constitute both subjectivity and power relations. Discourses are 'practices that systematically form the objects of which they speak . . . Discourses are not about objects; they do not identify objects, they constitute them and in the practice of doing so conceal their own invention' (Foucault 1974: 49).
>
> (Ball, 1990, p. 2)

Invent the category, create the student. The category floats around waiting to 'gobble up' victims (Mehan, 1996):

> the possibilities for meaning and for definition are pre-empted through the social and institutional position held by those who use them. Meanings thus arise not from language but from institutional practices, from power relations. Words and concepts change their meaning and their effects as they are deployed within different discourses. Discourses constrain the possibility of thought. They order and combine words in particular ways and exclude or displace other combinations.
>
> (Ball, 1990, p. 2)

Between 1945 and 1960, the numbers of students classified as 'maladjusted' rose from 0 to 1,742. By 1975, there were 13,000 'maladjusted' students (Furlong, 1985).

Critical views

Early sociological studies in education, for example, in the UK in the 1950s, were primarily concerned with the extent to which students from different social classes experienced equal opportunities in the educational system as measured by inputs and outputs. Later, the trend towards qualitative research, beginning in the 1960s, enabled the focus to shift onto processes within schools in order to study further the concern with social class inequalities. Later still, other researchers also working from a qualitative orientation argued that a concentration on the distribution of opportunities in education was insufficient to explain inequality. Attention should also be given to the nature of school knowledge and students' learning and the question of who has the power of decision-making within the educational system.

Beginning in the 1970s a new tradition of 'critical' educational research emerged which continued to expose class inequalities in education and developed to explore ways in which the education system serves to reinforce inequalities in society as a whole by, for example, separating certain sectors of the child population into special forms of educational provision and, in this way, maintaining or reproducing the social class structure. This tradition has broadened to include other domains of inequality, for example, sexism and racism.

Issues relating to which societal groups are most likely to be represented in the 'special' sector in education have often been raised from a critical perspective relating to issues of power and control in society (Tomlinson, 1982; Armstrong, 1995):

- Difficulties in learning have been attributed to the characteristics of the individual student rather than to the school and societal context in which the difficulties have arisen. One of the criticisms made of the Warnock Report (1978) is that it neglected the importance of social factors in the creation of learning difficulties.
- Many students categorised as 'having emotional and behavioural difficulties' and removed from mainstream education into special segregated provision come from working-class families whose parents find it much harder to negotiate with professionals than middle-class parents (Tomlinson, 1982, p. 5).
- Society maintains a state of equilibrium between its interrelated parts. From this viewpoint, special education is seen as a safety valve for the rest of the education system. Order within the education system is

maintained . . . by removing potentially troublesome children which upset the smooth running [of schools] (Tomlinson, 1981, p. 209).

- Special education is used as a form of social control: 'Is the establishment of special educational facilities, particularly those concerned with problems of behaviour, a pernicious system of social control?' (Ford *et al.*, 1982, p. 27).

Educational institutions maintain social stratification by reinforcing class identities among young people. In this way they contribute to the production and reproduction of social and cultural inequality (Wexler, 1987). Tomlinson concludes that in this respect traditional and existing practices benefit the current social order:

> any form of special education or exclusion is as much to do with the political economy and class structures of the society as with the 'benevolent humanitarianism' of those who undoubtedly wish to help young people with difficulties.
>
> . . . the exclusion of the difficult, the disaffected, the troubled and troublesome from the kinds of education considered important will continue. A labour market that took in unskilled special school leavers and low attainers has disappeared, and mainstream education cannot deal with the increasing numbers of young people unable or unwilling to develop their 'human capital' in a system where academic and technological qualifications reign supreme.
>
> (Tomlinson, 2001, pp. 191–2)

Other writers have taken a similarly highly critical view of the role of special education in stigmatising and marginalising particular groups of students and 'condemning' them to 'voicelessness' (Thomas and Loxley, 2001, p. 57).

A critical view has both strengths and weaknesses in its ability to explain the development of special educational provision. Particular strengths are its analysis of:

- the implications of the existence of a special system side by side with a mainstream (Booth, 1981);
- provision developed for pupils whose behaviour is seen as disruptive and therefore challenging to the social order;
- the societal and organisational factors which prevent some students from learning and produces barriers for others.

It also has a number of weaknesses (Copeland, 1993). It cannot explain the following:

- How and why change arises in the special system. The move towards integration into mainstream cannot be explained by dysfunction within the special sector alone. Factors in a larger social system beyond and outside the educational must have facilitated this development which otherwise could not have occurred.
- The diversity of trends within special education and the development of every type of special provision made. For example, in the case of special provision for pupils who choose to truant, it is unclear how social control is operating when all that is taking place is a change of location for pupils' actions rather than the actions themselves.

Clark *et al.* point out that this orientation tends to be preoccupied with critique: 'substantially unchanged recycling of their critiques continues to appear on a regular basis' (1998, p. 162). A fundamental claim that students' special learning needs are a social product rather than descriptions of what students' experiences are really like means that 'there are, therefore, no really-existing "special needs" which necessarily cause problems for educators and call for some carefully worked-out response' distinction (ibid., p. 162). Once the special–ordinary distinction is shown through critical analysis to be irrational, mainstream practices, it is argued, should be shown capable of supporting the learning of all students. This argument represents a binary, either–or, position, however. Individual student needs exist and are acted upon in the context of educational institutions. Student learning and behaviour are dynamic in an interactive relationship with the environment in which they occur.

Conclusion

As Cole (2004) has commented, a number of interlinking dilemmas affecting the development of policy and practice in the area of special provision for students whose behaviour is problematic in schools have recurred over time:

- the tensions between social control, therapy, welfare or education as the underpinning principles of any particular institution or service;
- the extent to which a special curriculum should replicate the mainstream in order effectively to address a child-rights perspective;
- the optimum balance between reducing the student's difficulties encountered in current learning contexts and developing curricula aimed at encouraging personal independence;
- the extent to which the needs of the individual student in a school community can be reconciled with the needs of the larger group. Deschenes *et al.* (2001) argue that in the USA schools always have, and likely will continue to exclude students who 'don't fit'. Criteria for exclusion have ranged from student character defects, poor preparation for school by

families from certain cultural backgrounds, school structures and systems that are insufficiently differentiated and school cultures that differ from the cultures of these students. Solutions advocated by Deschenes *et al.* incorporate fitting the school and the school system to the student, involving the community in the life of the school and involving the school in the life of the community.

• the extent to which adults should impose their will in relation to personal, social and educational development when students are resistant to what is proposed.

Cole and Visser (1998) noted that different officials and individuals within institutions offer contrasting answers to these questions. In history, balancing conflicting opinion on these key issues has led to shifting compromises that on occasion have advanced practice in one direction while forcing retreat in others.

However sympathetic a view is taken of humanitarian and therapeutic rationales underpinning special forms of provision, the fact remains that the very existence of these forms of provision 'inhibits any genuine discussion of the needs and interests actually being served by the expansion of special education' (Armstrong, 1994, p. 141). Adequate explanation for 'a whole sub-section of special education has developed and expanded, which is backed by legal enforcement and caters largely for the children of the manual working class' (Tomlinson, 1985: 164) is not yet forthcoming. Armstrong notes:

> The conceptualization of educational failure, disturbing behaviour and disablement in terms of personal deficits, for which a humanitarian concern is appropriate, serves to marginalize and contain opposition to structural changes in society. The legacy of the humanitarian conceptualization of 'needs', divorced as it is from an analysis of the social power of those who are affected directly and indirectly by it, may be legitimation of the disempowerment of the 'needy' by denying them the opportunity to negotiate a definition of their own needs in terms of their political and social origins.
>
> Professionals working with children who are experiencing difficulties within educational contexts may feel constrained to define the problem in terms of the difficulties a child presents to others despite being sensitive to the influence of wider social and political contexts. When a child is referred for assessment it is unlikely to be the result solely of a disinterested concern to identify a child's special educational needs.
>
> (1994, pp. 141–2)

The policy literature and discussions on special education raised in this chapter, and their linkages with societal structures and preferences, while clearly vocal with respect to issues of social class, are strangely silent with respect to culture. A similar observation was noted by Moore *et al.* (1999) in their review of special education paradigms and provisions in New Zealand. It is clear that students from cultural backgrounds different from those of teachers and management at the schools they attend will experience challenges to their values, beliefs and preferred ways of living and acting, in short, to their whole world-view. School rules, behaviour management policies and strategies and preferred pedagogies are highly likely to advantage students and communities from cultural backgrounds similar to those of teachers. Further, when the challenging behaviours displayed by students from indigenous, migrant or refugee groups are labelled as 'unacceptable', 'disruptive' or 'emotionally disturbed' by teachers and policy-makers from the mainstream culture, serious concern over power and control are revealed. These concerns are exacerbated when the members of the mainstream culture determine and control the nature of a school's response to these behaviours, especially when that response might include temporary or permanent exclusion. We address cultural issues and concerns such as these in Chapter 4.

Cultural understandings of learning and behaviour

Introduction

Viewing difficult behaviour in schools as stemming from the student, the context or the interaction between them leads to different kinds of interventions. In addition, different ways of conceptualising the human mind, the development of learning and how learning impacts on behaviour also lead to different approaches and different interventions for dealing with issues schools have about learning and behaviour.

As Bruner (1996) notes, there are two 'strikingly different' ways of thinking about how the mind works. One of these is to conceptualise the mind in cognitive terms, as operating like a computer in processing the information it receives. Information processing systems of any kind are governed by procedures that control the flow of incoming information, what should be done with it, how it should be categorised, and so on. For this conceptualisation of mind, one appropriate pedagogy is, as Bruner comments, 'drill'. This conceptualisation cannot account for processes of individual human meaning-making which are 'messy' (Frederickson, 1993), ambiguous and sensitive to context (Bruner, 1996). We consider cognitive approaches to an understanding of behaviour later on, in Chapter 6. Here, however, we are concerned with the second conceptualisation, what Bruner terms 'culturalism', which has rather different implications for addressing issues of learning and behaviour.

'Culturalism' assumes that the development of the human mind depends on its evolution within a society where the 'reality' of individual experience is represented through a shared symbolism, for example, verbal or written language, where the community's way of life is organised and understood through that symbolism. The cultural context in which a child is reared shapes his or her thinking and provides tools, a 'cultural toolkit' (Bruner, 1996) for organising meaning in ways that can be communicated to others. In Bruner's view, meaning-making is situated in a cultural context as well as in the prior conceptions that learners bring with them into new situations as a result of previous learning in other contexts. New learning is a product of the 'interplay' between them.

Bruner raises a number of issues relevant to education generally, and to student behaviour that arise from this view of learning and behaviour. For example:

- Where learning is assumed to occur through engagement in society, pedagogy needs to be interactive and 'intersubjective' to take account of individual meaning-making and allow for the production of shared task outcomes. It is the reverse of the transmission-of-knowledge view of teaching.
- Schools need to recognise that they exist in societies where issues of power, status and rewards are very influential. Educational policies and practices need to take account of this.
- Schooling plays a critical part in shaping a student's sense of 'self'; that is, in her or his belief in her or his ability, responsibility and skill in initiating and completing actions and tasks. The way in which schools mediate success and failure is crucial to the development of a sense of personal agency. Schooling is an integral part of the culture, not simply a way of preparing for entry to the culture. Teachers should therefore reflect continuously on the impact of school processes and practices on young people's sense of agency and ability.
- Failing to support the development of students' understanding and ability to act in a cultural context risks marginalising and alienating young people and rendering them incompetent, with the consequent threat to the stability of society as a whole.

The challenge for pedagogy to be interactive and inter-subjective to take account of individual meaning-making, and to mediate success and failure, is as important for understanding behaviour as it is for understanding learning. To respond appropriately to challenging behaviour at school requires us to understand how the cultural contexts of home and school can create challenges for many students. In this chapter we examine some of the evidence related to the relative under-achievement and disaffection with the education system by students from particular minority ethnic groups, and discuss only the proportionately high exclusion rate among the same students has been a focus of investigation in the educational research of some countries for a considerable time (Rampton, 1981; Swann, 1985; Smith, 1995; Bishop and Glynn, 1999). We go on to investigate a number of theories that attempt to explain these phenomena, and we examine practical ways suggested by some researchers to address them.

Research evidence

The happiness and success experienced by students in schools depend to a large extent on the way in which they respond to the expectations of family, friends and school. These expectations stem from the goals and norms of the community. Communities impose significant demands on students. These demands vary from one community to another. Students growing up in the UK, for example, face a number of demands which are specific to the UK and also others which are shared by students in other countries. For example, the British Psychological Society notes that 'formalised education, commencing at the age of five years, imposes a whole range of requirements including the need for compliance, focused concentration and the willingness to listen and reflect' (BPS, 1996, p. 13). It also comments that the hurdles facing students in the UK's education system 'reflect, in part, modern society's emphasis on competition and achievement' (ibid., p. 13). It is inevitable that students who experience difficulties in meeting these demands must face 'a range of social, educational and psychological consequences' which will be 'compounded by personal unhappiness' (ibid., p.?). The problems confronting the minority of students who do not meet these demands may stem from a variety of causes including membership of different groups which may have competing values (Bruner, 1996).

As Gillborn and Youdell (2000) note, the relative under-achievement of students from particular minority ethnic groups and the proportionately high exclusion rate among the same students have been a focus of investigation in educational research in the UK (Rampton, 1981; Swann, 1985) and also in research from New Zealand (Bishop, 1996a; Bishop and Glynn, 1999; Smith, 1995). Following the 1988 Education Act in England and Wales, attention focused more on the issue of racism in schools, tending to concentrate on small-scale qualitative studies (Mac an Ghaill, 1988; Sewell, 1997; Troyna and Hatcher, 1992) and switched away from overall patterns of achievement, making it difficult to examine the educational successes of different ethnic groups. However, findings from the Youth Cohort Study (YCS) of England and Wales (DfE, 1994a) confirms the trend of growing gaps by gender and ethnicity:

> The YCS data paint a clear picture of growing inequalities of achievement between the white group and pupils from several minority ethnic backgrounds. Only two of the different ethnic categories covered in the study enjoyed a year-on-year improvement: the white and Indian groups. The consequence is a growing gap between the majority white group and pupils classified as 'Black', 'Pakistani' and 'Bangladeshi'.
>
> (Gillborn and Youdell, 2000, p. 38)

As Gillborn and Youdell go on to point out, inequalities in achievement between ethnic groups were mirrored by growing gaps between the social classes. They conclude that 'It is clear that social class remains a hugely important factor associated with significant and increasing inequalities of achievement' (ibid., p. 40).

Rarely in the past have statistics on school truanting and exclusion rates been analysed, other than by school phase, and then not usually for special schools. It is the careful analysis of school exclusions which has begun to inform debate on the associated features and factors (Gillborn, 2001). Statistics on exclusions (DfES, 2002), are now presented nationally and regionally, for gender, ethnicity and for those with statements of special educational needs, as well as for age of student and type of school. The proportion of students excluded from school is relatively small. Gillborn (2001) notes that in 2000/1 the number of students excluded was 9,135, about 0.12 per cent of the school population. Boys account for 83 per cent of all exclusions and of these almost three-quarters are between the ages of 12 and 16. The exclusion rate for black students is significantly disproportionate to their numbers in the school population. In 2000/1 the exclusion rate for black Afro-Caribbean students was three times that for white students.

Gillborn comments on the first report of the Social Exclusion Unit (SEU) (1998) which was concerned with truancy and exclusion from schools. In 1998 the Social Exclusion Unit reported that around 13,000 students had been excluded from school permanently, a disproportionate number of whom were from minority ethnic families. The report indicated that African-Caribbean students were over six times more likely to be excluded than their white peers.

Similar issues of under-achievement and alienation as outlined by Majors (2001) and Osborne (2004) apply to all communities in some respects, both in the UK and around the world. In New Zealand the exclusion rate of Māori students is also disproportionately higher in comparison with their numbers in the school population (Ministry of Education, 2003). The position of Māori in mainstream schools in New Zealand has been a growing focus of research in recent years. Māori students make up approximately 20 per cent of the school student population. However, in comparison to non-Māori students, three times more Māori are suspended from school. Further, 38 per cent leave school without any school qualifications as opposed to 19 per cent of non-Māori students (Ministry of Education, 2001a).

Explaining disaffection and under-achievement

Disaffection and under-achievement have been explained in a number of ways by different researchers over the years. Inevitably, high levels of exclusion affect academic performance:

> The DfE Youth Cohort Study (1994) revealed that Blacks were academically the least successful when compared to Whites and other ethnic groups. Only 21 per cent of Blacks achieved five or more GCSEs at grades A to C. In contrast, 45 per cent of Indians and Whites achieved five or

more GCSEs at grades A to C, and 51 per cent of the other Asians gained five or more GCSEs at grades A to C. Furthermore, the *Raising the Attainment of Minority Ethnic Pupils* report (OFSTED, 1999) noted that 25 local authorities revealed serious underachievement among ethnic minorities. The report noted that Black Caribbean and Travellers' children were well behind other groups by the end of secondary school.

(Majors, 2001, p. 3)

Commenting on his perception of the reasons for the exclusion of so many black students, Majors states:

So why are so many Black children excluded? There is evidence that some are excluded for conduct and behavioural problems (although far too many students in this category are excluded for trivial and relatively minor offences). However, many are also excluded simply for exhibiting culture-specific behaviours (wearing dreadlocks, braids, having one's hair too short, having tramlines shaved on one's head, demonstrating 'inappropriate' walking styles or eye contact behaviour.

Many of these exclusions occur because of a lack of cultural aware-ness, miscommunication, racism and negative stereotyping. Teachers often label or view a Black child who demonstrates certain culture-specific behaviours as 'having an attitude problem' or even as being 'ignorant' rather than characterising the child as one who has pride, confidence and a positive sense of self-esteem and cultural identity (Majors and Billson, 1992). As Irvine (1990) reported, because the culture of Black pupils is (in most instances) so different from that of their teachers, teachers often misunderstand, ignore, or discount Black children's language, non-verbal cues, learning styles and worldview.

When teachers are colour-blind to the culture of others, and therefore ignore or are unwilling to affirm another's culture, it often leads to hostility and conflict between White teachers and Black pupils. Qualitative research, such as that cited by the Office for Standards in Education (OFSTED) in 1996, has frequently highlighted the high level of tension between White teachers and Black pupils, in particular Black boys.

(ibid., pp. 2–3)

The combination of gender and race-specific stereotypes is perceived as making success particularly problematic for black boys:

Many racist behaviours and attitudes are manifested in the form of stereotypes, lower expectations and differential treatment toward minorities, particularly Black males (Blair and Bourne, 1998). Wrench and Hassan (1996) reported that young African-Caribbean males felt that teachers often had negative views of them. As Irvine (1990) reported, overt and subtle messages are communicated by teachers to students about their reliability and ability to succeed and do well. Sewell (1997) found that not only were Black boys negatively stereotyped by teachers, but also feared by them. He reported that teachers said that they were afraid of Black boys because of their physical size and their views that they were more troublesome than other pupils.

Black pupils are consistently the subject of differential treatment and the victims of double standards. For example, Black pupils have reported that they have observed differential treatment with regard, among other things, to teacher bullying (e.g. harassment, over-monitoring) discipline, length of punishment, the choice of who is to speak in class, and how they are communicated with (Foster, 1995; Sewell, 1997).

A recent study conducted by Watt, Sheriffe and Majors (1999) on mentoring with Black boys found support for Black pupils' views of differential and inappropriate treatment from teachers. The study found that Black boys believed that they were more likely than their White classmates to be disrespected, talked down to, over-monitored, blamed for things they did not do, and to have limited chances to tell their side of the story. Hence, too many social inclusion initiatives focus on pupils' deficits rather than equally addressing teachers' deficits.

Black students also experience differential expectations from teachers in the area of academic ability. When Black and White males are compared, teachers tend to predict higher test results for White males than they do for Black males (Irvine, 1990). Teachers' assessments of Blacks are in fact consistently lower than their actual test results (OFSTED, 1999[a]). One Black pupil, Renaldo LaRose, who is taking three A levels, provides evidence regarding the lack of confidence which many teachers display in Black pupils' academic ability. 'After we got our GCSE results', he stated, 'teachers were going up to Black pupils and saying they were surprised they had done so well. They used to put Black pupils down' (Judd, 1999).

(ibid., p. 5)

Majors notes the limited amount of formal research that has been conducted on the long-term consequences of such stereotyping. However, he feels that:

given their interactions with teachers, many Black pupils become disappointed and overburdened and 'learn helplessness', or just lose interest in school altogether (White and Cones, 1999). In various studies, students have repeatedly pointed out the disregard teachers have for social justice and civil rights (Alderson and Arnold, 1999; Watt, Sheriffe and Majors, 1999) . . . The fact is, we are obsessed with controlling, monitoring, disciplining, punishment, excluding and labelling rather than focusing on relationships, communication and social justice.

(ibid., p. 6)

Majors' work illustrates how important it is to look at students' school and classroom experiences, and not just at the students themselves in order to understand behaviours that teachers find difficult and challenging. In a study of exclusions from schools in Enfield, England *et al.* (2000) claim that some of the factors associated with the disproportionate number of black students excluded are practices that have either excluded black children from the mainstream of academic achievement or have denied them comprehensive education. Particularly notable are the community attitudes that generally regard black people as unwanted visitors. Teachers are equally susceptible to adopting these attitudes. Grant and Brooks quote evidence to support the claim that training and socialisation of teachers tend to leave them holding negative perceptions and expectations of black students which results in an unequal conflict between teachers and black students and which disenfranchised parents cannot win. If teachers do not know their local communities, and are not visible in these communities outwith school hours, and do not shop or socialise in these communities, then it is difficult to see how they can be recognised as anything but strangers to community members (Ladson-Billings, 1995).

Similar findings have been noted by Bishop *et al.* (2001) in their study of effective Māori medium teachers in New Zealand. Bishop *et al.* identified that these effective teachers understood that teaching and learning within the culture of their students and families were crucial to their students' social and educational success. The impact of traditional cultural practices for the most effective teachers was embedded in all they did; in their interactions with people, with places and with things. Relationships and responsibilities were reciprocal and truly collaborative and lasted long after the student's time in that classroom. These teachers acknowledged the need to be competent cultural practitioners and would themselves actively seek the advice of experts (community elders) in matters that they did not fully comprehend or where they were not the most appropriate person to undertake the task.

Gillborn and Gipps (1996) have drawn attention to the lack of ethnic monitoring of exclusions by LEAs and the disproportionate under-achievement of black students compared to white students. Together with a lack of monitoring of data related to exclusions, the market-oriented policies of recent governments and the publication of league tables of comparative school performance as measured by national tests have also had a severe impact on black students. For example, Gillborn claims that:

Where equity is not monitored and crude notions of league table 'standards' are prioritised, the outcome is frequently a worsening of existing inequality. In the decade following the 1998 Act, for example, there was a dramatic rise in the proportion of young people ending compulsory schooling with five or more higher grade (A* to C) passes in their General Certificate of Education (GCSE) examinations: from around 30 per cent in 1988 to just over 46 per cent in 1998. At the same time, however, the inequality of attainment between black and white students worsened. In 1985 only 7 per cent of black students attained five or more higher grades, compared with 21 per cent of whites (a gap of 14 percentage points). By 1996 the gap had grown to 22 percentage points, with 23 per cent of black, and 45 per cent of whites attaining the same level (Commission for Racial Equality 1998; Drew 1995; Gillborn and Youdell 1998 p. 226).

(2001, p. 20)

Gillborn and Gipps, echoing Majors (2001), point out that New Labour (the 1997 Labour government), while accepting that there were inequalities in experience and attainment, produced no specific targets for raising minority attainment nor reducing black exclusions. However, Circular 10/99 states that: 'Schools should be aware of so called "colour blind policies" that can lead to the persistence of inequalities between ethnic groups' (DfEE, 1999a, p. 13). 'Colour blind' policies, such as asserting that 'all students be treated the same' can contribute to further inequalities in achievement when students from different cultural backgrounds have different pedagogical needs at school. Nevertheless, the circular does promote the ethnic monitoring of exclusions by schools and LEAs (DfEE, 1999b).

School or student?

Connors (2004) has outlined a comparison of explanations for school under-achievement of some minority ethnic groups, particularly African or Caribbean black boys, in the UK as offered by Osborne (2004) and Blair (2004) and the responses they propose in relation to these understandings. Blair suggests an examination of successful schooling for black children while Osborne is perhaps more concerned with social and psychological factors associated with under-achievement.

Osborne argues that all children enter school with positive attitudes, what Osborne refers to as 'identification with academics', but black boys are at high risk of developing a resistance to, or 'disidentification' with, school as the result of poor academic results, and retreat into a negative group stereotype. Both Blair and Osborne recognise that explanations have been sought within the children themselves and their culture.

Osborne examines in some detail three theoretical areas within social psychology, in some detail, and argues for the notion of school resistance ('disidentification' with academic learning). A stereotype threat theory (Steele,

1997) proposes that the school environment is aversive to members of groups with negative group stereotypes. A cultural-ecological theory (Ogbu, 1997) distinguishes between members of a minority culture whose forebears chose to live in the predominant culture and who seek education within that culture as the path to success, and involuntary immigrants. The latter, it is claimed, are more likely to develop social or collective identity in opposition to the predominant culture. A 'cool pose' theory (Majors and Billson, 1992) claims that survival in an environment of social oppression and racism leads to the adoption of flamboyant and non-conformist behaviour, leading to punishment in school settings.

Osborne claims that all three theories imply that black youngsters are at high risk of resistance to, or disidentification with, school education. He concludes that:

- disidentification is more likely from black boys;
- disidentification is a developmental process;
- identification with school learning is related to successful outcomes and that the social dynamics of an environment, for example, acceptance of difference, can affect academic outcomes.

It is perhaps this third conclusion that comes closest to the factors with which Blair is concerned: the effect of an 'aversive' school environment. Although Blair accepts that black children who behave badly, as with any other adolescents, are placed in lower academic sets (achievement groupings), she is more concerned with the institutional context as a factor and why they behave badly in a particular school. Osborne argues that black youngsters develop resistance to school, hence choosing to remove themselves from the source of their frustration and 'negative evaluation' to reduce their anxiety and to improve their self-esteem. Blair refers to 'cultural dissonance' in which white teachers do not understand black youngsters or their learning styles. Blair might claim children are as they are and that the institution and the individual both have a responsibility to respond to the culture, experiences, interests and needs of the whole range of children, hence the notion that for black youngsters racism is structural to an institution.

Similar challenges are faced by many New Zealand mainstream classroom teachers who find it hard to respond effectively to the cultural needs of Māori (Bishop *et al.*, 2003) and other minority culture students. Bevan-Brown (2003) in discussing Māori learners with special needs proposes a cultural checklist, framework and audit process to identify cultural gaps within the school's programme. School staff members then work collaboratively with Boards of Trustee and family members to embed aspects of the minority culture into the life of the school.

Addressing the issues

Gillborn (2004) argues that, in the UK, mainstream education policy has never been concerned to address racial inequality and racism. Policy strategies have been marginal and based on notions of increasing tolerance and understanding. Current approaches of British education policy, for a school population which he claims has always been ethnically diverse, are to be understood by reference to policies since the end of the Second World War.

Historical responses

Gillborn claims that migration to the UK from the Caribbean and the Indian subcontinent in the immediate post-war period, was followed by attempts to restrict immigration and to 'assimilate' black and Asian migrants into the existing culture, evidenced by the emphasis on the teaching of English as a second language and the dispersal of pupils around a number of schools to protect existing provision and respond to the concerns of white parents. He goes on to note that the late 1960s to late 1970s recognised cultural diversity, with inequality expressed through the growth of programmes to compensate for assumed cultural deficits. 'Tolerance' and 'diversity' were the rhetoric, but the new policy, as previously maintained, established educational arrangements and practices.

'Tolerance' and 'diversity' also figured from the late 1970s to late 1980s, but Gillborn argues that assumptions of differences in innate potential between races were challenged along with the suggestion that teachers might be implicated in race inequality. Gillborn claims that anti-racist perspectives and criticism of pedagogy were the result of resistance to the trend of existing public policy, marked, for example, by attempts to understand the racialised effects of education provision and the development of anti-racist policies in LEAs and schools, but anti-racist initiatives as such were never influential.

The mid-1980s to 1997, under successive Thatcherite Tory governments, were marked by 'education reform' in favour of a market in education where the majority predominate: a so-called 'colour-blind' approach where the interests of the white community become the priority and race inequalities were ignored, creating what Gillborn refers to as the 'new racism'. 1997 saw 'New Labour' maintain the education reforms of the previous administration, but declare high standards for all and a commitment to equality of opportunity which actually recognised ethnic inequalities in attainment and opportunity. However, discussions of racial inequalities did not influence the broad sweep of education policy.

Within a target-setting strategy, no targets existed for raising minority attainment. However, separate schooling for ethnic and religious groups was extended with surprisingly little debate, probably as an attempt to increase access and equity. Gillborn refers to this period as 'naïve multi-culturalism', marked by a failure to acknowledge and respond to more profound and structural forms of inequality.

Misunderstandings within the UK appear to have parallels in New Zealand. Institutions that do not work to ensure equity of participation for all groups may well be creating barriers to student achievement. Where these barriers work to disadvantage specific ethnic groups, those groups may issue challenges of institutional racism. When equity issues are not fully understood, cultural awareness programmes for non-minority groups cannot ensure equity of participation for all. A much greater structural response is needed in New Zealand schools than producing and delivering programmes and professional development that merely celebrate cultural diversity. Instead what is required are programmes and professional development to address and reduce the institutional racism. New Zealand is in a position to learn from the harsh experiences of some schools in the UK.

In 1999, following the racist attack and murder in South London of Stephen Lawrence, a black teenager, by several white youths, the Macpherson Report was commissioned to address the issues this tragedy raised (Macpherson, 1999). It indicated that less than half the schools it studied monitored achievement by ethnicity. With regard to the issue of racism, the report suggested that:

> the national curriculum should aim towards 'valuing cultural diversity and preventing racism'. These efforts should not duplicate the superficial multiculturalism of the 1970s that focused on dress, food, religion, holidays, festivals and events. This multicultural model is inappropriate for understanding deeper and more profound aspects of cultures (Majors, Gillborn and Sewell, 1998). Anti-racism should be about challenging and educating individuals about racism, rather than celebrating and reinforcing stereotypes (Blair and Gillborn, 1999).
>
> (Majors, 2001, p. 4)

Events at the time, such as the murder of Stephen Lawrence and the resulting inquiry (Macpherson, 1999), thrust the issue of racism to the forefront, but mainstream education policy was to reaffirm the existing National Curriculum as appropriate for the diverse nature of British society. On the margins, it did strengthen provision for citizenship education to yet again develop 'tolerance' and 'understanding' but without targeting anti-racist strategies in education.

The Ministry of Education in New Zealand is attempting to address issues such as these by placing a stronger emphasis on the system to assume greater responsibility for the success of Māori students and to increase the quality of educational services (early childhood through to tertiary) which are provided to Māori. This aim is embedded within overarching beliefs about the education system. In the New Zealand educational context, schools are now required to monitor the achievement of Māori students, in order to ensure that policies and practices are serving to enhance the achievement of Māori students. In talking about this, the Secretary of Education, Howard Fancy stated:

> I see the Ministry, as a whole, focused on building, and being part of an education system that looks to see every learner achieve to the best of their abilities:
>
> I would see learning success being characterised in three broad measures of achievement, namely:
>
> • strong foundation skills;
> • development of the highest possible levels of metacognitive skills;
> • strength in identity, culture, values, interpersonal and social skills.
>
> Together these would add up to an individual being 'educated for life'.
>
> I see the Ministry needing to respond to changes in the wider context in which we work. The context in which we work is being shaped by wider societal and international influences. We need to be both taking these factors into account in our work, and adapting to them.
>
> In some cases we also have a role in contributing to shifts in wider societal change such as attitudes to disability, discrimination and diverse cultures.
>
> We are looking to build a system unambiguously focused on raising the achievement of all students.
>
> (Fancy, 2003, verbal presentation)

In practice, for Māori, this has meant:

> The importance of a range of high quality education pathways for Māori students is emphasised as is the need to view quality as a broader concept valuing both Māori and global concepts.
>
> Increasing the responsibility and authority Māori exercise in relation to education has continued to be a high priority. More iwi [tribal] and other Māori organisations are working more directly with the Ministry and government through formal partnerships and other relationships.
>
> (Ministry of Education, 2003a)

Disley, the Group Leader of the New Zealand Ministry of Education's Group Special Education, sees this in practical terms as being able to ensure that:

> [in] every part of the organisation where decisions are made there are Māori voices.

We need to strengthen our ability to work in Māori spaces . . . as a group being able to better meet the needs of Māori families and students.

(2004, verbal presentation)

Current practice

Gillborn claims that racism and race inequality continue to be features of the British education system. Majors (2001) notes that the Labour government in the UK has prioritised what it terms 'social exclusion' for action. In terms of education, this includes school exclusions, truancy and under-achievement (ibid.). The Labour government in the UK in 1997 and 2000 set targets for reducing exclusions but no particular targets for reducing black exclusions. Majors claims that this is a failure of expressed national policy to reduce exclusions.

In some local areas in the UK, there have been particular efforts to address the issues of under-achievement and disaffection of minority ethnic groups. Community mentoring schemes and 'high quality' home–school liaison work are promoted by Circular 10/99 (DfEE, 1999a). The Minority Parents and Governors Group in Enfield has supported and been involved in the mentoring scheme in which mentors from the local black community work on a one-to-one basis with students to explore areas of difficulty and improve achievement (Grant and Brooks, 2000). A common experience is of the black parents having difficulties communicating with school. Parents and other members of the community, through the schools Mediation Service in Enfield, offer assistance to students, parents and teachers where there is a shared agreement that there are difficulties at school. Mediators can be in the school and mediation can last for three months before exclusion is contemplated. The LEA has tried to strengthen the power of the student and parent in the process by utilising pairs of mediators interviewing appropriate school staff separately and in the presence of parents and students.

However, Grant and Brooks (2000, p. 20) argue that black students will continue to be excluded disproportionately from mainstream schools because of:

- the absence of any radical government proposal to eliminate exclusions, not just to reduce them to current national average;
- the colour blind approach to the analysis of problems leading to exclusions;
- the new sanction of 'full-time' education other than at school.

Similar schemes in New Zealand schools have been implemented on the basis of consultation, collaboration and implementation by Māori groups. For example, He Ara Tika (the Right Pathway) provide additional youth mentoring support to Māori secondary students, their teachers and families in order to engage Māori students in learning. The initiative which is managed by seventeen Māori community providers across the country has also been found to reduce stand-downs (temporary exclusions) and suspensions among Māori students. The Annual Report on Māori Education reports that:

> The providers promote mentoring to schools, teachers, students and their families/whānau, recruit suitable people as mentors, match mentors to students, and monitor and support mentors and students in their mentoring relationships.
>
> (Ministry of Education, 2003b, p. 57)

Two alternative proposals

In considering steps that could be taken to address the issues of disaffection and under-achievement of minority ethnic groups, Osborne (2004) and Blair (2004) propose approaches related to their views on the causes of such phenomena. Their proposals therefore have rather different emphases. Osborne highlights the notion of overcoming students' 'resistance' to schooling, while Blair highlights the responsive, 'inclusive schooling'. A feature of one unsuccessful school, studied by Blair, was little recognition of minority cultures in the curriculum of those schools. As a part of a strategy for respecting all cultures, Blair describes a successful school which provided six-week courses of Afrikaans and Irish studies for all students to develop understanding and respect across the school. In contrast, Osborne criticises 'ethnic studies' additions to Eurocentric curricula. In a 'true' multicultural curriculum, he claims, the contributions of people of colour are infused throughout. However, Osborne also implies changing the attitudes and behaviour of black students through the teaching of black values in Europe (Afro-centric socialisation): mutual respect and cooperation, commitment and love of family, race, community and country, in contrast to what he sees as individualism and competition in white European culture. In New Zealand, Smith (1990) criticised an earlier Ministry of Education policy initiative to introduce a 'Māori dimension' (Taha Māori) into all schools to provide better information about Māori culture and language for the benefit of Māori students. However, Smith indicated that this policy instead resulted in an unfortunate 'capture' and selective modification of this knowledge to better serve the interests of the non-Māori community.

Osborne recommends promoting intelligence as developmental and the replacement of remedial teaching arrangements for black students, with a supportive and collaborative learning and teaching environment in which black youngsters are seen to cope within the mainstream school curriculum. This approach seems to avoid deficit theorising embedded in remedial approaches and moves instead to changing the pedagogical practices of the mainstream school. Blair perceives black boys in lower sets because they behave badly in response to inappropriate and unsuccessful school provision.

Both Blair and Osborne argue for closer links between secondary school and post-school institutions. The purpose, for Osborne, is to encourage secondary school completion. For Blair, the purpose is to recognise that black youngsters are disadvantaged in post-school opportunities.

Osborne's suggestions for changes within black children, in contrast to Blair's emphasis on changes within institutions, are also noticeable with respect to interventions in black communities. Interventions are suggested to change community and family norms to emphasise academic achievement and encourage black students to identify with education and school learning: 'accommodation without assimilation'. Osborne argues for a number of strategies to allow students to behave according to school norms while at school, and community norms while at home. For example, minority community youngsters might receive special counselling. Respected members and leaders of the community are to reinforce attitudes and behaviours that lead to academic success alongside attitudes and behaviours that maintain ethnic identity. The community ought to demonstrate, through examples, that academic achievement is valued equally with other activities such as sporting achievements. Members of the community, usually people who have voluntarily moved into the dominant culture, who use their academic success to leave, should be encouraged to remain within the community.

In contrast, Blair's suggestions are conceived from the outset in an inclusive 'whole-school' response. For her, the issue is change within schools in order to respond to a wider variety of student needs. Black children need to know that they are not only wanted but are also welcome in school. Black children will know this through seeing their culture respected and through awareness that the school understands the political issues that beset them as black people. The hopes of black parents that their children will benefit from education and school are the same as any other parents. A partnership with black parents would treat parents of minority ethnic groups with respect by listening to their concerns, consulting with them and giving them a voice. In the successful school that Blair describes, there is a commitment to work with black parents and to forge strong relationships between the school and the black community, with consultation on policies and school governance.

Blair places strong emphasis on a school climate and ethos in which the views of black students, along with those of all students, are listened to and respected. The essential factor is having teachers who respect diversity and who are open to learn and understand the issues that affect the students, including their political and social concerns. Students' needs and concerns as adolescents should be recognised alongside needs arising from their ethnic and racial identities. In the successful school, the views of black students on poor behaviour and poor relations within school were sought and respected.

The commitment of teachers was essential to success and this required their participation in frank discussions about the basic philosophy and culture of the school, staff development on equality of opportunity and consultations with students to decide what they want from school. Teachers were encouraged to develop their understanding of adolescence for young people and particularly the different needs of black adolescents.

Osborne and Blair take different views of adolescence as a complicating factor, which affects both black and white students in secondary schools. Osborne, for example, although not making explicit reference to the complications of adolescence, implies that there is a conflict between the norms of the black community and the norms of education and schooling for black youngsters. The 'cool pose' theory suggests that black youngsters, for survival in a school or society environment of 'social oppression and racism', adopt 'flamboyant and non-conformist behaviour'. Blair points out that black youngsters are adolescents in a different situation from white youngsters, both within the culture of the school and the wider society. For example, black adolescent boys are growing up in the context of being negatively stereotyped according to what people think black boys are like.

Harnessing students' understandings

One way of addressing problematic student behaviour that is integral to a socio-cultural view of learning and behaviour, but has often been lacking in schools, is through engaging with the views of the students themselves. Among the salient features of a socio-cultural approach, according to Davies (2004), is an emphasis on the 'indivisibility' of human action, both internal and external to the individual, and of the context in which it occurs. Learning is viewed as taking place through 'participation' and as transforming the individual learner's identity. The sense of belonging to, or marginalisation from, a community affects every aspect of participation and, therefore, learning within it, and also affects a student's behaviour and self-perception. Notions of 'inclusion' from this perspective can be interpreted as the extent to which students are able to participate in the school community on the basis of who they are, without having to leave their cultural identity at the gate.

Some of the issues Davies raises are fundamental to understanding and addressing behavioural concerns in schools. Among them is an understanding that a basic human need is the sense of belonging and acceptance in a social group which shows care and respect for its members. The identity of community members is influenced by the extent to which the group engages and acknowledges them. It may not be easy to engage with and acknowledge students whose behaviour in schools is experienced as challenging or threatening, but nevertheless they have the same basic needs as any other student.

In New Zealand, Glynn, Berryman, Atvars and Harawira (1997) worked with Māori students themselves in order to enhance conditions for other students who experience behavioural and learning challenges. This research suggests ways of developing positive, bi-cultural partnerships between parents, their children, other family members and the teachers themselves. Students suggested an approach that promotes co-operation and collaboration between families and teachers through the sharing of detailed information as well as human resources and skills. This approach capitalises on the strengths available within families, children and teachers, that will enable them to take joint responsibility for overcoming the behaviour and learning difficulties encountered. Working with Years 9 and 10 Māori students in mainstream schools, Bishop, Berryman, Richardson and Tiakiwai (2003) also learned from the students. These students talked openly about how they saw their teachers positioning themselves in relation to Māori students. According to the majority of Māori students who were interviewed in each of the schools, teachers' perceptions of Māori students were extremely problematic.

Students said:

> We are nothing Māori if we are good in class, but we are Māori if we smoke pot or whatever. (Engaged students, School 2)

> Some of us have good answers and we never get to say them. Yeah but the teacher doesn't know that! They just think all Māori will answer questions stupid.
>
> Some teachers are racist. They say bad things about us, We're thick. We smell. Our uniforms are paru (dirty). They shame us in class. Put us down . . . Say things about our whānau (family). They blame us for stealing when things go missing. Just because we are Māori. (Non-engaged students, School 1)
>
> (Bishop *et al.*, 2003, p. 47)

They also provided discourses rich in solutions regarding the kinds of relationships, interactions and strategies that would help teachers to facilitate Māori students' engagement with their learning:

> They have to laugh with you instead of just sitting there, but still keeping us in line. Keep the class in order, but still laughing with you . . . that helps you like the subject.
>
> The marking should tell us what we are doing wrong and how we can do it better . . . Even when it is a cross, they should tell us how we can fix it and explain it to us because a cross doesn't mean anything to me because I won't even remember what the question was, I have just got the answer and it is wrong. That does not help me learn from that mistake. (Engaged students, School 1)
>
> (ibid., pp. 52–3)

When this effective teacher profile was applied in a professional development process with teachers from four secondary schools, the classroom results supported the conclusion that the students' suggestions were valid.

In reporting on student change as a result of the effective teacher profile and associated professional development, the authors conclude:

> Māori students' on task engagement increases, their absenteeism reduces, their work completion increases, the cognitive levels of the classroom are able to increase, and their short-term achievements increase; in many cases dramatically so.
>
> (ibid., p. 2)

Conclusion

Clearly there are important challenges for schools who seek to address issues of the under-achievement of groups of students who experience alienation from the education system as a result of cultural difference. As Bruner (1996) notes, one of the prime responsibilities of schools is to support the construction of a student's sense of self through an acknowledgement of agency and the development of self-esteem. Within an institution, both educators and students are defined by that institution's social practices. Participation in a community is 'transformative' both for participants and for the group (Davies, 2004). It is essential, therefore, to examine the way in which school practices contribute to a student's sense of agency and personal esteem and, therefore, to the construction of a concept of self, and his/her feelings about being able to cope with the world both during and after the years of compulsory schooling.

Chapter 5

Biological and medical explanations of behaviour

Introduction

Biological and medical explanations of behaviour theorise problems as emanating from within the individuals themselves. Difficult or challenging behaviour, from a medical perspective, is the result of an underlying condition, disease or dysfunction which an individual has and which requires treatment. A behaviour problem is seen as an inherent characteristic of an individual. However, because behaviour is also located within a social context, establishing the existence of a condition or disease of 'difficult behaviour' or 'emotional disorder' as relating to the individual alone and not to the context in which it occurs is fraught with problems.

In this chapter we first discuss two biologically and medically based understandings of behaviour and the implications of these understandings for practice in schools. We go on to outline a fundamentally different understanding of behaviour within a holistic view of well-being.

Attention Deficit/Hyperactivity Disorder (AD/HD)

Among the ways of conceptualising behaviour experienced as challenging to teachers and (often) to parents also is the medically based notion of Attention Deficit/Hyperactivity Disorder (AD/HD). This is described by Norwich *et al.*:

> AD/HD is a medical diagnosis of the American Psychiatric Association. It is characterised by chronic and pervasive (to home and school) problems of inattention, impulsiveness, and/or excessive motor activity which have seriously debilitating effects on individuals' social, emotional and educational development, and are sometimes disruptive to the home and/or school environment. Between two and five per cent of British school children are believed to experience this condition (BPS, 1996). The coming of this diagnosis has revived traditional conflicts between

medical and educational perspectives on EBD, which affect the way in which practitioners approach problems surrounding childhood attention and activity problems.

(2002, p. 182)

Norwich *et al.* reflect on the differences in the reported incidence of AD/HD internationally, and possible reasons for this:

> up to 9% of US children diagnosed as AD/HD in certain regions compared to only 0.007% in the UK (Hinshaw, 1994; Prendergast *et al.*, 1988; Schachar, 1991; Taylor, 1994; Holowenko and Pashute, 2000). These variations reflect several factors, including how the diagnostic systems are interpreted and used in practice by professionals, and cultural practices as regards diagnosis in this field.
>
> (ibid.)

It may be assumed from these comments that the use and interpretation of a diagnosis of AD/HD may vary in relation to the sensitivity of the professionals in assessing how far different contexts encourage behaviour that is impulsive and inattentive.

Another possible reason for the variations in incidence of the AD/HD diagnosis may lie in the differential access to funding provision for students with AD/HD in different parts of the USA and the UK, and, indeed, other parts of the world also. There is a 'perverse' incentive to individualise behaviour problems, and to categorise and label in order to attract funding to schools where this is supported by statute.

The category AD/HD originated in the USA but is now in widespread international use. As the British Psychological Society (BPS) notes, the 'defining feature' of AD/HD is students' behaviour which 'appears inattentive, impulsive and overactive to an extent that is unwarranted for their developmental age and is a significant hindrance to their social and educational success' (1996, p. 13). In Britain and Europe, unlike the USA, the tradition has been 'to use the diagnostic systems of the International Classification of Diseases (ICD) published by the World Health Organisation' (1990) and to assume a 'hyperkinetic disorder'. There is a strict requirement for 'pervasiveness and persistence'. This means that behaviour which is seen largely only in one context only does not constitute grounds for a diagnosis.

The criteria for diagnosis of hyperkinetic disorder in the ICD-10 manual, for example, are as follows (BPS, 1996, p. 16):

A. Demonstrates abnormality of attention and activity at home, for the age and developmental level of the child, as evidenced by at least three of the following attention problems:

a. Short duration to spontaneous activity.
b. Often leaving play activities unfinished.
c. Over-frequent changes between activities.
d. Undue lack of persistence at tasks set by adults.
e. Unduly high distractibility during study.

and by at least two of the following activity problems:

f. Continuous motor restlessness.
g. Markedly excessive fidgeting or wriggling during spontaneous activities.
h. Markedly excessive activity in situations requiring relative stillness.
i. Difficulty in remaining seated when required.

B. Demonstrates abnormality of attention and activity at school or nursery, for the age and developmental level of the child, as evidenced by at least two of the following attention problems:

a. Undue lack of persistence at tasks.
b. Unduly high distractibility, i.e. often orienting towards extrinsic stimuli.
c. Over-frequent changes between activities when choice is allowed.
d. Excessively short duration of play activities.

and by at least two of the following activity problems:

e. Continuous and excessive motor restlessness in school.
f. Markedly excessive fidgeting and wriggling in structured situations.
g. Excessive levels of off-task activity.
h. Unduly often out of seat when required to be sitting.

C. Directly observed abnormalities of attention or activity. This must be excessive for the child's age and developmental level. The evidence may be any of the following:

a. Direct observation of the criteria in A or B above.
b. Observation of abnormal levels of motor activity, or off-task behaviour, or lack of persistence in activities, in a setting outside home or school.
c. Significant impairment of performance on psychometric tests of attention.

D. Does not meet criteria for pervasive development disorder, mania, depressive or anxiety disorder.

E. Onset before the age of 6 years.

F. Duration of at least 6 months.

G. IQ above 50.

However, while behavioural rating scales are an accessible, expedient way to quantify adult perception of students' behaviour, behaviour assessment which is intended to lead to intervention in the context of a student's education needs to take account of a comprehensive range of factors that influence the student's behaviour in the context of school. This assessment is seen as its most constructive when it includes an assumption that the student will be actively involved and participating in the process (BPS, 1996).

Defining AD/HD as a mental disorder is problematic:

> We have evidence that children given the diagnosis AD/HD don't attend, don't wait and don't sit still. But just because they don't do all these things does not mean that they cannot do them. The pattern of AD/HD-type behaviour might be maladaptive to environmental requirements, but it is not necessarily the result of psychological dysfunction.
>
> The adoption of a disease model may of course have advantages in helping those with severe, persistent and pervasive hyperkinetic problems conceptualise their difficulties in a way that aids therapy (Taylor, personal communication). But when it comes to the large and heterogeneous group of children subsumed under the heading AD/HD, advantages may be outweighed by:
>
> • A lack of evidence that ADHD is the result of a fixed psychological dysfunction;
> • The potentially limiting effect of the language of mental disorder in developing environmental approaches to intervention; and
> • The possibility of stigmatisation.
>
> (BPS, 1996, p. 23)

There is also some evidence that some students experience intolerance to particular foods and there is the suggestion of a link between this and difficult behaviour. 'Common allergens included additives, chocolate, dairy products, wheat, oranges and other fruit. These particular substances are found in many commercially produced foods and medicines' (ibid., p. 52). The area of the influence of diet over behaviour is largely under-researched and controversial:

> There is evidence to suggest that diet may influence difficulties with attention and overactivity. For some children reducing access to certain substances appears to result in increased attention span, reductions in levels of motor activity and other behavioural changes. However, for other children dietary manipulation effects no change. Controlled diet, under the advice of a nutritionist, should not be dismissed if it is part of a multimodal intervention programme. Neither should we assume

it is an appropriate intervention for all children with ADHD-type behaviour.

(ibid., p. 53)

As we discuss in Chapter 8, in some cases, a medical diagnosis of problematic behaviour may result in a prescription for medication. There is research to indicate that psychostimulant medication, combined with psychological, social and educational support, may encourage student behaviour that is socially acceptable in schools. Of the three most commonly used psycho-stimulants, methylphenidate (Ritalin) is most widely prescribed. Where teachers and/or other educators are involved in the use of chemical forms of behaviour management, there are obviously ethical questions to be addressed, as we outline also in Chapter 8.

The concept of 'autism'

Autism is a medical explanation of behaviour that relates very closely to a within-person perspective. Sheehy (2004) describes how Kanner (1943) noted that a pattern of behaviour in a small group of young children seemed apparently inward-looking. Kanner termed this 'early infantile autism' after the Greek 'autos' (self). Separately, Asperger (1944), described older children whose behaviour was in some ways similar to that discussed in by Kanner's ideas. Asperger also used the term 'autistic' to describe this behaviour. Asperger Syndrome is commonly used now to refer to a 'form of autism used to describe people at the higher functioning end of the autistic spectrum' (National Autistic Society, 2004).

The National Autistic Society in the UK indicates that 'autistic spectrum disorders are estimated to touch the lives of over 500,000 families throughout the UK'. Autism is described as:

a lifelong developmental disability that affects the way a person communicates and relates to people around them. Children and adults with autism are unable to relate to others in a meaningful way. Their ability to develop friendships is impaired as is their capacity to understand other people's feelings.

People with autism can often have accompanying learning disabilities but everyone with the condition shares a difficulty in making sense of the world . . .

Reality to an autistic person is a confusing, interacting mass of events, people, places, sounds and sights. There seems to be no clear boundaries, order or meaning to anything. A large part of my life is spent just trying to work out the pattern behind everything.

A person with autism

(http://www.nas.org.uk/nas/jsp/polopoly.jps?d=211)

Wing and Gould (1979) identified a broader group of 'autistic' children, about 15 in 10,000, showing a 'triad of impairments' in the areas of social interaction, communication and imagination. 'These children experience difficulties in both verbal and non-verbal communication, and in important aspects of their play activities' (Sheehy, 2004, p. 339):

> *Social interaction* (difficulty with social relationships, for example, appearing aloof and indifferent to other people).

> *Social communication* (difficulty with verbal and non-verbal communication, for example, not really understanding the meaning of gestures, facial expressions or tone of voice).

> *Imagination* (difficulty in the development of play and imagination, for example, having a limited range of imaginative activities, possibly copied and pursued rigidly and repetitively).

> In addition to this triad, repetitive behaviour patterns are a notable feature and a resistance to change in routine.
>
> (http://www.nas.org.uk/nas/jsp/polopoly.jps?d=211)

Sheehy notes the occurrence of difficulties in learning among autistic young people:

> Eighty percent of children with autism score below 70 on the psychometric tests of intelligence (Peeters and Gilberg, 1999) and increasingly severe general learning difficulties are correlated with an increasing occurrence of autism. Consequently, a high proportion of children with autism have severe or profound learning difficulties and it becomes difficult to separate out the effects of autism and those of having profound learning difficulties (Jordan, 1999).
>
> (2004, p. 339)

Agreed diagnostic criteria consisting of a profile of symptoms and characteristics of autistic behaviour are used to identify autism in young people. The *Diagnostic and Statistical Manual of the American Psychiatric Association* (DSM-IV) lists the criteria for autism:

A. A total of six (or more) items from (1), (2), and (3), with at least two from (1), and one each from (2) and (3)

(1) qualitative impairment in social interaction, as manifested by at least two of the following:

---

a) marked impairments in the use of multiple nonverbal behaviors such as eye-to-eye gaze, facial expression, body posture, and gestures to regulate social interaction

b) failure to develop peer relationships appropriate to developmental level

c) a lack of spontaneous seeking to share enjoyment, interests, or achievements with other people (e.g. by a lack of showing, bringing, or pointing out objects of interest to other people)

d) lack of social or emotional reciprocity (note: in the description, it gives the following as examples: not actively participating in simple social play or games, preferring solitary activities, or involving others in activities only as tools or 'mechanical' aids)

(2) qualitative impairments in communication as manifested by at least one of the following:

a) delay in, or total lack of, the development of spoken language (not accompanied by an attempt to compensate through alternative modes of communication such as gesture or mime)

b) in individuals with adequate speech, marked impairment in the ability to initiate or sustain a conversation with others

c) stereotyped and repetitive use of language or idiosyncratic language

d) lack of varied, spontaneous make-believe play or social imitative play appropriate to developmental level

(3) restricted repetitive and stereotyped patterns of behavior, interests and activities, as manifested by at least two of the following:

a) encompassing preoccupation with one or more stereotyped and restricted patterns of interest that is abnormal either in intensity or focus

b) apparently inflexible adherence to specific, nonfunctional routines or rituals

c) stereotyped and repetitive motor mannerisms (e.g. hand or finger flapping or twisting, or complex whole-body movements)

d) persistent preoccupation with parts of objects

B. Delays or abnormal functioning in at least one of the following areas, with onset prior to age 3 years:

(1) social interaction

(2) language as used in social communication

(3) symbolic or imaginative play

C. The disturbance is not better accounted for by Rett's Disorder or Childhood Disintegrative Disorder

According to the National Autistic Society in the UK (2004), the exact causes of autism are still not known, although there is evidence that genetic factors are implicated. Research also indicates that a variety of conditions affecting brain development which occur before, at, or soon after birth are associated with autism. According to the UK National Autistic Society, what is needed in educational terms to support the learning of such students is a 'specialist' approach and 'structured support' (http://www.nas.org.uk/nas/jsp/polopoly. jps?d=211).

Autism is a medical diagnosis of a 'condition'. However, the three most common approaches are designed to address the behaviour in context through manipulating the environment, not through administering medication. These approaches are: behavioural, cultural and social (Sheehy, 2004). An example of the first is applied behavioural analysis (ABA) which we discuss further in Chapter 6. 'ABA is built on behavioural methods such as reducing identified tasks into small discrete "teachable" steps reinforcing appropriate behaviours associated with each step, and using highly structured intensive teaching strategies' (Sheehy, 2004, p. 342).

An example of what might be described as a 'cultural' approach is 'TEACCH' (Treatment and Education of Autistic and Related Communication Handicapped Children) (TEACCH, 1998) in which parental involvement is seen as an important element:

> TEACCH's unique approach is that it considers the way the child 'reads' their environment, rather than looking simply for environmental stimuli that might trigger particular behaviours. TEACCH considers the environment in terms of how the child will be able to interact and learn from it, and how the child him/herself will see the environment. Therefore a TEACCH-influenced classroom places a large emphasis on physically structuring the room to facilitate learning interactions within it.
>
> (Sheehy, 2004, p. 347)

An example of a social interactive approach is 'intensive interaction' where the child is seen as struggling to grasp the meanings embedded in his/her social world. In 'intensive interaction' interpersonal relationships are used to build and develop this meaning. The interaction between two people, the educator and the child, is assumed to generate the social interactions from which human abilities are constructed (Nind and Kellett, 2002). Key to this approach are:

- Responding to the behaviour of the child with autism 'as if' they had an intentional purpose.
- Adjusting one's own behaviours to establish social interplay and rapport.

- Allowing the person with autism to 'take the lead' in social interactions.
- Use rhythm and timing to give the interactions flow.
- Allowing the sessions to be enjoyable.

(Sheehy, 2004, p. 350)

Conflicting world-views

Oakley (2002) notes how the tensions between medicine and educational practice, and the differing professional roles can clash. In the following extract, Oakley describes what happened to Ravitch, a Research Professor in Education, who thought she might have a pulmonary embolism after a long flight and went to hospital:

> There Ravitch listened to the doctors discussing her condition, and she began to fantasise about what would happen if the doctors who were gathered round her bed discussing her treatment were to be replaced with education experts. The first thing that would happen would be the disappearance of the doctors' certainty that she had a problem. The education experts would argue about whether anything was actually wrong with her at all – after all, illness is a socially constructed experience. Some would point out that attributing problems to people is simply to blame the victim. In Ravitch's fantasy (or nightmare) the hospital administrator walks in at this point and announces that the hospital has just received a large grant to treat people like her. Immediately the experts decide that her symptoms are real after all, but now they are unable to agree on what to do. Each has their favorite cure, and each cites different sets of research 'findings' to support their case. Ravitch, who did get better, because there is an established and effective treatment for her complaint, was left wondering why medicine and education should behave so differently (Ravitch, 1999).

(Oakley, 2002, pp. 281–2)

In the context of school the differences in world-views held by different professional groups and their different ways of working may make it difficult for those groups to negotiate effective working partnerships based on reciprocal understandings. These differences may also have a very important influence on students' educational experiences in schools. The behaviour of children and young people in a school environment is judged by outside professionals, staff, peers and parents. Where a student has a particular disability, it is easy to assume that difficult behaviour relates to that disability alone, and cannot be regarded as understandable in the same way as any other student's behaviour. It is also easy to abnegate the responsibility for reflecting on ways in which the learning environment creates barriers to positive learning experiences for those students.

In the section below, a former teacher reflects on her own experiences of dealing with a student, Sara, who had Down Syndrome. Sara was involved in the process of integration into a mainstream primary school in 1987, prior to the shift towards inclusive education policies and practices. Her inclusion in the primary school was under threat, owing to what was perceived to be her 'behaviour difficulty' in the classroom:

> Sara, aged 5, had been attending a school for two terms. Her mother had insisted on the local authority placing her in this school, refusing to send her to a special school. I attended the annual review for this child before I started my post. The staff were suggesting that the placement was not suitable for Sara as she was hitting the children in the playground and that this was not appropriate behaviour and indicated that she would be better off in a special school. I interrupted, having observed Sara in the classroom, and being an experienced teacher in a special school I suggested that the special school would not be a 'better place' for her and that once in post I would be able to change her behaviour. I suggested that rather than view her behaviour as disturbed, she was trying to communicate with her peers, but did not know how to do this in an acceptable way. Once she was able to be taught this and could learn how to communicate in an appropriate way, she would be able to play with her peers. Her mother became very emotional and thanked me for my positive view. I was asked by the head teacher how I would implement these changes. I suggested a behaviour modification approach of rewards and clear instructions about how she would be expected to communicate with her peers in the playground. I also explained that this would be done in co-operation with the class teacher and the assistant. After a few weeks, Sara's behaviour had improved. She had learnt how to make friends and how to touch others appropriately. She also had a selection of activities to do at playtime if she became bored. Later she went on to secondary school with her peers to study for her A-level Art.
>
> (Paige Smith, unpublished)

Furlong suggests that an explanation for Sara's behaviour might be:

> schooling is a highly demanding experience which inevitably gives rise to many emotional injuries. Most children live with these 'injuries' – they repress the emotion and carry on with the business of schooling, perhaps finding another more acceptable outlet for their feelings.
>
> (1991, p. 305)

According to Furlong, there are two groups of students who will not find an acceptable outlet for their feelings. Students will challenge those in authority and will show aggression if they have been affected by their school experience and will draw on their friendship groups for support and will oppose school. Other students are emotionally vulnerable, the demands of school will be overwhelming for them and hence they experience conflict and reject their school. If these students reject their school, they still require support for coping with their high degree of emotionality. Furlong suggests that the latter students are in the minority, but students who suffer 'injuries' at school cope by forming a subculture and 'evolve a social solution to their psychological problem' (ibid., p. 306). This gives them a rationale for rejecting school as a way of dealing with their experience of schooling. This way of explaining their experiences has been frequently documented in the literature on students' perspectives on their deviant behaviour. Sara would have been unable to express her reasons for her 'deviant' behaviour due to her learning difficulty.

Holistic views of well-being

Alongside biological and medical understandings is the acknowledgement by some cultures that these elements are only one part of a more holistic understanding of well-being. Fundamental to the underlying beliefs of these cultural foundations is the need to respect the uniqueness and integrity of all people, and the interconnectedness of people in extended family groups.

In the New Zealand context, for example, Durie (1994) presents a Māori model of well-being that is conceptualised in terms of the four walls of a house (*te whare tapa whā*), each wall providing a key foundation for one's holistic well-being. The four walls are made up of a spiritual side (*taha wairua*), a physical side (*taha tinana*), a side to do with intellect and feelings (*taha hinengaro*), and a side to do with relationships and social support (the family), the extended family and the community (*taha whānau*). The core values concerned with identity, self-esteem and sense of purpose are held intact, and the person is in a state of well-being (*oranga*) when all four sides of the house are strong. The *whare tapa whā* model locates well-being both within the individual and in the social and cultural contexts.

While Pere (1994) agrees that *wairua* or spirituality is an important component of an individual's well-being, Macfarlane (1998) points out that educational environments also have a *wairua* or ethos which is influenced by the mana (prestige, authority, charisma) of educators. The institutional ethos (*wairua*), represented in the values, actions and intentions of staff and students, can work to enhance or undermine the well-being of cultural minority students. In a New Zealand context, behaviour interventions with Māori students require attention to all four elements (both within person and environmental factors) if holistic well-being is to be addressed effectively.

Durie (1994) goes further to suggest that there are also four key cultural foundations that must underpin work with Māori. These are:

- *Mauriora* (open and full access to one's indigeneity). Separation from traditional knowledge, language and land has led to ongoing and increasing reclamation movements to relearn and revitalise practices that historically led to the well-being of indigenous populations.
- *Waiora* (environmental protection and well-being). This is linked to the spiritual element that directly connects the wellness of Māori as a people to their relationships with cosmic, terrestrial and water environments. In general terms it is easy to see how pollution or any lack of respect for the physical environment impacts upon human well-being.
- *Toiora* (healthy positive lifestyles). This denotes healthy and positive lifestyles which are focused against risks that pose a threat to well-being of self, family or communities. In the modern world this would include things such as drugs and alcohol but would also include social environments that generate or foster abusive relationships.
- *Te oranga* (well-being, participation in society). *Te oranga* is dependent on the terms upon which one participates in society and the authority with which one is legitimated and has access to society's benefits. As the gap in educational achievement between Māori and non-Māori continues to increase, and as disproportionately more Māori students find themselves excluded from schooling, Māori people are asserting the need for different classroom and school approaches to behaviour management. They argue that such approaches should build on the four elements of well-being that come from within a Māori world-view.

Conclusion

In what are often referred to as 'medical' or 'functional deficit models' of problematic behaviour, explanations involve a process of expert diagnosis based on specific symptoms to identify the existence of an underlying condition or illness and then remedial intervention or treatment to provide a cure. Sometimes the underlying condition is 'real' in the sense of having a genetic or physical base. Even so, the behaviour associated with these causes occurs in a social context. Hence the learning environment and pedagogy exert strong influences even over student behaviour associated with biological damage or disfunction. For example, one common treatment for AD/HD may be the prescription of a chemical psychostimulant. However, as noted by the British Psychological Society (1996), apart from all the ethical considerations, prescribing a drug provides an insufficient response. Also needed are appropriate social support mechanisms in school and outside, including ways to address barriers to learning within the classroom or school context.

Focusing on the medical and/or biological bases alone to explain behaviour is likely to provide an insufficient remedy because it ignores the holistic nature of well-being and, therefore, all those other elements which contribute to it.

Students' core values associated with self-identity, self-esteem and a sense of purpose as a functioning member of a social and cultural group must also be considered in addressing overall well-being. These core values and associated preferred behaviour interaction patterns vary extensively between different cultural groups, and may either align with, or conflict with, prevailing values and patterns of interactions within classrooms and schools. There is a great deal of room for exploring ways in which more inclusive pedagogies within classrooms and schools might improve the learning and behaviour of students who are diagnosed as AD/HD or as autistic.

Chapter 6

Psychological understandings of behaviour

Introduction

Bruner (1996) notes, from a socio-cultural view of the human mind, that the meaning of any proposition is relative to the frame of reference in which it is conceptualised. Each culture has its own ways of constructing reality. The degree to which understanding a concept in any specific way is right or wrong has to be judged against its own frame of reference. Psychological interpretations of behaviour have profound effects on conceptualisations of the behavioural interventions in common use in schools, and need to be seen as cultural constructs (Bruner, 1996) and not as universal givens. It is easy for psychological constructs of a dominant cultural group to be understood as normal and universal. This is a very important issue in schools because different psychological approaches are underpinned by different ways of understanding human learning and behaviour and legitimise different ways of engaging with students and attempting to change their behaviour. The psychological discourses of educators reveal the theoretical constructs by which they position themselves, and from which they operate. However, these constructs and operations can lead to deficit theorising and positioning others as problematic. One crucial component of deficit theorising and positioning others as problematic within psychological discourses is the lack of attention to culture. Neglect of the importance of cultural values, practices and preferences as both antecedents (setting events) as well as providing specific consequences for behaviour in classrooms and schools severely limits the power of psychology to contribute to the improvement of learning and behaviour in minority student education.

This chapter outlines a range of different psychological approaches to understanding and changing behaviour in educational contexts. A number of these share a common focus from the field of applied behavioural analysis which Sulzer-Azaroff and Meyer (1977) identify as a systematic method of changing behaviour that is performance-based and self-evaluative. It can be used for preventing and treating of behavioural 'problems' and in learning programmes.

Characteristic of an applied behavioural analysis approach includes assessing and intervening in behaviour within the context where it occurs, focusing on observable events through the use of systemic gathering and recording of data over time, employing research design that explore relationships between behaviour, contextual factors and reinforcement contingencies (Baer *et al.*, 1968). In the New Zealand educational context these elements have provided the conceptual framework for ten operational principles for changing behaviour in school, home and community settings (Berryman and Glynn, 2001). These principles (see Chapter 9) include four that are aimed at changing contextual factors (antecedents of behaviour) and six that are aimed at changing the timing, frequency and form of reinforcing contingencies (consequences of behaviour). Many different procedures and strategies can be constructed on the basis of these principles. [Challenges of cultural appropriateness and cultural responsiveness of behaviour management procedures and strategies arise when teachers and pupils come from different cultural contexts.] These challenges will be addressed in this chapter and in the following chapters.

Understanding 'emotional and behavioural difficulties'

Efforts to understand and change students' behaviours that are seen as problematic are fraught with difficulties arising from the way in which language is used to label those behaviours. Kauffman (1995) observes that the changing terminology employed reflects a growing consensus that both emotions and behaviour are involved in the notion of a behavioural disorder. Indeed, many labels used to describe behaviour are emotionally laden. Some labels locate the problem or disorder entirely within the individual, for example, emotionally disturbed, emotionally disabled, or behaviourally disordered. Other labels are used which convey a sense of judgement in terms of some accepted position on what behaviours are normal or acceptable and what are not, for example, delinquent, maladaptive, and anti-social. Still other labels convey more about the effects of specific behaviours on the individuals using them than they do about the behaviours themselves, for example, hurtful, distressing, disturbing, undesirable, and intolerable.

Behavioural researchers strive to find ways of talking about behaviour that minimise these labelling problems. The approach taken to describing and changing behaviour in a New Zealand school and community programme known as Hei Āwhina Mātua (supporting parents) (Glynn *et al.*, 1997) follows the behaviour interactionist perspective (Wheldall and Glynn, 1989). In this perspective behaviour is observed and analysed within the social, cultural and physical contexts in which it occurs. Behaviour is interpreted and understood in terms of the social interactions with other people around shared tasks and challenges. The place to begin a search for understandings and solutions to the problems generated by students' behaviour is with the students themselves. Input from students into the design and evaluation of the resources and programme in Hei Āwhina Mātua is one of its most distinctive features. Involving students themselves in this way provides a means of addressing issues of power and control that can arise between dominant culture schools and minority culture pupils, when schools do not respond to the language and cultural needs of their students.

Bennathan (2000, pp. 3–5) discusses the problematic status of students with emotional and behavioural difficulties (EBD) as a special educational need in the UK and notes that:

> Historically, individual differences in children had been seen as the main cause of differing educational progress, but the idea that individual differences in schools may be just as important is one that has been gaining ground over the last generation and is now centre stage. Rutter and colleagues (1979), in their landmark research, *Fifteen Thousand Hours: Secondary Schools and Their Effects on Children*, showed how schools with students from comparable backgrounds achieved widely varying educational outcomes. The (UK) Elton Report (DES, 1989), *Discipline in Schools*, also put the emphasis not on individual children and their circumstances but on the importance of creating a positive atmosphere in schools for all children and for their teachers.

This recognition makes it impossible to hold that all children who show EBD are a discrete group requiring special treatment. The situation is more complex than that, as is now officially recognized by central government, notably in the guidance which accompanied the 1993 Education Act . . . The Department for Education circular, *The Education of Children with Emotional and Behavioural Difficulties* (DfE, 1994b), is an admirable survey of the present state of thinking about such children. Of EBD as a special educational need, it states, 'There is no absolute definition . . . The difficulties are genuine. But EBD is often engendered or worsened by the environment, including schools' or teachers' responses'.

Some children have been so affected by extremely adverse experiences in their early years that they need more skilled help than can be offered by even the best mainstream schools. But the dangers in rushing to categorize children as EBD need to be underlined . . . First, the demand for special placement would be high, which goes against the well-accepted policy first stated by the Warnock Report and reinforced by the 1993 Act that, with few exceptions, children should have the opportunity of mainstream education as the best preparation for adult life. Secondly, special placement is extremely expensive, using resources for a few that might enhance educational standards for the many. Thirdly, and this is perhaps in the long run the most important caveat, children with EBD should not be seen as a race apart . . . Understanding the processes that make a few children incontrovertibly 'EBD' helps to a greater awareness of the potential hazards for many more of the children in our schools. It can lead to an increased awareness of the emotional needs of all children, an understanding which ought to be part of the professional competence of all teachers.

(Bennathan, 2000, pp. 3–5)

Bennathan's discussion highlights five issues of crucial importance which are also emphasised by Galloway *et al.* (1994, p. 112):

1   Discourses which locate EBD as an individual attribute can marginalise or render invisible notions that teachers and schools need to change in order to include rather than exclude such students. Where the problem is located determines the location of the solution.
2   The issue of mainstream or special provision as the most appropriate form of organising support for students whose behaviour is of concern needs to be under continual review.
3   It is important for all teachers to take into account the emotional needs of all students and to address concerns about their self-esteem.
4   It is important for all teachers to take into account the impact of inter-cultural contact and different understandings of the behaviour of both students and teachers.
5   There is no commonly agreed understanding of what an 'EBD' child is, except that EBD relies on the subjective judgements of teachers and other professionals rather than on any agreed objective criteria. The nearest professionals come to agreement is that while a child's behaviour may be both disturbed and disturbing, there are likely to be psychological or medical factors associated with the behaviour.

Teachers can make a difference

Armstrong and Galloway (1994) carried out research in three local education authorities (LEAs) in England and looked at the assessment process of 29 children, aged 5 to 16, referred to educational psychologists because of emotional and behavioural difficulties. They found that there was a significant difference in the way that teachers viewed children with disturbed behaviour and children with disruptive behaviour. Children with disturbed behaviour were considered to be unmanageable by the school or classroom practices, and it is understood that their needs 'cannot be met in mainstream schools'; this view was also expressed by the Elton Report on Discipline in Schools (DES, 1989). However the teachers in this research stated that 'if they had the opportunity to teach on a one-to-one basis they could easily cope with an emotionally disturbed child' (Armstrong and Galloway, 1994, p. 183). Armstrong and Galloway identified strategies used by teachers to legitimise the high rates of exclusion by placing an emphasis on disturbed, rather than disruptive behaviour 'and on the professional role of teachers being concerned with educating "normal" children' (ibid., p. 192). In contrast, inclusive pedagogies emphasise the teachers' role in varying their teaching strategies in order to meet the needs of increasingly diverse student populations. An emotionally disturbed child takes away the focus from the teacher's responsibility, as the label assumes that the child's personality and emotional or family history make it difficult for the child to be able to manage in a classroom. This again highlights the issue of how problematic behaviour is understood (as an individual attribute or as being associated with the learning environment). This strongly influences the way teachers view their own ability to address it.

Poulou and Norwich (2002, p. 112) comment on a review of international studies which 'reveals that children with EBD add to teachers' concerns and threaten their teaching authority. Dealing with children with EBD is considered to be a frustrating task for teachers and can generate feelings of helplessness and incompetence (Lennox, 1991; Bennett, 1992; Leadbetter and Leadbetter, 1993; Chazan et al., 1994; Gray et al., 1996).' Poulou and Norwich investigated the relationship between teachers' attribution of the causes of student behaviour that they found disturbing and their emotional, cognitive and behavioural reactions to that behaviour. Poulou and Norwich concluded that:

> ascribing children's problems to factors originating from teachers themselves, like 'their personality', 'manners towards the child with EBD', or 'teaching style', predicted the perceived nature of EBD as remediable. It appears that since teachers can control the cause of a difficulty, they perceive that they can also sufficiently treat it. In addition, they perceived themselves in such cases as even more responsible for finding an effective solution for the child's problem . . . It was also found that the more they attributed EBD to child factors, such as 'child wants to attract attention', 'child's innate personality' or 'inability to cope with school demands', the more they experienced feelings of 'stress', 'offence' and even 'helplessness', especially for conduct and mixed behaviour difficulties.
>
> (2002, p. 125)

Behavioural management approaches

Understanding the principles underlying behavioural approaches is particularly important in the area of special educational needs in schools because of the dominance of these approaches in generating interventions over a long period of time. Dwivedi and Gupta (2000, p. 76) comment that much of the research work on individual students' behaviour that is perceived as disturbing by teachers has been based on behavioural management approaches. The field of applied behaviour analysis employs strategies based on behavioural principles such as positive reinforcement, negative reinforcement, response cost, extinction, generalisation and discrimination. When behavioural principles are applied in classroom or school settings, the reinforcing conditions or consequences of behaviour as well as the physical and social context in which the behaviour occurs are systematically modified in order to improve students' behaviour.

Almost all of these behavioural principles have been derived from work with laboratory animals, for example, Skinner (1938). However, these same principles have been successfully applied to behavioural interactions between teachers and pupils in classroom and school contexts. Wheldall and Glynn (1989) present a range of such studies carried out in UK and New Zealand schools. They describe a behavioural interactionist perspective which emphasises the interdependence of student and teacher behaviour in classrooms, and provides clear evidence that much unacceptable or inappropriate student behaviour can result from the social reinforcement contingencies provided by teachers themselves. This behavioural interactionist perspective, while employing the observational methodology and behavioural strategies of applied behaviour analysis, also recognises the importance of working in natural settings and contexts, and using naturally occurring reinforcers. This perspective draws on theoretical constructs from different disciplines, and emphasises the interactive nature of learning, and the interdependence between teaching and learning roles. It seeks to assist students to take a greater degree of control over their own learning (self-management) and prioritises student initiation of learning interactions over teacher initiation, and values the learning opportunities provided by errors (rather than devising error-free learning tasks). Finally, the behaviour interactionist perspective acknowledges the complex professional skills required of teachers and rejects attempts to produce 'teacher-proof' materials and tasks, which would degrade the professional expertise of teachers. Instead, this perspective aims to enhance teachers' professional expertise through assisting them to create responsive, social contexts for students' independent learning (Glynn, 1985, 1987), and assisting them to work in collaborative partnership with parents and communities.

Merrett (1985) notes that the application of behavioural methods in the classroom is relatively recent, reaching the UK in the 1970s. Merrett observes that behavioural methodologies do not focus on identifying 'inner' causes of behaviour but hold that all behaviour is learned and, therefore, behaviour can be modified through intervening in the environment.

Because behavioural methodology is a scientifically based technology, the first requirement is an operational definition of the target behaviour which is of interest. For instance, if a child is thought to be 'hyperactive' Merrett suggests an operational definition of behaviours such as 'out of seat' will be required. Once the behaviour has been identified and operationally defined, Merrett then discusses the need for systematic observational sampling across times of day, situations, nature of activity, person in charge, and so on. Such observations need to be taken over a period of about five days to establish the baseline or operant level of responding. Once the operant level of responding can be clearly seen, Merrett recommends carrying out a functional analysis detailing the three stages or events to be considered in this analysis. These are:

A – the antecedent event(s), that is, whatever starts off or prompts
B – the behaviour, which is followed in turn by
C – the consequence(s).

In any particular situation or setting or when some particular signal or prompt is given, the child behaves in some way which we have identified by our definition. This is followed by a consequence or outcome, frequently provided by an adult and this either increases or decreases the likelihood that that response will be repeated in the same circumstances another time. If it is possible to identify the setting or the prompt then it may be possible to change the behaviour by changing one or the other of these. Alternatively, identification of the consequences, whether positively reinforcing or aversive, which are controlling the behaviour also allows us to intervene with a good chance of success.

(Merrett, 1985, p. 8)

Merrett discusses different interventions teachers might plan in response to the analysis of A–B–C contingencies.

Teachers are professionally involved in bringing about changes in children's behaviour both by changing their responses to stimuli about them (by teaching them to read for example) and by teaching them new responses. The reasoning is very direct. Teachers aim to change their pupil's behaviour. Behaviours are changed chiefly by changing the consequences. Therefore, teachers change their pupil's behaviours by changing the consequences of classroom behaviour.

Changes in the rate of responding can also be brought about by removing or changing the antecedents. A child who is stimulated by the activity and bustle of the classroom can be put to work in a more private 'carrell' or booth so that he is not distracted by the others.

(ibid.)

Merrett explains that when:

> A consequence of a behaviour is shown to be maintaining that behaviour at a high level then that consequence is, by definition, and regardless of its nature, reinforcing it positively. Sometimes teachers 'tell children off' for certain behaviours which are temporarily choked off but recur after a very short time, just a few minutes perhaps. This is very frustrating for the teacher but it may be the teacher's chiding which is maintaining the child's behaviour. By definition 'ticking off' is positively reinforcing the child's 'attention-seeking' behaviour. If that positive reinforcement is removed then the rate of occurrence of the behaviour will be reduced. It will eventually become extinguished.

Merrett then describes a range of procedures or strategies to maximise students' learning of new behaviours. These include 'shaping' or successive approximations either through forward chaining or backward chaining, which break complex tasks down into compound steps, and ensure that each step is reinforced in a particular sequence. Other procedures include modelling (where students are reinforced for matching the behaviour being displayed for them. Merrett (ibid., p. 11) presents four reasons for choosing positive reinforcement contingencies rather than aversive (punishment) contingencies in reducing the rate of acceptable or unacceptable behaviour in educational settings.

1 Punishment 'tends to become less effective the more it is used. Thus, the harshness of the punishment has to be increased by degrees to maintain its effectiveness'.
2 Although punishment 'may inhibit some responses', it does little to signal or reinforce behaviours that are acceptable or appropriate.
3 Punishment motivates 'escape and/or avoidance responses' such as lying and truanting.
4 Punishment 'becomes associated with fear, anxiety and guilt' which are completely out of place in educational settings. Furthermore, the teachers who dispense punishment reduce their effectiveness as dispensers of positive reinforcement.
5 Punishment both models and reinforces behaviours such as aggression and violence.

Rules

Classroom and school rules are examples of antecedent conditions (or setting events) that are intended to signify behaviour that is acceptable or appropriate. However, many such rules are negatively stated, and specify behaviours that are not acceptable or not to be tolerated in classroom or school contexts. Unfortunately such rules can also serve as antecedent conditions for teacher monitoring and providing punishing consequences for behaviour that is unacceptable. This can result in pupils receiving excessive teacher and peer attention for rule breaking and minimal reinforcement for rule compliance. Merrett (ibid., p. 12) points out that in order to be effective in teaching a new behaviour, positive reinforcement must be applied:

1 contingently (and only contingently)
2 immediately
3 consistently and
4 abundantly.

Merrett goes on to describe different types of reinforcers used by teachers and parents, such as tangible rewards, token reinforcers (for example, points exchangeable for tangible reinforcers) and social reinforcers (for example, smiles, praise, social attention but also access to enjoyable social interaction or shared activities with adults or peers). He also addresses issues of group-contingent reinforcement (for example, when pupils in small groups compete with other groups in teams to access positive reinforcers of any type).

However, what is more important than teacher or pupil choice of type of reinforcer is the specific behaviours signalled as appropriate, acceptable, eligible for reinforcement or for punishment. This is an area where cultural values, preferences and practices may be crucial in behaviour management. Some Pacific Island cultures value pupils' avoidance of eye contact with teachers or other authority figures as a means of showing respect. However, many teachers of European descent may regard students' avoidance of eye contact as showing disrespect. Some cultural groups value and facilitate individual achievement in a competitive context and teachers from these cultures may choose to reinforce high achieving or top scoring individuals. However, some Māori and Pacific Island cultures may value more highly, and facilitate pupil behaviours that contribute to the well-being and achievement of the group, and may choose to reinforce these behaviours. Clearly a considerable level of cultural knowledge and cultural competence is required of teachers intending to implement behaviour management procedures with students from cultural backgrounds different from their own.

Functional assessment of behaviour

One of the applications of a behavioural approach based on applied behaviour analysis is to enable an assessment of the functions served by particular behaviours. The purpose of functional assessment of behaviour that is causing concern in schools is to enable more clearly targeted planning for, and design of, interventions which are likely to be more effective. For example, if a student's challenging and aggressive behaviours serve the function of escape from a boring classroom context, then teachers sending him out of the classroom (as an intended punishment) will act as a positive reinforcer.

Moore (2004) describes functional analysis as an experimental approach to behavioural assessment in which variables hypothesised to maintain the target behaviour are systematically examined one independent variable at a time in order to isolate effects. For example, curricular expectations, tasks and instructional practices within the classroom are understood as antecedent events that involve students for a major part of their school day. When these curricular and instructional variables can be proven to be associated with the occurrence of undesirable behaviour, then a clear functional relationship can be established to link disruptive behaviour in the classroom to a mismatch with the curriculum tasks or teaching practices.

Functional assessment therefore aims to discover the antecedents, setting events and consequences that cause or maintain challenging behaviours. In order to do this, Moore argues, functional assessment must involve precise, objective procedures and be aimed at developing and selecting effective and efficient treatments. The functional analysis of such assessments then attempts to explain why a particular individual engages in such behaviour in a particular context. The analysis can then be used as a direct and reliable means for identifying the functional relationships between particular behaviours and specific antecedent or consequent events.

> The underlying assumption of a functional assessment is that if interventions and behavioural support plans are based on the function that the target behaviour serves for a given individual, interventions will be more effective and efficient in controlling and reducing levels of challenging behaviours.
>
> (ibid., p. 296)

Functional assessment has been criticised for being too labour-intensive, and requiring knowledge and/or resources beyond what school personnel or regular caregivers can be expected to give and for being too impractical to carry out in the home and/or school environmental conditions. However, Moore describes a range of non-experimental but practical, functional assessment procedures that have been designed to identify functional relationships between events in the natural environment and the occurrence or non-occurrence of a target behaviour.

Moore also describes a large and increasingly growing body of research, using functional analysis procedures published since 1982 and claims:

> While functional analysis procedures have been used primarily for children with intellectual and developmental disabilities in restrictive settings, these procedures have been extended recently to the population

of 'typically-developing' children exhibiting more high incidence inappropriate behaviour in less restrictive settings.

This work demonstrates conclusively that the identification of the function/s of problem behaviour is crucial in the design and implementation of successful behavioural interventions for low incidence, severe or persistent behaviour difficulties.

(ibid., p. 295)

Moore further claims that functional analysis procedures provide 'the most conclusive information of all assessment techniques' (ibid.).

He concludes that recent developments in curriculum-based assessment (CBA) procedures which directly link assessment to the curriculum and instruction (thus providing a measure of fit between instructional expectations and students' performance capability) could usefully be incorporated into functional assessment procedures. This would allow assessment of student performance levels, and simultaneously guide theorising about the function of disruptive behaviour in the classroom.

Challenges for behavioural approaches

We have noted that implementing behavioural management strategies while ignoring issues of culture will seriously limit their effectiveness. However, behavioural approaches are often criticised also for failing to take adequate account of the emotions. As Hanko comments:

Yapp (1991) points out, for children with problems, emotional factors affect learning, especially if we see only their provocative or withdrawn facade which usually hides children in constant misery, loneliness, self-loathing and fear

. . . teachers are frequently baffled by children who 'don't respond even to praise', 'spoil their work the moment I praise it', 'just shrug it off' and 'don't seem to care'. . . . There is a danger in perceiving praise and encouragement as synonymous. When children are praised, are they necessarily encouraged?

(1994, pp. 125–37, 166)

In Hanko's view, inappropriate use of praise can be damaging to some students:

Discouraged children, trapped in a self-concept created by past experiences of failure, will lose out in a particularly disheartening way when a praising teacher fails to understand, and thus to address, the effects of such painful experiences on their low self-image as learners.

Consequently, a praise-refusing student's determination not to be lured into the risks of failing yet again may be further reinforced.

(ibid., p. 166)

In operant terms, an effective positive reinforcer is what works to change behaviour. However, some teachers may actually have become aversive or frightening to some children. Hence any attention or praise from them may not be reinforcing at all. Crucial to an understanding of students' behaviour is an acknowledgement of the students' cognitive perspective on behaviour. This lack of understanding of the students' cognitive perspective can complicate things further when teachers come from different cultural backgrounds from their students.

> The emphasis on behavioural *techniques* as classroom management *skills*, when divorced from such understanding, raises the whole gamut of issues concerned with the concept of training as a legitimate part of the educational process. Evaluations of 'positive teaching' strategies (whether applied for the purpose of classroom management or to target specific children) point to hazards, such as mere conditioning through wanting to 'shape' children's behaviour, a process which ignores the emotional factors that influence learning and the failure to learn, and the crucial cognitive part of education, ie, which is thus not education (Hargreaves, 1972; Peters, 1967).
>
> (ibid., p. 166)

Hanko is critical of behavioural approaches as, potentially, purely technicist approaches which may serve teachers' wishes to manage students rather than encouraging teachers to teach their students through responding to individual needs:

> Furthermore, praise may be used as a ruse to meet the teacher's managerial needs without addressing the student's specific difficulties, and will not work if it is perceived by students as insincere.
>   . . . It may lead children into praise-dependent, even praise-hungry, conformity, and the ability to analyse problems only with deference to authority (Milgram, 1974). The disagreements voiced against the advocates of 'assertive discipline' (Hanko, 1993; Robinson & Maines, 1994), are similar to those raised by Rowe (1994) who warns that when children are taught: '. . . it is the adults who decide what will be rewarded, with no allowance for the differences in the way children and adults perceive the situation . . . [children may] lose, not only much of their creativity, but their appreciation of [its] importance'. . . . Hargreaves (1972) commented on the contrasting and potentially damaging tendency of any teacher 'to load all his reactions to pupils with

approval and disapproval'. He consequently suggested that teachers need . . . to learn how to help students to evaluate as much as possible their own efforts, abilities and achievements, and to be their 'own judge . . . with the help of the teacher where this is necessary'.

(Hanko, 1994, p. 166)

Cultural differences are crucial in this context also. Where teachers are from different cultural groups than their students, they may 'mis-cue' in their application of behaviour management strategies. Gee (1990) illustrates this point vividly with an example of a small African-American girl who tells a story at the class 'sharing time'. The story was full of rhythm, pattern and repetition and had the other children's appreciation. The child was basing her story on an oral discourse which was valued in her community, namely that a story should be a good performance, an entertainment. The teacher, however, was looking for a different (unarticulated) discourse, that of being informative, linear and to the point, and did not appreciate the child's own poetic or entertainment discourse. This child was eventually sent to the school psychologist for telling tall tales.

Gee goes on to make the point the teacher failed to see that in another school-based discourse, a high school literature class or a creative writing class, this discourse would be closer to what was valued. Unfortunately this little girl may by that time have accepted a negative, deficit view of the worth of her community values and of her own self-esteem.

In her critique of behavioural approaches in general, Hanko advocates that instead of training students through behavioural techniques, support them to reflect on their behaviour and potential for success, for example, by using 'attunement strategies' (Hastings, 1992) which are

. . . geared to alerting children with disabling beliefs about themselves to their own untapped or negated resources. By eliciting the child's view of a given task through verbalising questions which children may be asking silently ('Do I know what this task is about?' 'Do I know how to go about it?' 'Am I able to complete it?') teachers help children in supportive pre-task and on-task discussions as they proceed towards their completion.

Hanko suggests that:

[T]hrough similarly therapeutic strategies, teachers can address not only emotional and cognitive factors affecting a child's failure to progress.
. . . Children may not try as they do not believe that they can succeed . . . having come to see themselves as stupid. They may also not make the effort in order not to disprove the teachers' view that they 'could do better'. They, therefore, require differently 'attuned' evidence from their

teachers than children who believe their failure to be due to external sources such as discouraging relationships ('nobody likes me!') at home or at school.

(1994, pp. 166–7)

Hanko observes that many experienced teachers appear to attune themselves instinctively, while others may lack the confidence to try out strategies if they are unsure of the student's response.

Hanko critiques behavioural approaches on a number of grounds. Among these are that behavioural approaches fail to address adequately either the emotions or students' sense of self-efficacy and ability to reflect on their own behaviour and achievement.

Cognitive-behavioural approaches

Cognitive-behavioural approaches have emerged from behavioural psychology and have a number of additional key characteristics: 'a problem-solving, change-focused approach to working with clients; a respect for scientific values; and close attention to the cognitive processes through which people monitor and control their behaviour' (McLeod, 1998, p. 62).

Cognitive-behavioural approaches can incorporate a wide range of cognitive processes including the use of perception, language, problem solving, memory, decision making and imagery. For example, in the school situation when students begin to pay attention to 'the stream of automatic thoughts which accompany and guide their behaviour, they can learn to make choices about the appropriateness of these self-statements, and if necessary introduce new thoughts and ideas' (ibid., p.72), which result in behaviour more appropriate to the school context and leads to a higher level of academic achievement.

Encouraging meta-cognitive awareness

In the area of student behaviour in schools, a number of researchers have employed the concept of meta-cognitive awareness (that is, awareness of one's own thinking, feelings and emotions) in the area of emotional regulation, or self-management, in order to cope with feelings such as violence, bullying, disaffection or isolation (Meichenbaum and Turk, 1976; Shapiro and Cole, 1994). Teaching student self-management skills aims to encourage independence and self-reliance and thus serves to avoid the ethical concerns associated with a behavioural approach of external management of individuals' behaviour (Dwivedi and Gupta, 2000; Shapiro and Cole, 1994).

Dwivedi and Gupta divide self-management training into two categories: training in self-instruction, and training in stress inoculation.

Self-Instruction Training is a cognitive approach aimed at 'teaching a child verbal behaviour that will guide his or her non-verbal actions' (Shapiro and Cole, 1994). Stress Inoculation Training is a cognitive-behavioural approach for developing a child's 'competence to adapt to stressful events in such a way that stress is manageable and the child able to function more productively in his or her environment' (Shapiro and Cole, 1994). It is used for the management of anger, anxiety or pain, usually in clinical settings.

(2000, pp. 76–7)

Conventionally, Stress Inoculation Training consists of three phases (ibid., p. 77):

1   *Conceptualisation of the problem area/cognitive preparation.* This involves describing a model of how the inappropriate response arises, identification of internal and external triggers and the choice of response.
2   *Skill acquisition.* Skills are acquired to deal with stressful encounters. These exist at a behavioural and cognitive level.
3   *Skill use.* Skill use is gradually generalised to genuine encounters.

Approaches such as these are intended to take account of feelings in ways that tend to be ignored by many behavioural strategies. Dwivedi and Gupta consider that:

if children are able to better manage their feelings, this will have an impact on their behaviour, because of the systemic connection between cognition, affect and behaviour. Through such a system, feelings are also thought to be influenced through cognitive components (such as automatic thoughts, appraisal and beliefs).

(ibid.)

Dwivedi (2004) argues that the many factors associated with emotional and behavioural difficulties are found in the surroundings, habits and modes of living of individuals and groups. These factors are likely to prevent some children from developing emotional competence (for example, the capacity to tolerate emotions, the use of emotional energy to solve problems, and so on) which would enable them to take responsibility for their own behaviour. Dwivedi states that the development of emotional competence depends not only on individual potential but on the quality of training an individual receives from those around. Because emotions have a direct effect on teaching and learning, Dwivedi argues for specific strategies in schools to improve emotional competence of all children.

In recent years the cognitive-behavioural approach has extended into constructivism with its focus on ways in which individuals construct their understanding of the reality in which they live. There is recognition that 'the emotional and behavioural difficulties which people experience in their lives are not caused directly by events but by the way they interpret and make sense of these events' (McLeod, 1998, pp. 71–2).

> Constructivism can perhaps be characterized as resting on three basic assumptions. First, the person is regarded as an active knower, as purposefully engaged in making sense of his or her world. Second, language functions as the primary means through which the person constructs an understanding of the world. Constructivist therapists are therefore particularly interested in linguistic products such as stories and metaphors, which are seen as ways of structuring experience. Third, there is a developmental dimension to the person's capacity to construct their world.
>
> (ibid., pp. 81–2)

A particular strength of constructivist approaches to understanding and modifying behaviour lies in its affirmation and validation of the language, stories and metaphors of all people in their efforts to make sense of their world. However, this places considerable demands on teachers to know and understand something of the stories, metaphors and language of the students they teach.

The ecosystemic approach

In contrast to individualistic approaches, the ecosystemic approach shifts the focus away from a traditional view that problem behaviour resides with the student to a view that students engage in problem behaviour because the school and general environment have become dysfunctional in some respect. Addressing problematic student behaviour thus requires addressing problems within the interactions between students and their learning environment. Cooper and Upton (1991) locate the origins of ecosystemic approaches within general system theory (von Bertalanffy, 1968), in the work of Gregory Bateson (1972, 1979) in the areas of epistemology and psychiatry, and in the field of family therapy. Family therapy now has widespread international recognition through a growing body of literature indicating the efficacy of family therapy approaches in the treatment of psychiatric disorders and emotional and behavioural difficulties (de Shazer, 1985; Hoffman, 1981; Minuchin, 1974; Selvini, 1988).

Family therapists and educationists have begun to understand the school behaviour problems in terms of dysfunctions in the family system, in the school system, or in the family–school relationship system (Campion, 1985; Dowling and Osbourne, 1985). Most recently, attention has turned to the use of ecosystemic techniques by teachers and others to tackle behaviour problems in school (Molnar and Lindquist, 1989). The vast majority of this work has been carried out in the USA. However, there has been little evaluative work on these approaches in the school context.

Cooper and Upton (1991) comment that:

> the ecosystemic approach is based on the idea that human interactional structures, such as families, schools and other organisations, are self-regulating systems, which function in a way which is analogous to the natural ecosystem. Such systems are sustained by repeating interactional patterns among the participants (subsystems), which are shaped and continually modified by the survival needs of the system as a whole. Systems are in continual interaction with other systems which form elements in their environment (the social ecosystem). Changes in any one part of the ecosystem have the result of changing the whole ecosystem. Difficulties for individuals arise when they become caught up in interactional patterns which serve the needs of the system as a whole at their personal expense.
>
> (1991, p. 22)

Cooper and Upton (ibid., p. 23) identify four key concepts underlying the ecosystemic approach (see also Upton and Cooper, 1990).

1   Problem behaviour does not originate from within the individual who displays the behaviour, but from within the interaction between that individual and other individuals . . . each individual has a rational basis for behaving as they do, based on their perception of the situation . . . There are many valid viewpoints, and it is often possible for a particular interpretation of events to be found that will serve the interests of different parties, without need for conflict.
2   Causation patterns in interactional behaviour are circular (or 'recursive'), rather than lineal.
    The behaviour of individuals cannot be accounted for in terms of a simple cause–effect model . . . It is the systemic, problem-maintaining function of the behaviour which is of importance.
3   Change in any part of a system will change the whole system, and reverberate through related systems.
4   Intervention strategies must be based on a recognition of the contribution made to a problem situation by *all* participating parties in the interactions surrounding the problem. Anyone whose involvement in the situation is not helping to solve the problem is part of the cause of the problem: there is no neutral position.

One example of an ecosystemic approach is the 'Quality Circle Time Model' of Mosley and Tew (1999) who acknowledge that:

> The theoretical origins of applying a systemic approach to human behaviour rests in the work of Ludwig Von Bertalanffy (1950, 1968) and

Gregory Bateson (1972, 1979) and in the clinical practice of pioneering family therapists such as Selvini-Palazzoli *et al*. (1973), Minuchin (1974) and De Shazer (1982, 1985).

(1999, p. 12)

While Molnar and Lindquist (1989) developed an application in the school context, Mosley and Tew (1999) argue that people are not wholly free to behave as they choose, but are constrained by, and have an influence on, the social network in which they operate. Similarly to Cooper and Upton (1991), Mosley and Tew (1999) also explain how a change in any one part of a system has a 'knock-on' effect throughout the whole system and may lead to reverberations in allied systems. Mosley and Tew observe that belonging to a social group meets people's needs for personal identity and for a sense of belonging. The central focus of activity is the social group, which in the secondary school context is the tutorial (or home room) group.

From an ecosystemic perspective:

> If the cause of the problem behaviour is perceived to reside in the student, the 'cure' will be in dealing with the individual and the school need not question its structures, relationships and systems. Systemic approaches (in contrast) see behaviour as a product of interaction. Consequently if teachers wish to change the behaviour of students, they need to consider whether the behaviour is in any way a product of the environment which exists in the classroom, the school, or in the teacher–pupil interaction (Hanko 1985). The view produces a shift towards collaborative approaches to problem-solving. Student behaviour, which is defined as problematic, is always goal directed. This means that from the student's viewpoint it is understandable, rational and, above all, necessary . . . In a systemic approach it becomes important then to hear how each individual perceives a situation in order to understand the interaction and explore alternative, more effective means of achieving the goals which the behaviour is perceived to serve. The circle meeting in this model provides a place for listening to individual perceptions and exploring alternative solutions. It permits pupils and teachers to view one another differently and so to reframe both 'problems' and 'solutions' while providing an image of the individual as a worthy and valuable human being.
>
> For instance, creating Circle Time as a respectful forum for listening might well generate difficulties in the sanction system because young people now question whether it is fair. Similarly implementing ground rules for good communication in PSHE [personal, social and health education] may well generate hot debate about the way students are spoken to in other lessons.
>
> Molnar and Lindquist (1989) put it succinctly when they suggest 'when you want something to change, you must change something'.

Changing one part of the system alters the interactional meaning with repercussions throughout the whole.

(Mosley and Tew, 1999, pp. 13–14)

The work of Cooper and Upton (1991) and Mosley and Tew (1999) is of great importance to the development and implementation of behavioural interventions at the school-wide, and at school, home and community levels where there are several systems in continual interaction with each other. Examples of interventions in these settings are examined in Chapters 10, 11 and 12.

Attachment theory

One psychological theory of human development that has had considerable influence on educational provision for young children whose behaviour is of concern to teachers is that of attachment theory (Bowlby, 1952). Central to Bowlby's work is the view that:

> children deprived of maternal care . . . may be seriously affected in their physical, intellectual, emotional and social development . . . Bowlby asserts that 'prolonged separation of a child from his mother (or mother substitute) during the first five years of life stands foremost among the causes of delinquent character development' (Bowlby, 1944; Bowlby, 1952).
>
> (Holmes, 1993, p. 39)

Bowlby, who trained as a psychoanalyst, draws together two different traditions: child psychiatry and ethology, the study of animal behaviour. As a child psychiatrist, he made the connection between the lack of consistent and caring relationships in early childhood and later development, and published an article called 'Forty-four juvenile thieves: their characters and home life' (Bowlby, 1944). Later, he was influenced by the work of the ethologist Lorenz, who had noted the significance of 'imprinting', that is the bonding processes between mother and young of a species, in his book *King Solomon's Ring* (Lorenz, 1952). In it he describes how he gave signals to a clutch of hatching ducklings which persuaded them that he was their mother, so that they waddled after him in a line. Support for the view of the devastating effects on their later social relationships of being reared in social isolation was indicated in the work of other ethologists, for example, Harlow's famous study of rhesus monkeys (Harlow and Harlow, 1972).

There have been criticisms of Bowlby's hypotheses from psychoanalytic circles and from others. However, the scientific study of early childhood is now well established. It is accepted that babies quickly attach themselves emotionally to their adult carers and progress through well-recognised stages of development towards maturity. Moving successfully to the next stage depends on needs having been adequately met at the earlier stage. If this is not the case, then:

> Unless there is skilful intervention they will persist in inappropriate attachment behaviour, whether over-anxious, or avoidant and aggressive, or will become quite incapable of warm attachment and therefore indifferent to human relationships (Harris-Hendriks and Figueroa, 1995).
>
> (Bennathan, 2000, p. 11)

Greenhalgh (1994) draws on attachment theory to argue that feelings affect the capacity to learn, and the interplay of inner and outer worlds (Capra, 1982). The capacity for learning, that is the individual construction of the meaning of reality gained through experiences of operating in the world, depends on emotional growth. Relationships and sense of place in the wider world depend on emotional maturity (Salmon, 1998b). The capacity for effective learning, Greenhalgh claims, depends on the development of:

- emotional safety and trust in others (Winnicott, 1984; Hirschorn, 1998) which has an essential implication for teacher and learner relationships;
- internal confidence or strength to perceive oneself as a separate person (Winnicott, 1984; Hirschorn, 1998) which has an implication for teachers to use transitional objects or strategies to enable learners to move from feelings of incompetence to competence, dependence to independence;
- a sense of inner security gained from attachment to a significant figure, enabling some detached exploration of the world (Bowlby, 1988), in which a secure feeling of attachment to a teacher is necessary for autonomous exploration of the world and to feel that independent exploration is respected and encouraged.

Recently, attachment theory has influenced education in the early years through the development of 'nurture groups' in some infant schools. The underlying assumption of the nurture group is that children who have fared badly though the learning processes of early childhood need extra support and appropriate experiences before they can interact and learn in a normal school setting. The emphasis within nurture groups is 'on growth not on pathology' (Bennathan, 2000, p. 11). In this way participation in nurture groups is understood as facilitated social interaction and development and not as a permanent withdrawal from regular classroom settings with the consequential deficit labelling.

Bennathan (2000) argues that nurture groups allow children with serious social behaviour developmental difficulties to be included in mainstream schooling. The nurture groups accept and work with children who present major challenges to regular class teachers and other students. The critical challenge for nurture groups will be to ensure that their role remains a short-term developmental one and that students will be included in regular classrooms after a relatively short time.

A group of Inner London Education Authority (ILEA) head teachers of primary schools with nurture groups commented on the way in which, following the 1981 Education Act in England and Wales, nurture groups were able to support the inclusion of young children who might otherwise not have coped in mainstream schools as a result of behaviour perceived as worrying (Bennathan, 2000). These head teachers noted that:

- Nature groups cater for children who need total environmental support, much more than peripatetic [itinerant] help can provide.
- Their developmental rationale makes sense and provides a purposeful framework for the teaching of all primary school staff.
- Nurture groups are an integrated provision and their operation is based on detailed observation and planning.
- They are located within the mainstream of good educational practice and contribute to it through their engagement and interaction with regular classroom teachers.
- They emphasise positive learning experiences, so that the developmental progress of the child is more apparent.
- They generate effective teaching strategies that are immediately available to other school staff and so generate optimism and cooperative nurturing attitudes throughout the school.
- To a major extent they eliminate the need for sanctions, suspensions and Statements of Special Educational Need.
- For parents nurture groups are an acceptable and positive provision. Some have refused other forms of help for their children and have requested nurture group placement. Many parents maintain daily contact with the group and value the teacher and welcome advice that is offered.

Boxall (2000) argues that learning, personality and behaviour difficulties, which are more likely in the young children of families experiencing dis-advantage and deprivation, are the result of inadequate early care and support from parents who struggle with poverty, damaged relationships and harsh and stressful living conditions.

The nurture group attempts to create the features of adequate parenting within school. Opportunities are provided to develop trust, security, positive mood and identity through attachment to a reliable, attentive and caring adult and to develop autonomy through the provision of secure, controlled and graduated experiences in a familiar environment.

Some features to be found in nurture groups include easy physical contact between adult and child; warmth and intimacy and a family atmosphere;

good-humoured acceptance of the children and their behaviour; familiar and reassuring routines; a focus on tidying up and putting away; the provision of food in structured contexts; opportunities to play and the appropriate participation of the adults; adults talking about and encouraging reflection by children on trouble-provoking situations and their own feelings and opportunities for children to develop increasing autonomy. These opportunities incorporate visits outside the nurture group, participation in games, visits to regular classrooms leading to children's eventual return to a full-time class.

Counselling approaches

Counselling is a complex learning process which takes place 'at a physical, bodily level and through language, and in the thoughts, feelings and memories of each participant' (McLeod, 1998, p. xvii) simultaneously. In part, it is psychological, 'but it is also social, cultural, spiritual, philosophical, aesthetic and much more' (ibid., p. xvii).

Mahrer (1989) notes three 'core' approaches to counselling which represent fundamentally different ways of regarding human emotions and behaviour: psychodynamic, cognitive-behavioural and humanistic. Other academic disciplines are also actively involved in counselling. For example, moral philosophy offers a framework for ethical issues. Ideas and practices from various religions permeate counselling. The arts, for example, drama, sculpture, dance, painting and literature-based techniques, such as autobiography also have a strong influence on practice.

As McLeod (1998) comments, within the broad tradition initiated by Freud and developed and modified by other practitioners, there are many counsellors who call themselves psychodynamic in orientation and who make similar assumptions about the root causes of emotional and behavioural difficulties. Some of the distinctive features are (ibid., p. 33):

1 An assumption that the client's difficulties have their ultimate origins in childhood experiences.
2 An assumption that the client may not be consciously aware of the true motives or impulses behind his or her actions.
3 The use in counselling and therapy of techniques such as dream analysis and interpretation of the transference relationship.

We have already noted above how one writer who stresses the psycho-social events of childhood is the British psychoanalyst John Bowlby who researched the way in which the experience and loss of attachment in childhood can influence later adult relationships.

Some of the aims of counselling can be summarised (McLeod, 1998, p. 8) as assisting clients to acquire:

- *Insight.* An understanding of the origins and development of emotional difficulties, leading to an increased capacity to take rational control over feelings and actions (Freud: 'where id was, shall ego be').
- *Self-awareness.* Becoming more aware of thoughts and feelings which had been blocked off or denied, or developing a more accurate sense of how self is perceived by others.
- *Self-acceptance.* The development of a positive attitude towards self, marked by an ability to acknowledge areas of experience which had been the subject of self-criticism and rejection.
- *Self-actualisation or individuation.* Moving in the direction of fulfilling potential or achieving an integration of previously conflicting parts of self.
- *Enlightenment.* Assisting the client to arrive at a higher state of spiritual awakening.
- *Problem-solving.* Finding a solution to a specific problem which the client had not been able to resolve alone. Acquiring a general competence in problem-solving.
- *Psychological education.* Enabling the client to acquire ideas and techniques with which to understand and control behaviour.
- *Acquisition of social skills.* Learning and mastering social and inter-personal skills, such as maintenance of eye contact, turn-taking in conversations, assertiveness or anger control.
- *Cognitive change.* The modification or replacement of irrational beliefs or maladaptive thought patterns associated with self-destructive behaviour.
- *Behaviour change.* The modification or replacement of maladaptive or self-destructive patterns of behaviour.
- *Systemic change.* Introducing change into the way in which social systems (e.g. families) operate.
- *Empowerment.* Working on skills, awareness and knowledge which will enable the client to confront social inequalities.
- *Restitution.* Helping the client to make amends for previous destructive behaviour.

The emergence of the person-centred, humanistic approach by Rogers (1942) and also Maslow (1968), Buhler (1935, 1940) and Jourard (1963) has, at its centre, an image of the human being as 'self striving to find meaning and fulfilment in the world' (McLeod, 1998, p. 88). However, this approach does not constitute one coherent theoretical model. Instead, it consists of 'a broad set of theories and models connected by shared values and philosophical assumptions' (ibid., p. 89). Therapeutic change in the individual depends on the existence of a relationship between therapist and client characterised by three 'core conditions' of 'unconditional positive regard', empathy and genuineness (Rogers, 1957).

One of the criticisms of the practice of counselling is that it tends to be protracted. In recent years there has been an attempt to address this criticism by offering brief series of therapy sessions, 'on average in less than 5 sessions', from a solution-focused approach. This approach is justified as brief 'because it is future-focused and because it works with the strengths of those who come by making the best use of their resources' (http://www.brieftherapy. org.uk/).

Conclusion

It is problematic to assume that psychological understandings of behaviour from particular cultural groups are universal givens. Frequently, interventions designed to address issues of student behaviour in schools are underpinned by assumptions from particular psychological paradigms. However, these assumptions can position some students as deficient and problematic. As we have noted above, one important component of deficit theorising is the neglect of culture:

> the dilemma in the study of man is to grasp not only the causal prin-
> ciples of his biology and his evolution, but to understand these in the
> light of the interpretive processes involved in meaning making. To
> brush aside the biological constraints on human functioning is to commit
> hubris. To sneer at the power of culture to shape man's mind and to
> abandon our efforts to bring this power under human control is to com-
> mit moral suicide. A well-wrought psychology can help us avoid both of
> these disasters.
>
> (Bruner, 1996, pp. 184–5)

Chapter 7

Assessment of students' behaviour

Introduction

Students' behaviour in schools does not occur in a vacuum (Watkins and Wagner, 1995). Students are members of classrooms which function as aspects of the school system within particular neighbourhoods. Students also fulfil roles within their own families and communities. The demands of society at large impact on communities in different ways. In the UK, for example, 'formalised education, commencing at the age of five years, imposes a whole range of requirements including the need for compliance, focused concentration and the willingness to listen and reflect' (BPS, 1996, p. 13). These requirements do not sit easily with many students.

Difficult behaviour which seems to relate to a particular student may be indicative of a range of contextual issues associated with society, the family, ethnic or community group, school, classroom, peer group or teacher, as well as the individual student. In this chapter we address some of the challenges schools face in addressing behaviour seen as worrying or troubling.

A problem-solving approach

Watkins and Wagner (1995) advocate a problem-solving diagnostic approach to identify when the challenges presented by an individual student's behaviour require special consideration. In order to develop effective problem solving:

> a good definition of the problem is required at the start. For this the following 'ten important questions' provide a useful starting structure:
>
> *What behaviour is causing concern?*
>   specify clearly, do not merely re-label
>
> *In what situations does the behaviour occur?*
>   in what settings/contexts, with which others?
>
> *In what situations does the behaviour not occur?*
>   (this can often be the most illuminating question)

What happens before the behaviour?
a precipitating pattern? a build up? a trigger?

What follows the behaviour causing concern?
something which maintains the behaviour?

What skills does the person demonstrate?
social/communication skills? learning/classroom skills?

What skills does the person apparently not demonstrate?
and how may these be developed?

What view does the person have of their behaviour?
what does it mean to them?

What view does the person have of themselves?
and may their behaviour enhance that view?

What view do others have of the person?
how has this developed? is it self-fulfilling? can it change?

Who is most concerned by this behaviour?

The eleventh question in the above list is of a different style, but often has an important effect: in some cases it appropriately turns attention from the behaviour causing concern to the way the concern is being handled by the range of people around it.

(Watkins and Wagner, 1995, p. 59)

Watkins and Wagner (ibid., p. 68) go on to offer an example of a proforma that they have found useful as a tool for collecting information about students' behaviour (see page 112).

Issues in the assessment of 'special' groups

Underlying particular forms of assessment of students' 'special' learning needs there are assumptions which carry particular consequences. Some of these assumptions intrinsically contradict notions of inclusion. For example, available resources have often dictated the provision made for individual students (Cline, 1992). To determine eligibility for additional services, special educational provision typically depends on norm-referenced assessment designed to compare individual students' achievement with that of peers and, therefore, identify some students who are 'different'. Standardised tests of intelligence typically reflect Western/European constructions of intelligence as an innate quality, and they provide a statistical definition of need. The underlying assumption disallows a view of intelligence as having the potential to achieve anything, given the right learning opportunities. Norm-referenced tests of ability and attainment have the potential to 'determine selectively the

Diagnostic behaviour questionnaire

From: . . . .   To: . . . .   Subject: . . . .

Regarding: . . . .   Tutor Group: . . . .   Date: . . . .

Concern has been expressed about . . . .'s behaviour in a number of lessons. The following diagnostic questions are designed to help us get a picture of . . . . across all lessons so that we can make some sense of the behaviour overall, and then work out strategies to bring about change in lessons where there is concern. Whatever your view of . . . . I would value your answers. *Thank you for your help.*

What does s/he do that causes concern?

What precedes the behaviour that causes concern?

When does it NOT occur?

Which other pupils are involved, and what are their expectations?

What does s/he seem to gain from behaving this way?

What strategies do you find effective?

Add any other information you feel is relevant

way in which issues are discussed and solutions proposed' (Broadfoot, 1996). The influence of psychometrics on professional practice in education lends support to deterministic views of ability and achievement which not only can limit teachers' expectations of certain students but also restrict the development of different approaches to assessment.

In addition, Tomlinson (1988) argues that, for some students, for example, those from poor or disadvantaged backgrounds, lowered expectations can lead to a reproduction of underprivileged groups in schools and society. While special educational arrangements appear to be the result of rational and pragmatic assessment of students, this, however, is questionable. Tomlinson considers that the function that such assessment practices serve in maintaining the power of the privileged and dominant groups in society is a powerful determining factor in explaining their continued use:

> The ideas of critical theorists can suggest that the stupidity or dullness of some individuals or social groups is not necessarily self-evident or 'true'. Acquiring the label and being treated as 'less-able' is likely to be the result of complex social economic and political judgements and considerations.
>
> (ibid., p. 45)

Some commentators argue that schools help to reproduce the pattern of control and subordination within society which is linked to the economic context (Bourdieu and Passeron, 1973). There is a contradiction between the rhetoric of education to promote equality and the reality that the system of education functions to maintain the children of underprivileged groups in powerless positions in society. 'Success' and 'failure' are not objective 'givens' but social categories whose labels serve the vested interests of dominant, powerful groups in society. The reason why children fail in the education system can be understood as a function of the societal, economic and political status quo which requires some children to fail in the education system. This explains individual student failure as much as the supposition of a deficit in the child.

In a post-industrial age where achievements assessed through reading and writing are the prerequisites to obtaining a job with a salary above subsistence level, education is in a crisis. The inability of illiterate citizens to find well-paid employment is legitimised if they have been labelled in advance through special education: 'Special education reproduces and controls lower-status groups, and legitimates their life-long treatment, but is, in itself, an accept-able, legitimating, humane development' (Tomlinson, 1988, p. 49). Low scores on standardised tests of reading and spelling allow schools to 'blame' the child, the family, or the ethnic group and also absolve themselves from taking responsibility for that child's progress in school. 'The way the black and working-class Johnnys with reading problems are dealt with will usually ensure that they are reproduced into the low-status sections of society' (ibid., p. 55).

Tomlinson's views reflect in part some of the concerns about equity issues raised in previous chapters. On the one hand, identification and labelling of students with special educational needs or behaviour seen as problematic may bring additional resources, but on the other they may serve to perpetuate the existing social order.

One of the key issues in summative assessment is the selection of assessment strategies. Among the types of strategies often used to assess within-child factors related to poor achievement in literacy, as we have noted, are normative, psychometric tests. Norm-referenced tests, for example, standardised reading and spelling scores, imply measurement and the use of standardised instruments and typically produce measures in terms of ranked scores. While it might be important for a teacher to gain some understanding of the way in which a learner's comprehension of text, or ability to read individual words, or to spell accurately compares with that of peers, we have already noted problems around inclusion and the model of learning that it assumes. While this type of assessment has some uses, particularly for supporting requests for additional resourcing of individual students' learning needs, it must also be treated with some caution as the results of such norm-based tests may be misinterpreted and misused. They cannot, for example, determine appropriate intervention strategies because: 'the scores do not provide details of what the child knows or does not know, nor do they elucidate the processes that are involved in the child's difficulty' (Dockrell and McShane, 1993, p. 34). When students' scores are taken to indicate some innate quality such as intelligence or general ability, knowing that a student scores poorly provides little incentive or guidance as to how best to facilitate their learning.

Cultural context and assessment

Interventions designed to improve student behaviour can be centred on the child, on the environment, on the child and the environment, or on the interface between the child and their environment. Hence, the focus and process of assessment may need to include the effectiveness of teachers and other educational professionals in implementing pedagogical strategies that are culturally safe and effective, as a research report on sites of effective special education practice for Māori students with learning and behaviour needs concludes (Berryman et al., 2002).

In identifying key factors for the assessment of American Indian and Alaskan Native (AI/AN) pre-school children with special needs, Banks (1997) proposed seven criteria that are relevant to the assessment of young people in other contexts also. Banks suggests that appropriate assessment should be authentic, congruent, sensitive, collaborative, convergent, ecologically valid and equitable. What he found about assessment practices under each of these criteria, however, was not always compatible with his views of appropriate assessment practices. Banks' seven criteria are elaborated on below.

Authentic

Assessment should be gathered from a variety of sources that access real performance in real situations for the students who are being assessed. Parents and caregivers suggested that children's assessments should be based on knowledge of things from their environment and experiences. They suggest not using things from a totally different area because students should not necessarily be expected to know what is not in their own environment. They further suggest that if educators want to assess cultural minority students fairly, they should use tests that are familiar to the students and their families (Banks, 1997).

Congruent

Assessment should be field-tested on children whose circumstances match the child being tested. All professionals reported that the most frequently used tools included 'standardised norm referenced instruments' (Banks, 1997). Yet Neisworth and Bagnato (1992) point out that to administer standardised tests following the standardised manner with students whose behaviour is usually not standardised is highly suspect. Neisworth and Bagnato also caution that assessment practices using tests which have been standardised with school-aged children are inappropriate when used with very young children from culturally diverse populations who have not been exposed to the life experiences of similar-aged children on whom the test was standardised. Congruent assessment means ensuring that assessment content and practices are representative and relevant to the cultural group being assessed.

Sensitive

Assessment should be graded finely in order to track progress, by being sufficiently responsive to pick up small changes occurring over time (Banks, 1997). This is particularly important when assessment is being used to evaluate the effectiveness of modifications to teaching strategies. Teachers should not have to wait until the end of a school year when a standardised test can be administered in order to judge whether a new teaching programme is working.

Collaborative

Parental involvement in the observation of or assistance in students' assessments is rare. Some 60 per cent of parents reported that they did not know how many testing sessions their child had experienced. Of those who did know, 30 per cent reported one testing session, whereas the professionals reported that testing ranged from one to five sessions. Information was also gathered from parents through home inventories. However, again there was some discrepancy in perceptions of parents and professionals as to what actually took place. Some 30 per cent of parents reported being involved in this process, whereas 72.7 per cent of professionals reported parent involvement. But it was generally agreed that parental input in determining goals was seldom extensive. Collaboration between professionals and parents was rarely established (Banks, 1997). Similarly, Bevan-Brown and Bevan-Brown (1999) reporting on the assessment of New Zealand Māori students with special needs also identified that parents' knowledge of what was actually being 'done with their kids' was very limited.

Convergent

Assessments should be gathered from a variety of sources. All participants agreed that the community resources, their cultural perceptions of disabilities, the educational priorities of families, and educational priorities of the respective American Indian nations were rarely if ever addressed (Banks, 1997). Similarly, the New Zealand mainstream education system has rarely addressed the hopes and aspirations of Māori students and their families, typically expecting Māori students to succeed at school while leaving their language and culture at home (Bishop et al., 2003; Glynn, 1998b). Yet families and community hold key sources of information for making culturally safe educational assessments of children's strategies as well as their needs.

Ecologically valid

All those sampled agreed that family strengths and needs were rarely examined (Banks, 1997). Parents indicated that they were rarely satisfied with how information was obtained. Professionals relied heavily on standardised norm-referenced testing. There is a serious issue when the 'testing' has been validated with a different group. The issue is about who is the 'norm' and to whom this 'norm' is being applied. Banks reported that professionals listed only 11 per cent of screening instruments and 2 per cent of assessment instruments that were not standardised norm-referenced instruments. Other assessment strategies reported were observational techniques and informal interviews, regular classroom teachers' observations, observations of the child and interviews with teachers and parents. No professionals indicated using ecological-based assessment or dynamic assessment. Observations were largely judgement-based observations and informal interviews.

Equitable

Assessments should be fair and equitable for those being assessed. The English language was used in the majority of cases for assessment, yet as few as 35 per cent of parents and caregivers reported that English was the main language at home (Banks, 1997). Some 46 per cent of professionals reported that the child's primary language was only occasionally, or never, used in the assessment process. Berryman and Glynn (2003) report a study in which students, competent in reading and writing in Māori, were assessed in English upon entry to secondary school, and judged as having only minimal reading and writing achievement.

As previously discussed, there is a danger of teachers in the majority culture seeing their own assessment perspectives and practices as 'the norm'. This has been a long-standing problem for Māori in New Zealand and seemingly for other minority cultures elsewhere (Berryman et al., 2002). 'Norm referencing' has been a standard method for assessing students who may have special needs. The danger is that norms developed for the majority culture are likely to disadvantage minority cultures, because they encourage and support 'deficit' theorising by majority culture professionals in the explanation of learning and behaviour difficulties. Majority culture students are not measured against 'norms' generated from the performance of tasks at which minority culture students have strengths based on experience. Banks cites Brescia and Fortune (1989) who found that commonly used standardised testing underestimated the potential of the indigenous Americans being assessed.

Children in remote areas or children who have been educated in traditional language immersion programmes are likely to be more fluent in the traditional languages than in English. If the initial assessment is carried out in English, and is within a Western European world-view, many of these children may achieve low scores. In fact, the literature reviewed revealed that traditional languages were seldom used in assessments. The danger is that the performance of children assessed in this manner is likely to be understood or represented as evidence of low intelligence, specific learning disabilities, possibly hearing impairments, or maybe language deficiencies.

Where an unknown non-indigenous person, in a strange classroom, administers such 'foreign' tests, the child is quite likely to display anxious and stressed behaviour. There is a strong danger that these behaviours may be understood or interpreted as signs of emotional disturbance. An ethnic group tested in this way will most likely generate a high proportion of children with special needs. In one Navaho school studied (Mayhew et al.,

1966), one-third of the students assessed were identified as having special needs, yet over the following two years, when reassessment took into account language and cultural perspectives, the number dropped to 10 per cent, which is in line with the national average. Inappropriate assessment that does not take into account cultural factors may lead to wrong classification, which leads to faulty understanding or interpretation of the problem. It also leads to educators looking for solutions that try to remedy perceived deficits in individuals and families, rather than solutions that try to remedy deficits in the classroom and school learning contexts and practices. This in turn can lead to placing individual students in inappropriate and culturally unsafe programmes, with long-term adverse consequences.

Ladson-Billings (1995) points out that attempts by Western European educational professionals to educate children from minority cultures are shaped by theorising about principles such as cultural appropriateness, cultural congruence and cultural compatibility. However, these approaches aim to fit the child (and the parents) into the preconceived educational programme, by selecting those cultural aspects of the children's culture that seem most useful to the educator. Ladson-Billings seeks instead to operate from the principle of cultural responsiveness, a concept that reflects the need to respond to minority culture values, needs and preferences, and adapts the programme to the child. Bureaucracy often specifies in advance of any assessment or intervention what support is to be made available, instead of seeking to provide support that is designed to meet actual needs as identified by particular cultural communities.

There is much in the literature on students who come from minority cultures and who have learning and behavioural needs that provides clear indicators of effective practice. Although there are distinct cultural differences, there are a surprising number of problems and solutions common to many cultures, often owing to the common experiences these cultures have had of colonisation with its imposition of foreign educational values, beliefs and practices. One such common experience is that of having the domain and focus of educational achievement, and the criteria for success, defined and controlled by another cultural group.

Assessment of environmental factors

Compatible with the view of 'problematic' student behaviour being understood in terms of both the context and the attributes of the individual, is Birmingham Local Education Authority's three-level approach outlined in its strategy document *Behaviour in Schools: Framework for Intervention* (Birmingham City Council Education Department, 1998). In this approach, responses to problematic behaviour begin with an audit of the learning environment and considerations of alterations to that environment in order to maximise the positive impact on behaviour and learning. After this has been done, responses continue if necessary with a greater focus on the individual student within that environment, and then go on to involve external agencies.

For many teachers there seems to be an inherent conflict between meeting the needs of the student and meeting the demands of a prescribed curriculum. This needs to be taken into account in assessing ways in which the learning environment supports or militates against the learning needs of students whose behaviour is of concern in some way. Such assessment may uncover both structural and pedagogical barriers to improving learning environments for these students. Examples of structural barriers might be rigid timetabling and inflexible allocation of resources, while examples of pedagogical barriers might be lack of provision for on-site professional development of teachers in teaching strategies that promote effective inclusion in classrooms.

There are a number of ways of conceptualising the interactional relationship between the learning environment and the learner. For example, Bronfenbrenner (1979) identifies four levels that influence student outcomes:

1   the *microsystem*, the immediate context of the student – school, classrooms, home, neighbourhood;
2   the *mesosystem*, the links between two microsystems, for example, home–school relationships;
3   the *exosystem*, outside demands and influences in adults' lives that affect students;
4   the *macrosystem*, cultural beliefs and patterns or government or institutional policies that affect individuals' behaviour, including societal structure and organisation and prevailing value systems.

Royal Tangaere (1997) presents an analysis which illustrates the complexities in understanding Bronfenbrenner's ecosystemic model when applied to students and families from one culture and language when schooling practices and operations are provided by another culture and another language. For example, there would be two exosystems exerting independent influences on student behaviour and family well-being, even if one is nested inside (subsumed by) another. In the case of children attending a *kōhanga reo* (early childhood Māori language setting) Royal Tangaere suggests that:

> Both exosystems (Māori and non-Māori) impinge on the microsystems of the child's whānau and the kōhanga reo context. For the kōhanga reo and the Māori whānau, the child was the link, and because the kaupapa [agenda] of the kōhanga reo required commitment from the whole family to revitalise the Māori language and to support the kōhanga, the two settings were compatible. Therefore one could assume that positive learning would occur, not only for the child, but also for the family and the kōhanga reo.
>
> (1997, p. 67)

In their review of the literature on learning environments, Ysseldyke and Christenson (1987) identified three categories of environmental factors influencing instructional outcomes:

1 school district conditions (for example, policies on inclusion, or instruction in home languages);
2 within-school conditions (for example, school behaviour management strategies or different pedagogical strategies within classrooms);
3 general family characteristics (for example, families whose intellectual and cultural aspirations are different from those of the school).

Ysseldyke and Christenson (1987, 1993) argue that it is important to assess characteristics of the classroom learning environments in which students are placed because these can be changed to support more effective learning. They identify a number of instructional factors in the classroom environment that influence student outcomes. These authors argue that it is important also to focus assessment on current features of classroom practice because these can be changed to support more effective learning. On the basis of extensive literature reviews, they identify a number of instructional factors in the classroom that influence student outcomes:

• planning procedures;
• management procedures;
• teaching procedures;
• monitoring and evaluation procedures.

Ysseldyke and Christenson used their analysis of these features in the learning environment to design 'The Instructional Environment Scale' (TIES) as a framework for the systematic collection of data to analyse contextual barriers to students' learning. Data were gathered through classroom observation and interviews with both students and teachers on twelve components of teaching (Ysseldyke and Christenson, 1987, p. 21):

1 *Instructional presentation*: Instruction is presented in a clear and effective manner; directions contain sufficient information for the student to understand what kinds of behaviours or skills are to be demonstrated; and the student's understanding is checked before independent practice.
2 *Classroom environment*: The classroom is controlled efficiently and effectively; there is a positive, supportive classroom atmosphere; time is used productively.
3 *Teacher expectations*: There are realistic yet high expectations for both the amount and accuracy of work to be completed, and these are communicated clearly to the student.

4 *Cognitive emphasis*: Thinking skills needed to complete assignments are communicated explicitly to the student.
5 *Motivational strategies*: The teacher has and uses effective strategies for heightening student interest and effort.
6 *Relevant practice*: The student is given adequate opportunity to practise with appropriate materials. Classroom tasks are clearly important to achieving instructional goals.
7 *Academic engaged time*: The student is actively engaged in responding to academic content; the teacher monitors the extent to which the student is actively engaged and redirects the student when the student is not engaged.
8 *Informed feedback*: The student receives relatively immediate and specific information on his or her performance or behaviour; when the student makes mistakes, correction is provided.
9 *Adaptive instruction*: The curriculum is modified to accommodate the student's specific instructional needs.
10 *Progress evaluation*: There is direct, frequent measurement of the student's progress toward completion of instructional objectives; data on pupil performance and progress are used to plan future instruction.
11 *Instructional planning*: The student's needs have been assessed accurately and instruction is matched appropriately to the results of the instructional diagnosis.
12 *Student understanding*: The student demonstrates an accurate understanding of what is to be done in the classroom.

Collecting evidence through observation

Observing children in the environment of the classroom or school is something that is a part of teachers' everyday practice. It is rare, however, for teachers to find the time to stand back and closely observe the processes, relationships and behaviours involved in teaching and learning. For the purposes of assessment of individual students' behaviour, this process might need to be formalised. It should be systematic and there will need to be an effective means of recording and interpreting what is seen.

Bell (1999) points out that while observation is not an easy option – it requires careful organisation and practice – nonetheless, it can reveal characteristics of the behaviour of groups or individuals, which would have been impossible to discover by other means. Direct observation can be particularly useful to find out whether people do what they say they do, or behave in the way they claim to behave.

As Fisher *et al.* (2004) comment, there are a number of different formats that can be adopted. The first step is to make decisions about exactly *what* will be the focus of the observation: people, activities or events, or a combination of these. It might be important to observe an individual, a group, or a whole class in particular lessons or playground activities. If the problem-solving approach recommended by Watkins and Wagner (1995) is adopted, observations may take place in specific, pre-selected lessons or locations where individual students' behaviour has been identified as particularly problematic. Then, as Fisher et al. go on to note, there is a question about the time frames to be used: whether to sample what goes on during short pre-determined time periods or whether an individual student will be 'shadowed' for a longer period of time. The answers to these questions will, to a large extent, be dictated by the kinds of concerns raised in relation to the behaviour of individual students, the kinds of reflection that has already taken place in relation to the evidence already collected, and the extent to which an audit of the learning environment such as that framed by Ysseldyke and Christenson has already formed part of the collection of evidence.

Another choice to be made is whether the class teacher can be expected to collect evidence while also taking part in the activity as part of the teaching role, or whether others, for example, support teachers, might take the role of the 'non-participant observer', noting down observations at a distance. Whoever carries out the observations, it might be difficult to maintain a detached, non-participant stance. In the hurly-burly of classroom activity, an observer who has insufficient training in observation techniques might well be drawn into what is going on despite his/her best intentions. In any case it is likely that the presence of an observer is likely to have an effect on the activity or on the behaviour being observed. In New Zealand, Resource Teachers of Learning and Behaviour (RTLB) are education professionals (Brown et al., 2000; Thomson et al., 2000) who can provide teachers with in-class support in devising and implementing behaviour observation strategies that will generate data to improve teachers' understanding and management of the behaviour of either individuals or the whole class.

When conducting observations, it is usually more helpful to make notes at the time, even if systematic time sampling or event recording procedures are being implemented. These notes could be open-ended, where general points of interest are recorded, or can be focused on targeted events as and when they happen. A useful format is to write down what happened, and then to add a brief comment or interpretation later. For the teacher in the classroom it can be difficult to do this in any detail in the heat of the moment. It may be possible, however, to jot down a few brief notes, or even to make mental notes, which will need to expanded and reflected upon as soon as possible afterwards. If s/he is looking for particular events or behaviours which can be easily categorised, s/he could devise an 'observation schedule'. A number of illustrative UK and New Zealand studies involving the use of observation schedules to design and evaluate effective behaviour change strategies at pre-school, primary and secondary school levels are reported by Wheldall et al. (1986). Systematic observation procedures also contribute greatly to the effective design and evaluation of learning programmes such as tutoring reading (Glynn and McNaughton, 2002). This involves the construction of an appropriate grid in which instances of specified reader and tutor behaviours can be recorded as they occur.

Assessment at individual level

Functional assessment of behaviour

One of the questions posed by Watkins and Wagner in their proforma relates to the gain for the individual (that is, the function that is served) by behaving in a particular way. As we noted in Chapter 6, functional analysis can be seen as an experimental approach to behavioural assessment in which variables hypothesised to precede or to maintain the target behaviour are systematically examined in order to isolate their individual effects (Moore, 2004). For example, a mismatch between curriculum tasks or teaching practices and students' current achievement levels may be shown to be associated with the occurrence of undesirable behaviour, such as a student's verbal abuse towards a teacher, which may serve to facilitate his escape from an embarrassing and stressful situation.

Students' views

The assumption that students are active agents in their own learning raises serious questions about how we can expect students to participate positively in a process, if we do not understand how they feel about being identified as the focus of teachers' concerns for behavioural reasons. This issue creates major challenges facing those responsible for behaviour management and/or planning provision for individual students. On the one hand, there is an expectation that students' views will be sought regarding provision made for them and that teachers as well as students will be willing and able to engage in this activity, however much their interests may be in conflict. On the other hand, traditional school structures and bureaucracy often present barriers to the expression of student opinion. Teachers are professionals in the education industry. It is their role to make informed decisions based on their knowledge and experience. In many school staffrooms, attempting to claim the moral high ground by appealing to colleagues to respect the rights of the individual student is insufficient to establish effective student participation in decision-making processes. It is important, therefore, that a greater degree of student participation can clearly be justified and enacted. Moreover, the assumption that 'teachers know best' can be a barrier to student participation.

Dilemmas in encouraging student self-expression

During the development of a number of research initiatives in schools designed to support the development of active student participation in decision-making processes, Gersch (2001) noted the following dilemmas:

- how to deal with other colleagues who might feel that children should be seen and not heard;
- the question of whether some children are mature or capable enough to participate. (In Gersch's experience even very young children and students who experience severe difficulties in learning can make some choices about their educational programmes.)
- how to deal with parent–child dislike;
- how much scope children need to negotiate, try things and change their minds;
- how adults can distinguish what a child needs from what he or she prefers or wants;
- what status should be given to a student's views if the professional responsible for organising the special or additional provision comes into conflict with their head teacher over ways of meeting a student's needs.

Clearly there are no easy answers. These dilemmas represent conflict between the roles of the participants. Gersch does not offer a single answer. He comments that, if a positive way forward is to be found, then a mutually trusting, listening, open, non-judgemental relationship must be established between teacher and student. In the Republic of Ireland the *Learning Support Guidelines* (DES (Ireland), 2000) offer guidance on how this might be achieved:

> The involvement of students in the development, implementation and review of their own learning programmes is seen as crucial to effective supplementary teaching. Students can become more independent as learners if they perceive themselves to be stakeholders in the learning process. Students who are in receipt of supplementary teaching should, as appropriate:
>
> - become familiar with the medium- and short-term learning targets that have been set for them, and they should be given the opportunity to contribute to the setting of such targets;
> - contribute to the selection of texts and other learning materials that are relevant to the attainment of their learning targets;
> - develop 'ownership' of skills and strategies that are taught during supplementary teaching and learn to apply these learning strategies and skills to improve their own learning;

- contribute to the evaluation of their progress by participating in appropriate assessment activities, including self-assessment.

(DES (Ireland), 2000, in Open University, 2001, p. 94)

In recent years, as we have noted in previous chapters, in the special educational needs field there has been a move towards a view that students' difficulties in learning, including those difficulties associated with challenging behaviour, may arise as a result of aspects of the learning environment (Clark *et al.*, 1997, 1998; Cline, 1992; Cooper, 1993; Dyson, 1997). Sometimes the source of difficulties is described as stemming from the interaction between the characteristics of the learner and those of the context (Mittler, 2000; Wedell, 2000). Some researchers, however, have taken a view of learning as 'situated', dynamic and interactive between learner and context (Greeno, 1998; Lave and Wenger, 1991, 1999) and, therefore, a view of difficulties in learning as situated and dynamic also (Lave and Wenger, 1999; Mehan, 1996; McDermott, 1999). We should take account of how students make sense of their own circumstances and what impression they have of others' constructions of them. Glynn *et al.* (1997) reported on an effective school and community behaviour management programme in which students and family members participated in defining problematic behaviour and devising intervention strategies, and evaluating the outcomes. The process ensured students and family members remained active agents in their own behaviour management.

Engaging with students' views in schools

A school which endeavours to engage with the perspectives of disaffected young people has to recognise a number of constraints:

> Recent and current pressures on schools emanating from league tables of absence rates and academic results have made 'disruptive' students less tolerable . . . Including students whose behaviour seems threatening to the system is not easy . . . Exclusionary pressures resulting from the current competitive climate are very strong.
>
> (Wearmouth, 1999, p. 22)

Problems associated with a number of philosophical and practical issues surrounding self-advocacy have been identified by Garner and Sandow (1995). These issues suggest a conflict of values both within and between individuals. For example, student self-advocacy may conflict with professionals' values and assumptions both about themselves with the responsibility for maintaining control and direction in the classroom, and the school as a whole, and also about students' rights and abilities to express their own views. There are no easy solutions to this issue which represents, essentially, conflict between the roles of the participants within the system of the school. If, as in many schools, student self-advocacy, particularly for students whose behaviour may be challenging to schools, is not acceptable, then some professionals will need to take on the role of advocate on behalf of students.

'Talking Stones'

Wearmouth (2004b) describes the use of a projective interview technique, 'Talking Stones', as an interesting assessment strategy to help students represent problematic relationships and situations as they see them. This technique is derived from techniques related to Personal Construct Psychology and developed from Crosby's therapeutic work with adults (unpublished report, 1993, Centre for Personal Construct Education). 'Talking Stones' is designed to address the challenge of engaging with a student's perspective meaningfully in order to work through what are often difficult situations in schools, and matching provision to real needs. The assumption underpinning this technique is that, for the individual learner, everything is perceived and mediated by what is salient, socially and personally. This view of behaviour implies that it is possible for a person acting in support to enter the student's reality and hold a dialogue.

During an individual interview, a student is given a pile of stones of varying shapes, sizes, colours and textures and encouraged to explore thoughts and feelings about school and him/herself in relation to it by projection on to them. The individual selects one stone to represent him/herself in school and discusses his/her choice. Subsequently s/he selects more stones to represent significant others in the context about which there is current concern, describes why they have been chosen, and then places them on a rectangular white cloth or large sheet of paper. The edges of this set a boundary to the positioning of the stones and their distance from each other. Stones, their attributes and their positions in relation to each other can be understood as a student's representation of individually constructed meanings.

One way in which a procedure such as 'Talking Stones' can contribute to the process of assessment in schools is in the manner in which it can open up problematic relationships between, typically, teenagers and staff members, and facilitate dialogue or conversation. The student is not seen as 'mad' and therefore unintelligible and threatening, but engaging with life in an alternative mode.

'Talking Stones' is a powerful procedure. The ethics surrounding its use should therefore be taken into careful consideration. It should be used only where there is positive benefit to the student. Its use is ethically questionable unless there is a clear benefit for the student. Teachers using 'Talking Stones' should be aware of ethical principles associated with techniques of a counselling nature, for example those of 'non-maleficence' and 'beneficence'. As McLeod (1998, pp. 272–3) notes, 'non-maleficence' refers to the principle of not doing any harm, and 'beneficence' to promoting human welfare. Asking personal questions may be construed as prying into a student's privacy. It raises a question about what teachers and schools should do with sensitive information of this sort that is very important to understanding individuals, but may be used by some to belittle or stereotype students.

Raising self-esteem is frequently set as a target for students seen as having a low self-image. However, attempting to raise self-esteem may have little point if teachers are not aware of major factors driving students' behaviour. It also raises the question of who should decide whether the risks of using a technique such as this outweigh the benefits.

There are many instances in schools where students disclose very sensitive information about themselves to teachers. Before engaging in any activity where this is likely to happen, including using 'Talking Stones', teachers need to familiarise themselves very well with any guidelines that may exist in their own schools about handling information that may emerge from student self-disclosure, for example, information relating to sexual abuse.

The assessment of students' perceptions of, and feelings about, their own behaviour depends on very finely tuned listening skills as well as suspension of judgmental responses on the part of professionals. In terms of practice, it is important to recognise that:

> True listening is an art; children will make decisions about people they can talk to and trust, and those they cannot. We know from the counselling literature that good listeners offer time, support, non directive questions, acknowledgement of feelings, reflecting back, and such non-verbal behaviour as eye contact, sitting next to (rather than opposite, behind a desk), and a basically trusting atmosphere which communicates that it is all right to speak honestly.
>
> These are not easy situations to create in school.
>
> (Gersch, 1995, p. 48)

'Talking Stones' is a technique not to be used lightly. Once a student has begun to disclose personal information, it may be difficult for an inexperienced teacher-interviewer to bring about closure in a way that leaves the student in a frame of mind sufficiently comfortable to return to regular classroom activities.

Engaging with parents' or carers' perspectives

In some countries within the UK there is overt acknowledgement of effective working relationships between home and school in supporting the education of students who experience difficulties of some sort. For example, in England, the Department for Education (DfE), then the Department of Education and Science (DES), produced a document in the 'Citizen's Charter' series:

Children with Special Needs: A Guide for Parents, first published in 1992, supporting the rights of parents to be involved in decisions about their children's education. In New Zealand recent education policy documents are increasingly requiring of schools that they engage in full consultation with parents and communities, for example, the National Administration Guidelines (NAGs) (Ministry of Education, 2001b).

Effective communication with parents

It is important to bear in mind what families expect and need and what professionals aspire to in the parent–professional relationship. Russell (1997, p. 79) makes a plea to schools to take seriously their power to affect the lives of children and their families and carers through the kind of assessment and provision that they make:

> Please accept and value our children (and ourselves as families) as we are.
>
> Please celebrate difference.
>
> Please try and accept our children as children first. Don't attach labels to them unless you mean to do something.
>
> Please recognise your power over our lives. We live with the consequences of your opinions and decisions.
>
> Please understand the stress many families are under. The cancelled appointment, the waiting list no one gets to the top of, all the discussions about resources – it's our lives you're talking about.
>
> Don't put fashionable fads and treatments on to us unless you are going to be around to see them through. And don't forget families have many members, many responsibilities. Sometimes, we can't please everyone.
>
> Do recognise that sometimes we are right! Please believe us and listen to what we know that we and our children need.
>
> Sometimes we are sad, tired and depressed. Please value us as caring and committed families and try to go on working with us.

The following are suggestions for professionals dealing with parents in schools which have been adapted from Friend and Cook (1996, p. 232):

- Create an environment that is welcoming.
- Schedule the meeting at the convenience of the parent.

- Provide an advance summary of the topics to be covered and a list of questions that the parent might want to ask.
- Suggest the parent brings to school copies of work the child has done at home.
- Let the parent be seated at the meeting table first.
- Provide the parent with a file folder containing copies of the information that the professionals have in their folders.
- Use your communication skills to structure the meeting so the parent has opportunities to provide input throughout the meeting.

Suggestions for parents

- Review records on past meetings.
- Talk with other family members and friends about what questions to ask and what information to share.
- Make a list of questions to ask.
- Make a list of information to share.
- Ask another person to go to the meeting with you.
- Take all relevant records to the meeting.
- Take a pen and paper.
- Check the time and place of the meeting.

These suggestions and advice from Russell (1997) and Friend and Cook (1996) highlight the need for reciprocity and mutual respect between teachers and parents, whereby each acknowledges the expertise and competencies of the other. This issue is discussed further in Chapter 11.

Conclusion

The view of problematic student behaviour in schools seen as associated both with the context and with the attributes of the individual requires an approach to assessment at multiple levels: the individual student, the classroom, the school, and so on. A constructive and positive approach to assessment begins with an evaluation of the learning environment and considerations of how to modify to enhance behaviour and learning. The approach then continues if necessary with a greater focus on understanding the individual student as behaving 'normally' and actively engaged in making sense of the situation in which s/he finds him/herself. Such an approach is more likely to empower students to take an active part in the management of their own behaviour.

Chapter 8

Working at individual level

Introduction

For a small minority of students whose behaviour continues to be a focus of teachers' concerns, it may be seen as appropriate to investigate learning and behavioural issues at the level of the individual and draw up an individual intervention plan. Planning a curriculum to meet particular special learning needs of individual students should take place within the context of the same decision-making processes that relate to teaching and learning for all students in a school. In addition, it must take account of any formal and informal individual assessment of student learning that has taken place, and this should address any statutory requirements.

Curriculum planning for any learner or group needs to incorporate an overall long-term plan based on a global view of the learner and an awareness of the context within which the plan must take effect. From this long-term plan it is possible to draw up medium- and short-term plans. Formal planning for individuals should be dynamic and involve both the iterative process of planning the next steps in a student's learning programme on the basis of an analysis of student needs, and the compilation of a summative document (Tod *et al.*, 1998).

A flow chart that encompasses the initial assessment of a student's behaviour and learning within the curriculum context and leads to long-, medium- and short-term planning based on whole-school contextual factors might be as shown in the box on the facing page.

In this chapter we begin by discussing the process of planning individual interventions and go on to debate the kind of ethical considerations that need to be taken into account in any relationship where the role of a professional is to influence the behaviour of others. We then discuss a number of individualised interventions against their underpinning rationales.

Long-term learning and behaviour plan based on the student's aspirations and strengths with provision for access to the whole curriculum

Medium-term learning and behaviour plan outlined on the student's individual programme or intervention document which should incorporate:

- strategies appropriate to the context and the individual needs of the learner;
- termly and yearly achievable targets designed to lead to the learner's long-term goal;
- referral to the Key Stage (UK) and associated programmes of study;
- regular assessment opportunities.

Short-term, day-to-day behaviour planning which should incorporate:

- medium-term targets;
- opportunities for daily, formative assessment.

The planning process

In many countries, for example, England, Wales, Northern Ireland and New Zealand, the individual education plan (IEP), in some form, has become a major tool for planning programmes of study for individual students (DfE, 1994c; DfEE, 2001a; DENI, 1998a; Ministry of Education, 1998b). In the Republic of Ireland, the individual profile and learning programme, and in Scotland the Record of Need, serve the same purpose (Ireland, 2000; SEED, 2001). In general terms, these documents are expected to contain details of the nature of the child's learning difficulties, the special educational provision to be made and strategies to be used, specific programmes, activities, materials, and/or equipment, targets to be achieved in a specified time, monitoring and assessment arrangements and review arrangements and date. The details vary slightly from one country to another.

In England and Wales, the government's 'social inclusion' agenda has led to the issuing of further guidance to schools about ways to reduce pupil disaffection and truancy. In England, Circular 10/99, *Social Inclusion: Pupil Support*, identified certain groups of students as being at particular risk of exclusion from education:

- those with special educational needs;
- children in the care of local authorities;

- minority ethnic children;
- Travellers;
- young carers;
- those from families under stress;
- pregnant schoolgirls and teenage mothers.

(http://www.dfes.gov.uk/publications/guidanceonthelaw/
10-99/risk.htm)

This circular exhorted teachers to identify students who do not respond to actions in school to address disaffection and to design a Pastoral Support Programme (PSP) in liaison with external support services. A PSP 'should be automatically set up for a pupil who has several fixed period exclusions that may lead to a permanent exclusion or who has been otherwise identified as being at risk of failure at school through disaffection' (ibid.). However, it is not intended to replace the assessment and intervention stages of an IEP. Agencies external to the school are involved, as appropriate: social services and housing departments, voluntary organisations and the Youth Service, both statutory and voluntary, careers services and minority ethnic community groups.

Issues relating to planning for individual students

Planning for individual students within the context of the whole school and the whole class curriculum raises a number of issues which are not easy to resolve. Three major issues continue to be raised by researchers, by teachers in schools and, in England, by the government's inspection arm, OFSTED, in relation to the compilation and use of IEPs. These issues involve how to do the following:

- cope with the time demands on paperwork (OFSTED, 1997);
- embed IEPs into the curriculum;
- conceptualise appropriate targets.

The pressure on schools to comply with the procedures relating to IEPs, in particular the heavy demands on time, have been well documented (OFSTED, 1997). It is important therefore for schools, with the support of the school staff, to develop ways of working that keep this pressure to a minimum while at the same time considering how to develop systems for ensuring that the learning programme is carried out, monitored and evaluated. Attempts to reduce the bureaucratic demands on schools of the IEP process have been summarised below from Tod *et al.* (1998):

- allocating the meeting arrangements and collation and distribution of information to clerical staff;

- using in-service training to encourage class teachers and form teachers to prepare IEPs and to support all those involved in the education of students with IEPs to monitor progress;
- delegating responsibility for IEPs to one person in each subject area for overseeing the progress of all students experiencing difficulties in learning;
- training classroom assistants in aspects of the process;
- organising group learning plans which incorporate the monitoring of individual students' progress;
- increasing the involvement of parents or carers which can result in a higher degree of 'fit' for the individual student;
- using electronic means of communication (which has become increasingly common in schools) to generate reports for all students from, for example, banks of comments pre-existing in a data bank. Many of the issues relating to the use of pre-specified comments for all students apply equally to the use of computerised files of comments for the specific purpose of generating IEP documents, in particular that of time efficiency versus individuality of approach.

Target setting

In some institutions there may be a difference of opinion about the level of detail required for the targets that are set for students. This might be addressed by considering the purpose of the IEP or individual profile which, as Tod *et al.* (1998) note, is to facilitate student learning by means of the effective negotiation and planning of learning goals as well as the nature of the assessment it reflects.

Lessons may be planned to facilitate understanding of content, develop concepts or skills, practise problem solving, or encourage students' personal interests. Sometimes it happens that barriers are created to children's learning simply by the way in which material designed to facilitate understanding of a concept is presented. Where students experience difficulty, it is essential to tease out whether the problem lies at the level of conceptual understanding or is the result of the mode of communication, especially when this is reliant on written text.

Individual plans, profiles or records can only be as effective as the rigour of the thinking underlying their design. Similar issues arise in relation to target setting for IEPs and individual profiles within the national context. The strength of targets may be that they provide a focus for the combined efforts of all those concerned to support a learner's progress and highlight the need to link planning and provision. However, there are specific areas of the curriculum where it may be problematic to conceptualise measurable targets. These areas involve behaviour, the emotions and creativity.

Setting measurable targets is closely associated with behavioural approaches. A school and a national curriculum can be seen as a ladder of progression which children are expected to climb, with specific assessment learning goals at each rung. An inherent difficulty in this view, however, is that not all children learn the same way, so setting targets which follow in a similar sequence for all students is not necessarily appropriate. Dockrell and McShane (1993) highlight problems associated with this approach and note that: 'One of the major criticisms of task analysis and learning objectives is the conceptualization of the learning process.' They also comment that 'there may be a number of routes by which a child can acquire mastery, rather than a single instructional hierarchy that is common to all children'. They note that carrying out a task analysis assures that each child will 'learn the task components in the same order, because the task is analysed and not the learning processes or the learning context'. There is also the possibility that an 'over-reliance on task components can lead to a rigid application of prescriptive teaching, which takes no account of the knowledge a child brings to any given task or the specific strategies that a child utilizes' (Dockrell and McShane, in Open University, 2002, pp. 196–7). In addition, some areas lend themselves to this approach more easily than others. In the area of behaviour and emotional development, notions of task analysis and mastery learning are clearly problematic.

Interventions to support inclusion

Within the context of improving student behaviour in schools there is a wide range of intervention strategies that might be adopted. In a national context where inclusion of all students in mainstream schools is promoted, it is important for schools to choose behaviour management strategies which are compatible with inclusion rather than withdrawal.

Specific intervention strategies can promote inclusive teaching practices. Selection of strategies highlights essential differences between mainstreaming and inclusion. Mainstreaming focuses on the rights of all students to participate in regular education. It is concerned with issues such as equity of access and provision of resources. Inclusion, on the other hand, focuses on ways in which regular education needs to change in order to fully include more diverse students in classroom and school learning activities. The changes that regular education needs to make include modifications to curriculum delivery, to classroom pedagogies, and to the school systems and structures needed to promote these changes (for example, provision of on-site professional development to support all teachers to fully include more diverse students in their classes):

- Work within an educational/ecological paradigm prioritises interventions that enhance students' engagement in classroom activities and learning achievement, rather than interventions that focus on social work, lifestyle, or counselling issues. Educational/ecological interventions include class-wide or school-wide strategies to improve individual, small-group or whole-class teaching and learning. These strategies are implemented within specific curriculum areas and classroom contexts in which students are experiencing behavioural and learning difficulties. Their effectiveness is evaluated from data that assess not just student behaviour, but also the quality of the learning environments in which students are placed.

- Work within a collaborative/problem-solving model of professional work prioritises interventions which involve colleagues, teachers and students in:

  - defining what the challenging behaviours might be;
  - locating where those behaviours are occurring;
  - developing strategies for changing those behaviours;
  - identifying what counts as evidence to evaluate whether or not those strategies have been effective.

  Working within a collaborative problem-solving model typically results in teachers, colleagues, and students gaining additional professional expertise in managing behaviour, as well as achieving a positive behaviour outcome for an individual, group or class of students.

- Work within a cultural understanding of student behaviour prioritises improving challenging behaviour by taking into account the cultural contexts of that behaviour. Each culture has its own preferred strategies for meeting and greeting, for showing respect to people who are older than them or who hold positions of authority. Different cultures also have preferred ways of interacting, of learning and teaching, and of evaluating the quality of learning and teaching. Behaviour management strategies that incorporate culturally preferred ways of thinking and acting are especially important when class teachers come from ethnic or cultural groups that differ from those of their students. However, what is even more critical here is for teachers fully to understand their own cultural beliefs, values and practices, and how these impact upon students' cultural beliefs, values and practices. This impact is mediated primarily through the quality of the relationships and interactions they engender with their students.

- Work intended to improve the quality of theorising about behaviour is not confined to finding ways to increase or decrease specific targeted behaviours, but more importantly to gain a better understanding of the causes and functions of behaviour in different settings and contexts. Improving theorising leads to a more clearly stated rationale supported by appropriate evidence. Some interventions attempt to change behaviour by altering or manipulating aspects of the settings in which it occurs, while other interventions focus on altering behaviour by changing its consequences. Interventions employed in applied behaviour analysis and in the functional assessment of behaviour involve the use of careful observation and recording to try to uncover either remote or immediate antecedents or consequences of behaviour, some of which can be altered by teachers. This may well lead to better theorising, for example, about how both physical and/or social events (such as building positive teacher–student relationships) can combine to highlight powerful behavioural antecedents (contexts) and consequences (reinforcement contingencies). Such information will contribute to a better understanding of how a particular behaviour came about, how it is maintained, and how to go about changing it.

Ethical principles guiding behavioural interventions

McLeod believes that the ethical codes which underpin behavioural interventions with individuals 'are a set of core moral principles: autonomy, non-maleficence, beneficence, justice and fidelity' (1998, p. 289):

> One of the fundamental moral principles in our culture is the autonomy of individuals. People are understood as having the right to freedom of action and freedom of choice, in so far as the pursuit of these freedoms does not interfere with the freedom of others. . . . Another implication . . . of the concept of autonomy lies in the notion of informed consent . . .
> . . . freedom of choice and action . . . is also limited by a variety of practical circumstances. For example, few people would suppose that young children are capable of informed consent regarding the offer of counselling help, but it is difficult to decide at just what age a young person is able to give consent. . . .
> *Non-maleficence* refers to the instruction to all helpers or healers that they must 'above all do no harm'. *Beneficence* refers to the injunction to promote human welfare . . .
> The principle of *justice* is primarily concerned with the fair distribution of resources and services, . . . the principle of justice has particular relevance to the question of access to services . . .
> The principle of *fidelity* relates to the existence of loyalty, reliability, dependability and action in good faith. Lying, deception and exploitation are all examples of primary breaches of fidelity.

McLeod goes on to point out that, while autonomy, non-maleficence, beneficence, justice and fidelity are each important in most situations, they may conflict with each other in any particular situation. He cites Kitchener's (1984) review of theories of moral philosophy as suggesting a number of possible ways of resolving such dilemmas for practitioners. Utilitarianism (John Stuart Mill, 1868) for example, with its focus on the 'greatest good for the greatest number' suggests that a dilemma related to beneficence can be seen 'in the light of the costs and benefits for each participant in the event; for example, the client, the family of the client, other people who are involved and the counsellor' (McLeod, 1998, p. 273). Another philosophical approach derives from the work of Kant (1952), who proposed that 'ethical decisions should be *universalisable*. In other words, if it is right to breach confidentiality in this case, it must be right to do so in all similar cases in the future' (McLeod, 1998).

To these issues we would add cultural safety, that is, tolerance and respect for students' values and preferences, and providing learning contexts where they are seen as normal. One of the criticisms of behaviour interventions in schools is that they tend to ignore the importance of cultural and community contexts, together with the traditional values, in which behaviour is defined and understood (Glynn and Bishop, 1995; Macfarlane, 1997, 2000a, 2000b). As a result they tend to marginalise the voices of those whose behaviour is considered problematic by teachers. For example, programmes such as Assertive Discipline (Canter and Canter, 1992) are silent on the cultural contexts and understandings of behaviour. Hence we suggest additional ethical principles that should guide behavioural interventions when working with students and families from cultural minority groups. In a study seeking culturally appropriate ways to address Māori people's concerns about research into their lives, Bishop (1996a, 1996b), developed a framework to evaluate and guide investigations into Māori community research contexts that is relevant in considering behaviour interventions for individual students in schools. The framework consists of a series of questions around the five themes concerned with power and control. Applying Bishop's framework to evaluating behavioural interventions would pose questions such as:

1 *Initiation.* Who initiated the intervention with respect to an individual student's behaviour? How did this happen? Who set the goals? What were the goals? Who designed how they are to be addressed?

2 *Benefits.* What benefits will there be? Who will benefit? How does it support the aspirations of the student? What assessment criteria will be used to establish benefits? What assessment and evaluation systems will be used? Who decides on the methods and procedures of assessment and evaluation? How will this intervention benefit the student? Who else will benefit from the intervention?

3 *Representation.* Whose interests, needs and concerns are represented in the design and implementation of the intervention? How were the goals of the intervention established and by whom? How were the tasks allocated? What agency do individuals or groups have? Whose voice is heard in describing and reporting the intervention?

4 *Legitimation.* What authority do the authors of the intervention have? Who decides what is accurate? Who theorises the outcomes of the intervention? Who legitimates its results?

5   *Accountability.* To whom are the authors of the intervention account-
    able? Who owns the cultural knowledge being shared? Who can
    access this cultural knowledge? Who controls the distribution of new
    knowledge?

Undeniably, social pathological and deficit theorising approaches to behavioural interventions have been applied with some minority ethnic groups.
These approaches have perpetuated an ideology of cultural superiority that
have inhibited the development of power-sharing processes, and the
legitimation of diverse cultural world-views.

Designing interventions

Given the diversity of approaches to behavioural intervention with individual
students, it is important to have a clear understanding of which type of
intervention might be appropriate to address which need, as well as a clear
understanding of its theoretical rationale. Below we outline a number of
interventions from a range of psychological and medical perspectives.

'Multi-Element Planning' (MEP)

As noted in Moore's work on functional assessment of disruptive behaviour
(Chapter 6), the design and development of effective individual intervention
programmes based on behavioural principles require clear assessment of both
student performance and the learning environment. One practical approach
currently used in parts of the UK as well as in other areas of the world is that
of 'Multi-Element Planning' which takes account of a range of:

• potential causes of the problems experienced by the child;
• factors that appear to maintain the behaviour judged as problematic;
• strategies related to improving the learning environment, the teaching
  skills that will be useful to the child;
• strategies that will prevent the recurrence of the problematic behaviour
  or provide a way of safeguarding the child, peers and staff when the
  behaviour does recur.

Pitchford (2004, p. 323) sets his approach to multi-element planning within
a very clear ethical framework. He poses the following questions before any
assessment or intervention is devised:

• What gives us the right to manipulate or change someone's behaviour?
• How certain are we that the problem behaviour is not a perfectly
  reasonable response to unreasonable circumstances?

- If we do intervene, how ethically sound are our techniques and what is their record of effectiveness (Cooper *et al.*, 1987; Grant and Evans, 1994)?

Pitchford's questions take on a particular significance in the context of designing behavioural interventions for students from cultural groups different from that of the practitioner. Pitchford cites the Multi-Element Planning as described by LaVigna and Donnellan (1986) which has four main components:

1   *Ecological strategies* 'to examine whether there are mismatches between the child and his/her environment that require a change in the environment not a change in the child (Pitchford, 2004, p. 324). Change strategies should be considered in relation to a number of contexts: interpersonal, physical, and instructional.
2   *Positive programming* which involves teaching children skills that will have a positive impact on their lives working on the assumption that 'learning is empowering, gives dignity to the individual, helps them get their needs met and helps them cope with an imperfect world' (Pitchford, 2004, p. 325). Three areas of skill development are addressed within this framework, general, functionally equivalent and coping:

    (a)   General, that is 'academic or life skills that the child has not mastered that are having a negative impact on his/her quality of life' (Pitchford, 2004, p. 325).
    (b)   Functionally equivalent, that is, socially acceptable skills or behaviour that will serve the same purpose for the student as that which is seen as unacceptable. 'No matter how strange, behaviour always has a purpose or a function (LaVigna and Donnellan, 1986). If we understand that purpose or function we are more likely to be able to channel it in a constructive way' (Pitchford, 2004, p. 326). Pitchford offers examples of 'problem behaviours and their functions together with the functionally-equivalent skills that could be included in a multi-element plan to help the child achieve the same end' (see Table 8.1).
    (c)   Coping skills designed to help students 'manage and tolerate the frustrations and difficulties in their lives'.

3   *Preventive strategies*, comprising the antecedent control strategy and the use of reward strategies (LaVigna and Donnellan, 1986):

    (a)   Antecedent control strategies include removing those events that act as a direct trigger to problem behaviours (Glynn, 1982).
    (b)   Reward strategies only work well when they are used in the context of the types of positive programming and ecological strategies

described earlier. Rewards can be artificial. The teacher will not always be there to reward the child and since our aim is to teach the child to be independent, rewards may only be a short term expedient. From a behavioural perspective, basically there are three ways of rewarding children (LaVigna and Donnellan, 1986):

(i) rewarding children for being 'good';
(ii) rewarding children for not being 'naughty';
(iii) rewarding children for being 'naughty' less often than they were before. However, this technique, as Pitchford comments, may be inappropriate for behaviour seen as dangerous.

4 *Reactive strategies* which 'are included in the plan in order to safeguard the child, his or her peers and staff when things go wrong. . . . In particular we should know what safe non-punitive techniques will be used if the problem behaviour occurs and what support will be given to the child. Just as important is consideration of the practical and emotional help or support that should be given to the member of staff' (Pitchford, 2004, p. 333).

Table 8.1 Multi-element plan to help child gain functionally equivalent skill

Problem	Function	Functionally equivalent skill
Shouting out	Initiate social contact	Teach hand up and waiting quietly Teach hand up and saying, 'Excuse me, Miss, I've finished my work'
Aggression (bullying)	Obtain things or events (children are made to share or give sweets unwillingly)	Teach play skills, turn-taking skills and negotiation skills
Tantrums	Express emotion	Teach child to express emotions in writing or art or small world play
Tantrums	Avoid situations (e.g. repeated failure in maths)	Teach key maths skills Teach how to ask for help
Makes silly noises	To gain excitement (children laugh)	Teach child • how to tell jokes • right and wrong time and place to tell jokes

Three practical steps need to be taken before drawing up the plan:

1 Identify the frequency, seriousness and the contexts in which the behavioural problems occur.
2 Prioritise the problems.
3 Collect baseline data against which progress can be assessed. All data collected should be used to support the setting of targets for the MEP, reviewing progress and establishing appropriate criteria for rewards.

Behaviour modification and applied behaviour analysis

One of the most common applications of a behaviourist approach to improving student behaviour in schools is that of behaviour modification programmes for individuals. Behaviour modification is an approach which, as McLeod (1998) notes, takes as its starting point the work of Skinner (1938). That is, in response to any stimulus, an individual has a repertoire of possible responses. The behaviour that s/he performs is that which is reinforced or rewarded in the particular context. This principle is known as operant conditioning (see above, Chapter 6). When principles of operant conditioning are applied to the behaviour of individuals in the context of schools, they suggest that it is helpful to reward or reinforce desired or appropriate behaviour, and ignore inappropriate behaviour. If a behaviour or response is not rewarded, it will, according to Skinnerian principles, show a temporary increase in frequency of intensity and then fade out of the student's repertoire of behaviour.

A careful account of how the field of applied behaviour analysis employs operant conditioning principles to understanding and changing human behaviour in everyday home, school and community settings is provided in a seminal article by Baer *et al.* (1968). These authors introduced a new field of enquiry known as applied behaviour analysis which draws on the fields of psychology, education and human development.

The effectiveness of behaviour modification and applied behaviour analysis programmes in schools is highly dependent on 'the existence of a controlled social environment, in which the behaviour of the learner can be consistently reinforced in the intended direction' (McLeod, 1998, p. 66). This means that 'key participants' such as teachers and parents have to be trained in ways to apply the technique.

However, there are a number of caveats in adopting this approach:

It is essential . . . that whoever is supplying the behaviour modification is skilled and motivated, so that the client is not exposed to contradictory reinforcement schedules. Furthermore, because behaviour modification relies on the fact that the person supplying the reinforcement has real power to give or withhold commodities [as well as social reinforcers] which are highly valued by the client, there is the possibility of corruption and abuse . . .

Another way in which behaviour modification can be abusive in practice is by too much emphasis on the technique known as 'time out' . . . problematic behaviour patterns, such as aggressive and violent behaviour, can be interrupted by placing the person in a room to 'cool off'. The intention is that violence is not rewarded by attention from staff or other residents, but that resumption of rationality is rewarded, by the person being allowed out of the room. In principle, this can be a valuable intervention strategy, which can help some people to change behaviour that can lead them into severe trouble. The danger is that staff may use time out in a punitive manner . . . This technique may result in an abuse of . . . civil liberties.

(ibid., pp. 66–7)

The particular danger of using time out, as alluded to by McLeod, is that its effectiveness as a mild form of punishment (removal from opportunities to access reinforcement from ongoing positive events) depends upon the reinforcing quality of 'time in'. Temporary 'sin binning' of a football player for breaking a rule is likely to be effective. However, temporary 'sending out of the room' of a student who disrupts a boring and confusing lesson is not. Behavioural modification techniques can be very powerful and for that reason, if used, need to be considered very carefully within a clear ethical framework related to discussion of the best interests of students, as we have noted in the time out examples above. In other words, students' interests may be better served by professional input into improving the quality and interests of the classroom lessons ('time in'), rather than by professional input into training teachers and staff in the sole use of punitive time out.

Practice in classrooms

Rogers (1994a, 1994b) may be interpreted as presenting a behavioural self-management approach to encourage primary school students whom he describes as 'behaviourally-disordered' to take responsibility for their own behaviour:

> While a school needs to pursue appropriate counselling and welfare provisions for such students, they will often need to learn how to behave appropriately. While most students respond to the normal socialisation into rights-respecting behaviour, some will need to be *specifically taught* . . . learning targets can be developed as specific behaviour plans that involve teacher modelling, student-rehearsal and feedback and encouragement in the natural setting of the classroom.
>
> (Rogers, B., 1994, pp. 166–7)

There is an important general issue to be noted here. Students' inappropriate behaviour is conceptualised as a skills deficit to be addressed through modelling, instruction and reinforced practice so that students will acquire more appropriate behaviours. Students' behaviour is not conceptualised simply as a motivational (or performance) deficit which requires the application of positive and punitive consequences. In Rogers' view, a child's background is no 'excuse' for poor behaviour in school.

> There are children whose behaviour can be explained by 'causative pathologies' (Rogers, 1994b) such as home environment, socio-emotional deprivation, even abuse . . . we cannot simply allow their background to excuse them from:
>
> - taking ownership for their disruptive behaviour, or facing account-ability for such behaviour by facing appropriate consequences or
> - learning that behaviour is a 'choice' not merely an accident of birth, or location, and that one can learn to make better and more conscious choices about behaviour . . .
>
> [W]e will do them a disservice if we simply say they can't help it . . .
> Positive behaviour management (Rogers, 1991, 1994a) is not merely about controlling children but teaching children to repair and rebuild disordered patterns of behaviour.
>
> (Rogers, B., 1994, p. 167)

Hence, effective behaviour management is not simply about increasing and decreasing behaviours, but also about teaching students to discriminate between settings (times and places) where certain behaviours are appropriate and acceptable, and other settings where they are not.

Rogers goes on to advocate the use of individualised behaviour management strategies with some students. These strategies should make clear to the student what behaviours are unacceptable but should also provide the student with opportunities for modelling, rehearsing and reinforcement for behaviours that are acceptable.

> A key element of behaviour-teaching plans is explaining to the child what his current disordered behaviour looks and sounds like, and how it affects his peers . . . Teachers can illustrate the BD child's off-task behaviour on an A4-sized card prior to the meeting . . . The teacher can ask the student for permission to show them what it looks like when the student calls out, butts in, is motorically restless 'Do you mind if I show you what you do when . . . ?' This mirroring is brief, and purely illustrative . . . At this point the teacher is . . . raising awareness for the next step – the need to plan alternative behaviours which will increase social approval and increase the likelihood of positive learning outcomes . . . It is important to model the new behaviour to the child to enhance

specificity. This can be done by saying, 'Let me show you how I want you to:

- move through the room,
- put your hand up/ask questions in group discussion,
- speak in a reasonable voice,
- get teacher's attention and help.' . . .

Behaviour (like any 'skill') benefits from rehearsal. Having modelled the target behaviour, the child is encouraged to copy: 'OK, Jarrod, your turn – show me how you will come to the mat and sit quietly.' During rehearsal the student will need some fine tuning, descriptive feedback and encouragement . . . Such rehearsal may need to be spread over a couple of sessions, the first session being focused on the current behaviour and the need for a plan. . . . Back in the classroom the grade teacher will acknowledge the child's approximations to the plan with positive verbal encouragement.

(Rogers, B., 1994, pp. 167–9)

It is important to recognise that this type of intervention involves the skilful manipulation of both antecedents and consequences, and that training takes place in the context where problem behaviour occurs. However, it is important to note that Rogers' position on children's backgrounds providing 'no excuse' for 'unacceptable' behaviour in the classroom is a distinctly mono-cultural position. It is silent on the issue that behaviours that are unacceptable to the culture of the teacher and school may be functional and important to the well-being of the child's home culture.

Rogers' solution to repeated non-compliance with teachers' expectations of behaviour is time out from the classroom:

BD (behaviour difficulty) students need to know that if they continue to be disruptive in a group setting or cause another child to be hurt then they will go straight into cooling-off time (time out in the classroom) . . . Rather than emphasising punishment, the teacher will make clear that when students make it difficult for others to feel safe, or learn, or be treated with respect, they may have to face time out if they do not respond to teacher discipline . . . The primary emphasis of time out is temporary exclusion for the student to regain control and give the class time to regroup . . . This process needs proper planning with no imputation of failure to the initiating teacher. Time out, of itself, will not change disordered behaviour in the long term.

(Rogers, B., 1994, pp. 169–70)

In this instance, time out has been used as a contingent opportunity for the child to 'escape' from an unsafe or difficult setting. In contexts such as this, there is a serious risk that time out may be functioning as a positive reinforcer for the disruptive or dysfunctional behaviour being engaged in. However, as noted above, time out is also a withdrawal of opportunities to access reinforcement for on-going appropriate behaviours. The effectiveness of time out therefore, as noted earlier, depends on the qualities of 'time in'.

Behavioural responses to students with Attention Deficit/Hyperactive Disorder (AD/HD)

In the summary of 150 intervention studies of students with AD/HD (BPS, 1996), seven approaches are identified which are based on a cognitive-behavioural viewpoint. These approaches focus on the effects of consequences through positive reinforcement, response cost and training in the reduction of behaviour viewed as problematic (ibid., pp. 47–8):

1   *Positive reinforcement or token reinforcement*: These strategies appeared to result in reduced activity, increased 'time on task' and improved academic performance. It is argued that such methods were cost-effective, could be applied to individuals or groups fairly easily and were relatively familiar to most educators. However, evidence highlighted the common failure of behaviours to generalise. Several studies showed that behaviour management and medication were most effective when combined.

2   *Behaviour reduction strategies*: Mildly aversive short and immediate procedures (reprimands or redirection) seemed effective with primary age children, especially when combined with positive reinforcement [for alternative behaviours to those displayed by students identified as having AD/HD].

3   *Response cost*: A combination of positive and negative reinforcement procedures [and 'response cost' (a mild punishment which involves making the target, undesirable, behaviour more difficult and more effortful to perform)] through the use of token procedures was suggested as promising for educators. This [response cost] would represent a next step when positive reinforcement did not result in sufficient effects.

4   *Parent or family training*: Some studies have demonstrated effectiveness in reducing activity level, conflict and anger intensity and an increase in 'on task' behaviour and compliance. Parents have reported reduced stress and an improvement in the quality of parent–child interaction. However, all studies were clinic initiated and none were combined with inter-ventions by educators. Medication was part of most studies.

5   *Self-instruction or cognitive behaviour training*: The evidence remained unclear and contradictory, particularly when studies also involved medication.

6   *Task or environmental stimulation*: Given the laboratory context of studies on the exploration of optimal presentation features (e.g. colour, rate, response activity), the review reports little evidence which can be generalised to schools as yet.

7   *Biofeedback*: [This involves providing the child with some form of visual or auditory feedback on levels of physiological states (e.g. heart rate) with a view to the child learning to control and monitor those states] Because of the relatively improved outcome of other forms of intervention, any work in this area can only be regarded as experimental at present.

Engaging peer support to modify behaviour

Gable and Arllen (1995, pp. 25–8) illustrate how 'peer confrontation' might be used to modify individual students' disruptive behaviour in the classroom. They describe a student named Jimmie who exhibited frequent off-task behaviour and insulted his peers with hurtful or offensive names. His remarks disrupted the class and on occasions escalated into physical fights with classmates.

After amassing a range of information on the behaviour in context, Jimmie's teacher decided to introduce an intervention involving peer confrontation by a small group of students who were members of Jimmie's reading group. These students were chosen because they had demonstrated 'peer-group acceptance, willingness to participate, acceptable expressive and receptive language skills, compliance with teacher directions, responsiveness to adult reinforcement, and a satisfactory school attendance record', all skills important to the role of peer tutors (ibid.).

The teacher introduced the intervention by explaining that there are times when everyone needs to learn better ways to behave toward others. She defined the current problem as inappropriate comments and hurtful remarks towards classmates. Next, the teacher and the students engaged in a problem-solving exercise where she described a problem situation and asked the students how Jimmie might behave in ways that were more acceptable:

> For example, Jimmie needs a partner to practice reading sight words. Instead of making inflammatory remarks when Mike does not make room for him to sit down and practice, what could Jimmie do? The students brainstorm suggestions such as 'Jimmie could say, 'Can I be your partner,' or 'I'd like to work with you.'' Students practice prompting Jimmie to make these responses.

Finally, the teacher suggested several ways the group might respond when Jimmie behaves appropriately.

In five 30-minute sessions, students were taught to do the following:

> (a) identify the target behavior, (b) challenge the inappropriate behavior of a classmate ('I don't like being called names'), (c) ignore provocative acts (break eye contact, walk away), and (d) prompt and positively reinforce incompatible responses (e.g., smile and express verbal approval).

Explanation: The most effective strategies to prepare peer behavior modifiers include modelling the intervention procedure, student role-play/simulation, and adult feedback. In addition, accumulated research suggests that both students who serve as behavior modifiers and target youngsters themselves should be trained in the confrontation process.

The teacher also recognised that, when introducing an intervention to address challenging behaviour, it is essential to teach and reinforce alternative (incompatible) behaviour as well:

Because the target behavior consists of inappropriate verbalizations, Ms. Jones first teaches and then prompts and reinforces positive verbal initiations (e.g., 'I really like the way you draw, Mary'; or, 'That's a real sharp shirt, Phil').

Explanation: Research has shown that it is not enough to simply attempt to decrease or eliminate a noxious behavior. Teachers must promote an incompatible or replacement behavior, for which the student can gain positive reinforcement. As Nelson (1987) points out, in seeking to eliminate undesirable behavior, we must guard against unwittingly creating an aversive classroom environment.

The teacher acknowledged that students need to see a reason to commit themselves to helping their peers. She therefore encouraged students:

to view themselves as stakeholders and anticipate what might happen if Jimmie did use 'bad words' with another student(s). She helps the group to identify the results (or effects) of the target behavior – for example, 'If Jimmie starts calling names, we might have a fight and all lose recess.' When peer modifiers, or Jimmie, initiate an appropriate response, she says something like, 'You were really very helpful. Keep it up!'

The teacher realised that if peer confrontation is to work with a larger group, 'then she must provide an incentive to sustain student interest, for both target student(s) and peer change agents'. Therefore, she introduced:

a group contingency arrangement, to positively reinforce positive changes in Jimmie's behavior and the accomplishments of his classmates.

. . . She tells the reading group that for every day that Jimmie has fewer name-calling incidents, there would be 5 minutes of board-game play for all students at the end of the period.

After peer confrontation produces positive results during reading, Ms Jones implements the procedure for the entire day. She changes the contingency arrangement so the entire class receive 5 minutes of extra recess each day, contingent upon a reduction in the number of 'name calls.'

The teacher was aware of the problems that might occur when peers are responsible for deciding whether their classmates earn a reward so she observed the process and was prepared to change the intervention, as necessary:

> Once she has combined peer confrontation with a dependent group-oriented contingency, Ms. Jones decides to promote appropriate verbal exchanges with all of her students. She devises a bulletin board entitled 'Courtesy Cards.' In conjunction with a unit on creative writing, she encourages students to write something that is complimentary about another student and to place it on the board. At the end of the week, if everyone has received at least one compliment card, Ms. Jones schedules a card-sharing party, with refreshments. In this way, she incorporates an interdependent group-oriented contingency to highlight prosocial student behavior.
>
> (Gable and Arllen, 1995, pp. 25–8)

Cognitive-behavioural approaches

One way to address students' behaviour that teachers find challenging is to develop interventions built on a cognitive-behavioural approach (see Chapter 6). A common application of this approach is to the management of feelings of anger (Harris, 1976; Wilde, 1994, 1995). As Wilde (2001) notes, the first step is to encourage students to recognise bodily sensations that precede displays of anger.

> One of the simplest ways to teach children to identify their internal body cues is to ask them to respond to the query, 'What do you notice in your body just before you get angry?'
>
> Students often say they:
>
> - feel warm all over
> - notice their pulse is racing
> - make fists with their hands
> - have a clenched jaw and hold their teeth very tight
> - start shaking all over and
> - feel their muscles get tight, especially in their arms.
>
> (2001, pp. 192–3)

The intention is to give them the chance 'to distract themselves or walk away before they react' (ibid., p. 192). Distraction involves persuading students to think about something other than the focus of their anger. It can be done through helping them to remember in detail:

. . . the happiest, funniest, or most relaxing scene they can remember. For example:

- The time they hit a home run to win a game.
- The time they got the perfect present for Christmas.
- Their best birthday party.
- A great day at the beach.

(ibid., p. 193)

The assumption behind this is that: '*It is very difficult, if not impossible, for a client to think of a distraction scene and still become angry.* Since anger is produced by thinking demanding thoughts, . . . the distraction scene will buy them time' (ibid., p. 194).

A rational-emotive therapy example (RET)

The example below of one particular cognitive approach to 'managing behaviour' that is sometimes advocated for use by teachers is 'rational-emotive imaging' (REI). Wilde (2001) offers an example of REI in practice in the form of 'peer confrontation'. He advises starting a session with an individual student by asking him or her to visualise the scenario where the student's 'troublesome' behaviour is occurring and to ask him/her to describe all the details about the situation: what s/he hears, sees and does:

> Adult: Amy, I want you to listen very closely to what I'm going to tell you. I want you to be aware only of my voice and focus on what I say. Try to block everything else out of your mind for the time being.
>
> Imagine you are back in your class having problems with Mr. Smith. Picture the room in your mind. See all the posters on the walls and everything else that is in your class. Now go ahead and let yourself feel like you did that day. Feel all the anger you felt back then. Stay with that scene and try to feel just like you felt in the class. When you feel that way, wiggle your finger and let me know you're there.
>
> It is a good idea to look for behavioural signs confirming that the child is actually feeling angry (i.e., the jaw may tighten, brows furrow and some children even make fists).

The child is encouraged to continue to focus on the situation s/he has described for up to 40 seconds and to remain upset. Then the teacher might say:

> Now I want you to keep thinking you are in the class but I want you to calm yourself down. Stay in the classroom in your mind but try to calm down. Instead of being very upset, try to get calmer. Instead of being really mad, try to work toward only feeling irritated. Keep working at

it until you can calm yourself down. When you can make yourself calm, wiggle your finger again.

Students usually can reach a state of relative calm within a fairly short period of time (i.e., one to two minutes). Once a child has wiggled his or her finger, it is time to bring him or her back to the here and now. Simply say something like, 'Okay, now open your eyes.' Next ask, '*What did you say to yourself to calm yourself down?*' If the child was able to calm himself down, he had to be thinking calming thoughts. The only other way to calm down would be to mentally leave the situation (i.e., no longer visualize the classroom). This usually doesn't happen but if it does, try the exercise over encouraging the child to keep imagining the scene but working to calm down.

After completing the imagination game, clients should then be able to state the thought that allowed them to calm down. A typical calming thought that might have been produced from the above scenario would be, 'Even though I don't like the problems I've been having with my teacher, I can live with it. I don't have to like what he does.' Once the child has produced a calming thought, the therapist is wise to write it down. Now the client can practice this mental imagery several times a day and use this same calming thought each time. In effect, this technique allows kids to mentally practice dealing with a difficult situation in a new, more productive way. It is important that they practice this make believe game on a regular basis if they are going to learn to handle their anger in a more productive fashion.

Usually children can learn to do the Imagination Game by themselves after having been led through the technique a few times by the counsellor, teacher, or parent. It is also possible to make an audio tape recording of this intervention for the child to use at home as some students prefer using the tape rather than leading themselves through this technique. Both can be effective if used regularly.

(Wilde, 2001, pp. 194–5)

However, this approach faces serious challenges in terms of ethical issues involved in selecting behaviour change strategies. It is important to note that the intervention (training) in this approach takes place outside of the classroom context in which the problem behaviour occurs – thereby requiring the student to 'generalise' what he or she has learned back into the classroom. There is also the question of the 'safety' of such an approval for use by un-trained teachers. There seems to have been little or no emphasis to date on gathering data to ensure the child is implementing the procedures correctly, that the procedures are doing no harm to the child, and, finally, that there are clear positive behaviour outcomes for the child. In the absence of such data, it appears highly unwise and unprofessional to advocate or promote the use of RET by teachers within classrooms and schools.

An eco-systemic position

As we saw in Chapter 6, the behaviour of individuals can also be viewed as part of an ecosystem. Cooper and Upton (1991) illustrate this perspective through the example of John, an 11-year-old boy (Cooper, 1990, pp. 29–30, 222–3). John's home background was materially deprived and there was considerable conflict within the family which consisted of John, an older unemployed brother, and his mother, a sole parent. John's mother worked at night in a club and slept during the day. John was a student at a special school for students 'with emotional and behavioural difficulties' where he reported himself to be the victim of bullying. John responded to the bullying by running away from the school. Cooper and Upton (1991) note how John says that when he has done this before:

> he has phoned his mother, who has then 'come up [to the school] and really shout[ed] at them [the staff]' concerning their failure to look after her son effectively. However, John's mother dislikes, for obvious reasons, being woken in the daytime, and the phone calls become a focus for conflict between John and his mother. Therefore, when John next absconds, he does not telephone his mother. Concerned about his absence, however, a member of staff does telephone John's mother to inform her of his abscondence. John, interpreting this act by the teacher as being unnecessarily extreme and malicious, owing to the conflict it causes at home, returns to the school and assaults the teacher with a chair. Eventually John is transferred to a residential school some considerable distance from his home. . . .
>
> There is . . . an interactional pattern evident in these events. John's family difficulties have a powerful influence on his response to the teacher's behaviour, whilst the teacher's behaviour and John's behaviour have an influence on these very family difficulties . . . it is important to note the systemic function performed by the bullying. John claims that he never complained to the staff about being bullied, because he believed them to be powerless to stop it, and yet he repeatedly involves his mother in the situation, where she acts as his advocate. It is, therefore, reasonable to hypothesise that John is using the bullying as a means of eliciting this protective behaviour in his mother, which is such a contrast to the painful conflict which characterises their relationship at home. This would also begin to explain the ferocity of John's response to the teacher, who has clearly not only foiled the means by which John obtains what he sees as a positive reaction from his mother, but has elicited the complete reverse of the desired response. Furthermore, if the bullying problem were to be eliminated, it is likely that John would seek some other means of eliciting his mother's involvement, possibly in the form of another excuse for absconding from the school.

Such an analysis indicates that . . . what is required is an intervention strategy which enables the needs of all participants to be met, and leads to the development of co-operative relationships between the individuals concerned. Any proposed strategy which violates these requirements will meet with resistance from the interactional system.

(Cooper and Upton, 1991, p. 24)

From an ecosystemic approach, an appropriate intervention would need to aim to involve John and his mother in a collaborative relationship:

the first stage in developing an intervention strategy is the family–school interview (Aponte 1976, Fine and Holt 1983, Power and Bartholomew 1985). This is usually organised by a consultant family therapist. The purpose of the interview is to observe the pupil–parent–school relationship in action, and to involve all parties in the development of a solution. Such consultations may result in the adjustment of systemic structure (Minuchin 1974), in the form of an adjustment in the roles performed by members of one or other of the systems involved, or in the adjustment of systemic boundaries, whereby weakened boundaries are strengthened, or overstrong boundaries are relaxed (see, for example, Power and Bartholomew 1985). In the present example, for instance, it might be suggested that the home-based relationship between John and his mother is lacking in warmth, to the extent that John has to engineer the type of situation described above, in which his mother plays a protective role. A possible remedy for this might be to seek out a situation in which John's mother performs a protective role. The precise nature of this remedy would be dependent upon the outcome of meetings between the family and the therapist.

(ibid., p. 24)

Conceptualising interventions from a range of perspectives: the case of autism

As noted in Chapter 1, behaviour seen as problematic in schools can be understood from a number of different perspectives. Consequently, different interventions have been designed to address the same behaviour. Autism and interventions designed to meet the learning needs of students identified as autistic provide interesting examples of this.

Constructivist approaches

In recent years in the special educational needs field there has been a move towards acknowledging that the source of students' difficulties in learning, including those difficulties associated with challenging behaviour, can result from factors in the learning environment (Clark *et al.*, 1997, 1998; Cline, 1992; Cooper, 1993; Dyson, 1997). Sometimes the source of difficulties is described as stemming from the interaction between the characteristics of the learner and those of the context (Wedell, 2000; Mittler, 2000). Some researchers, however, have taken a view of learning as 'situated', dynamic and interactive between learner and context (Greeno, 1998; Lave and Wenger, 1991, 1999) and, therefore, of difficulties in learning as situated and dynamic also (Lave and Wenger, 1999; McDermott, 1999; Mehan, 1996). Following this line of thinking and understanding that children actively engage in construing themselves and their learning about the world through social interaction implies that teachers need to be concerned with what students themselves make of the circumstance in which they find themselves (Wearmouth, 2003). It is important therefore to understand how children make sense of their own circumstances and what impression is conveyed to students of others' constructions of them.

Bruner comments upon the link between low self-esteem and behaviour that can be experienced as challenging to the school system: 'sometimes it is accompanied by depression sometimes by defiant anger' (1996, p. 37). He notes the crucial importance of self-advocacy to the development of self-esteem: 'the management of self-esteem is never settled, and its state is affected powerfully by the availability of supports provided from outside. They include above all the chance for discourse' (ibid.).

One fast-growing group of students whose perspective it is particularly important to understand is those who are disaffected from school. Failure to address the 'problems' of non-engagement with their education of significant numbers of disaffected students costs society dearly 'both in terms of reduced economic contribution in adult life and, for some, of criminal activity and prison (DfEE, 1997, p. 78). The evidence submitted to the Elton Committee (1989) in the UK by the National Children's Bureau as to practical steps which should be taken with regard to improving discipline in schools included advocating that schools should find ways of listening to and heeding the views of students in relation to school procedures, policies and curricula. However, where students behave in ways that imply rejection of the unspoken values and assumptions on which formal schooling rests, professionals may feel their authority is being threatened and may experience particular challenges in engaging with students' perspectives (McDermott, 1999; Ravenette, 1984). This process is likely to be exacerbated when students, school staff, and professionals come from different cultural backgrounds.

It appears obvious that taking the young person's view seriously and attempting to understand his/her perspective is essential to any consideration of how we might reduce obstacles to students' learning (Hart, 1995). Learning programmes are likely to be more effective when students have some sense of ownership over them. Pragmatically it seems very strange not to involve young people in decision-making about their education when their opinions are sought over so many other things in which they have a strong interest, for example where commercial interests are concerned. As Gardner notes:

> It seems ironical that children's views are taken very seriously by those who wish to produce a new flavour of crisps or a different style of chocolate bar; in other words, where they, as a group, have some economic power to back their choices.
>
> (1987, p. 104)

The notion of student self-advocacy is supported by international law. In the United Nations Convention on the Rights of the Child (1989; available online [May 2000]: www.freethechildren.org/campaigns/cr_uncrcdoc.html), Article 12 states:

> Parties shall assure to the child who is capable of forming his or her own views the right to express those views freely in all matters affecting the child, the views of the child being given due weight in accordance with the age and maturity of the child.
>
> For this purpose the child shall in particular be provided the opportunity to be heard in any judicial or administrative proceedings affecting the child, either directly or through a representative or an appropriate body, in a manner consistent with the procedural rules of national law.

Article 13 (1) states:

> The child shall have the right to freedom of expression; this right shall include the freedom to seek, receive and impart information and ideas of all kinds, regardless of all frontiers, either orally or in print, in the form of art or any other media of the child's choice.

Students as experts

Faircloth and Tippeconnic III (2000) assert that special education is a collaborative process that involves students, parents and teachers. Some writers clearly recognise the students themselves as experts on their own behaviour and learning (Bishop et al., 2001a; Bishop et al., 2003; Glynn et al., 1997). Ladson-Billings (1995) suggests that students are experts in the area of curriculum while Gray (1984) views students as directors of their own programme. Habel et al. (1999) highlight students' ability to evaluate their own educational programmes while Ewing and Yong (1992) see them as experts in learning styles, and Glynn et al. (1996) and Peck (1978) identify students' expertise as literacy teachers of their peers.

Ladson-Billings (1995) reported on eight teachers who had been identified both by professionals and the local community as teachers evidencing best practice for black American students. A common feature was a teacher–student relationship that was balanced and reciprocal. This feature sits comfortably alongside Pere's (1982) notions of 'ako' as an essential principle of learning in that the teacher and learner's roles are regularly exchanged and each is able to learn from the other. Students of the best practice teachers in Ladson-Billing's research were also encouraged to work collaboratively and to teach and be responsible for each other, to buddy and peer tutor, formally and informally.

In studies of the needs of students from minority cultures who experienced learning and/or behaviour difficulties (Bishop et al., 2001a; Glynn et al., 1997; Habel et al., 1999) the researchers began by listening to the students themselves. These researchers found that students had both clear views of their problems, as well as practical suggestions for improving their learning programmes. Students were easily able to indicate where a programme was working well or where it was working badly. Students were also able to explain why this was so. Further, Glynn et al. (1997), interviewing Māori students, found these students were also able to suggest solutions that were worthwhile and fair as well as being culturally appropriate. More importantly, they recognised that students experiencing learning and behavioural difficulties needed to be able to build worthwhile relationships with their educational professionals before engaging in any other agenda. From the students' own perspective it appeared that the educational professionals with whom they worked were more concerned with the production and promotion of their curriculum agenda than getting to know their students.

Because recent special educational developments in the UK, in New Zealand, and in many other countries have seen a shift to working within an inclusive paradigm (Moore et al., 1999; Thomson et al., 2000; Thomson et al., 2003) teachers and other educators are now required to deal with greater cultural, physical and intellectual diversity. This presents challenges in terms of programme development, class structures, time-management and curriculum delivery. Teachers are pivotal components of an inclusive paradigm for they are the link between the specialist expertise of parents and community, on the one hand, and the specialist professional support team, on the other (Berryman et al., 2002). With these additional responsibilities, the task of the teacher can be considerably challenging but also increasingly satisfying and rewarding.

Challenges for student self-advocacy in schools

Recognising and responding to the insight and expertise that students have in understanding their own behaviour, creates major challenges for professionals responsible for assisting students whose behaviour is seen as problematic. On the one hand, students' views should be sought regarding provision made for him/her and that teachers, as well as students, will be willing and able to engage in this activity. However, often teacher and student interests may conflict. On the other, traditional school structures and bureaucracy often prevent the expression of student opinion. Institutionalised resistance to change is a well-known problem in schools (Hargreaves and Hopkins, 1991). Teachers are professionals and it is their role to make informed decisions based on their knowledge and experience. However, in many schools, appealing to colleagues to respect the rights of the individual child will not be enough to establish student participation in decision-making processes. It is important, therefore, that stronger arguments for student participation should be brought to bear. Moreover, the assertion that 'teachers know best' can also hinder student participation.

Wade and Moore (1993) suggest that teachers believe student consultation is time-consuming and of little value; that decisions are made at a higher level and preclude consultation; that, even if given the opportunity for participation, students would not take the task seriously; and that the range of perspectives within a given group would not be coherent.

Gersch (2001) lists a number of dilemmas encountered during the development of research initiatives designed to support active student participation in decision-making processes (see Chapter 7). These issues illustrate the extent of the conflict between the roles of the participants. As discussed in Chapter 7, Gersch himself does not offer a single answer but feels that, if a positive way forward is to be found, then a mutually trusting, listening, open, non-judgemental relationship must be established between teacher and student. This is the type of relationship established within the professional development strategies developed by Bishop *et al.* (2003) to address the behavioural and learning needs of Māori students in New Zealand mainstream schools.

While international law and current developments within the field of inclusion support student self-advocacy, at the same time there is also a clear recognition that 'ascertaining the child's views may not always be easy' (DfE, 1994c, 3:3). In many schools professionals will have encountered some students with whom communication has been difficult, who have, seemingly, shut themselves off:

> Many are socially isolated and, to judge by body language, feel appalled at their own loneliness yet just cannot do anything about it. I well remember the case of 'Peter', undernourished, dirty, smelly, and always alone, but hovering as close to the entrance of the school building as he could manage. Deliberation on the situation led me to try to get him involved in a lunchtime mutual-support group of students, but was told on the phone by his father: 'I'm not having my son associating with a load of drongos. He's not a drongo. I don't want him labelled.' . . . I

could never find a way to communicate with 'Peter' to see if there was anything the school could do to support him better.

(Wearmouth, 2003, p. 68)

Some, like Larry, interviewed in a study of adults' recollection of school, may reject any overture by teachers:

> I really didn't want teachers to know me . . . They just did their job and no more. I got help when I wanted it – eventually. I didn't want teachers hanging around me. Explain, then go away – that's what I preferred.

(Wearmouth, 2000)

Others, like Mark, interviewed in the same study, may feel that one-to-one discussion on a personal level is unwarranted intrusion into their privacy:

> The first time I saw an educational psychologist she made me so angry that I went away and got hold of some books on child psychology so I could see where she was coming from. She couldn't get through to me at all after that because I put up so many barriers against her.

(ibid.)

In the past twenty years there has been progress in involving children more actively in their education. However, 'such progress as has occurred has been patchy, unsystematic and slow' (Gersch, 2001). The ethos for listening has to be supportive; it will not take place automatically. Lack of progress in promoting student self-advocacy is a matter of regret because, in listening to what students say about their education and their needs provides a 'wealth of untapped resource for teachers, schools and other professionals'. Awaiting discovery there is a 'gold mine of ideas, views, feedback, information and motivational energy' (ibid.).

From both a human rights perspective and the perspective of the student having active agency in his/her learning, listening to students and taking serious note of what they say is not an optional extra in managing behaviour in schools, but, rather one of its core principles. From a constructivist viewpoint, there is no separation between learning and personal transactions. As noted earlier, students actively engage in construing themselves and learning about the world through social interaction which itself shapes the pattern of their thought processes (Wearmouth, 2003). Every act of learning, every act of deviance from social expectation, every refusal to co-operate is a personal engagement. However, understanding behaviour in this way may not make resistant or challenging behaviour any easier to tolerate in the mainstream classroom. Nevertheless, it does mean that this behaviour is understandable in the same way as any other. Furthermore, this position may make it easier to see the world more accurately through students' eyes and to engage in dialogue with them.

Whether any of us think we can trust students to tell us the truth about how they feel and what they have experienced may depend on our own construction of what we ourselves think young people are like as much as any objective 'reality', and it may be that young people merely reflect back the way they themselves have been treated (Freeman, 1993). One version of a constructivist approach that assumes a model of the learner as an active agent in his or her learning is that of 'solution-focused' narrative (de Shazer, 1985). Students are invited to talk about stories which result in a positive outcome to particular problems. They are then encouraged to use their narratives to learn ways of behaving more appropriately in school and/or achieve more highly in academic terms.

The use of medication

In some cases, a medical diagnosis of the cause of challenging or inappropriate behaviour in schools may result in a prescription for particular kinds of medication. There is evidence that psychostimulant medication, while not a cure for AD/HD, can, in conjunction with psychological, social and educational support, facilitate the educational process:

> The three most commonly used psychostimulants are methylphenidate (Ritalin), dextroamphetamine (Dexedrin) and pemoline (Volital). Of the three, methylphenidate (Ritalin) is most widely prescribed. Tricyclic antidepressants have also been prescribed as an alternative when children do not respond to the stimulants or exhibit motor tics and anxiety symptoms predictive of adverse stimulant response (Dupaul and Stoner, 1995).
>
> The use of stimulants is based on theories of biochemical imbalance . . . The medication stimulates areas of the brain regulating arousal and alertness and can result in immediate short-term improvements in concentration and impulse control. The precise mechanism is poorly understood and the specific locus of action within the central nervous system remains speculative.
>
> Psychostimulant medication is usually administered as tablets to be taken at regular intervals. Monitoring is critical both in terms of dosage and time intervals . . . Reactive time (how quickly it becomes effective) and effective time (how long it lasts) varies according to the metabolism of the individual . . . The monitoring and exact timing can be difficult to manage, particularly at school.

(BPS, 1996, pp. 50–2)

One major concern about the use of such psychostimulants has been the concern about the effects and side effects of these drugs:

Since the 1970s the number of American research reports on the various effects of stimulant medication has been voluminous (Hinshaw, 1994; Swanson *et al.*, 1993). Most are concerned with short-term results and very few document long-term consequences. The literature is convincing about immediate short-term benefits as perceived by parents, teachers and others involved. Where long-term outcomes are mentioned, both researchers and practitioners are unanimous about the importance of combining medication with other forms of intervention which enhance social adjustment and academic achievement. Psychostimulant medication is seen as a palliative and not sufficient on its own. By temporarily calming children down, it can enable them to take advantage of effective teaching. In addition, because they are able to control their behaviour better, they are better able to interact appropriately in social situations . . .

Although children make progress with the assistance of stimulant treatment, a substantial subgroup appear not to benefit and a minority may show adverse responses (Rapport *et al.*, 1994) . . . [E]ducational practitioners are concerned about the so-called 'zombie' effect (Sharron, 1995) which may be the result of inappropriate doses and poor monitoring. There is also evidence of 'behavioural rebound' in the afternoons when the medication wears off. These concerns illustrate the practical issues of managing medication at home and at school [as well as the ethical risks in relying on medication alone, without providing appropriate learning tasks and activities that attract positive reinforcement, to bring about behaviour change at school].

There is also an ethical issue concerning the lack of adequate monitoring of the day-to-day classroom learning and behavioural outcomes of medication prescribed for many students. Few studies provide evidence of positive learning outcomes to accompany evidence of reductions in frequency or intensity of specific challenging behaviours in the classroom.

Another issue concerns when a prescription should be given:

The decision if and when to prescribe stimulant medication clearly rests with the physicians involved although consumers of medical services retain the choice as to whether they wish to follow the professional advice. It is worth noting, however, that until April 1995 the British manufacturer of methylphenidate (Ritalin) only supplied it on a named person basis but the drug is now more widely available.

It is important to separate questions about the effectiveness of medication from arguments about whether to use the medication. The former questions are empirical, the latter ethical and sociological (Ideus, 1995) . . . Medication must not become the first, and definitely not the only, line of treatment.

(BPS, 1996, pp. 51–2)

Conclusion

Planning interventions to improve the learning and behaviour of individual students with special needs should address statutory requirements in national and regional policies on supporting these students within regular schools and classrooms. Preferred interventions are those which have an educational and ecological focus, and which adopt collaborative and problem-solving approaches between classroom teachers and other professionals. Preferred interventions must also take into account the cultural values and preferences of individual students, especially when these are different from those of the school and its teachers. Intervention strategies should be selected according to ethical principles such as promoting student autonomy and agency, and establishing supportive and preventive systems instead of relying on procedures that are simply merely reactive to behaviour seen as problematic, and the need to ensure the cultural safety of all students.

Various examples of different approaches to designing interventions with individuals were discussed. These include behaviour modification, applied behaviour analysis, cognitive behavioural approaches, constructivist approaches, ecosystemic approaches, and the use of medication. Successful interventions based on these different approaches highlight the importance of the relationship between student behaviour, self-advocacy and self-esteem. It is therefore vital for teachers to listen to their students, to engage them in planning and monitoring the interventions. and in discourses about behaviour.

Chapter 9

Working at class-wide level

Introduction

As we have discussed in previous chapters, student behaviour in schools does not occur in a vacuum. Students 'behave' within classrooms that are structured within the organisation and practices of schools, families and society at large. Within the school the learning contexts, including pedagogical approaches, clearly have a significant effect on the behaviour of individual students. Daniels *et al.* (1998) and Visser *et al.* (2002), for example, have found that in schools that successfully include students with behavioural difficulties, the emphasis is on teaching and learning rather than on responding to perceived deficits of the child.

In this chapter we focus specifically on class-wide behavioural approaches and examine a number that offer a clear conceptual framework for planning and organising activities to maximise student learning. Behavioural and learning interactions that occur within classrooms take on a special developmental importance when we consider them as real and significant life experiences, and not simply as some kind of preparation or rehearsal for use at a later stage in 'real life'.

Classroom management

In reporting on research into around 8,000 students' perceptions of classroom learning in about 15,000 classes, Hobby and Smith (2002) conclude that 'pupils' motivation and desire to learn will significantly affect their academic progress (as well as promoting more rounded, social development)' (2002, p. 8). Clearly, teachers are involved in creating learning environments, 'classroom climate', defined as:

> The collective perception of pupils of what it feels like, in intellectual, motivational and emotional terms, to be a pupil in any particular teacher's classroom; where those perceptions influence every pupil's motivation to learn and perform to the best of his or her ability.
>
> (ibid., p. 9)

Teachers' own behaviour and skills directly influence classroom climate. A pedagogical approach aimed at creating a positive learning climate in classrooms (constructing the antecedent contexts of behaviours) is more effective than control and sanctions as a means of managing behaviour difficulties in classrooms (Carpenter and McKee-Higgins, 1996).

Assessing the learning environment

Teachers in schools can begin to address challenging student behaviour by assessing characteristics of the classroom learning environments in which students are placed because these can be changed to support more effective learning (Ysseldyke and Christenson, 1987). Following an analysis of features in the learning environment that appeared to influence learning, Ysseldyke and Christenson designed 'The Instructional Environment Scale' (TIES) to collect systematic data for analysing contextual barriers to pupils' learning. Ysseldyke and Christenson (ibid., pp. 21–2) recommend that data should be gathered through classroom observation and interview with both student and teacher on twelve components of effective teaching: 'Instructional presentation', 'Classroom environment', 'Teacher expectations', 'Cognitive emphasis', 'Motivational strategies', 'Relevant practice', 'Academic engaged time', 'Informed feedback', 'Adaptive instruction', 'Progress evaluation', 'Instructional planning' and 'Student understanding'.

Applying behavioural principles

Most commonly, understandings and strategies in classroom management are based on operant behavioural principles (Skinner, 1938; Baer *et al.*, 1968). One very well-known framework that has been developed from these principles is that of 'Assertive Discipline' (Canter and Canter, 1992). According to Canter and Canter (ibid., p. 8), teachers are now expected to work with 'more and more students with more and more problems'. Canter and Canter's solution is to return to a type of behavioural approach which very clearly 'manages' students' behaviour in schools rather than challenging teachers to think more carefully on different ways to respond to the problems they experience in classrooms. From this perspective, students need to know 'without doubt' (ibid., p. 12) what teachers expect of them, what will happen if they choose not to comply, and that appropriate behaviour will be overtly reorganised. They also need to be taught 'how to choose responsible behavior' (ibid., p. 13). An 'assertive teacher' is one who communicates expectations to students clearly and assertively, and reinforces words with actions. At the same time, however, s/he 'in no way violates' what is in 'the best interest' of students (ibid., p. 14). This of course assumes that teachers do know what is in the best interests of their (increasingly diverse) students.

Canter and Canter offer a very highly structured approach to classroom management. They see the key to successfully managing classroom behaviour as a teacher's positive expectation that she or he will be able to do this. Conversely, a major factor preventing teachers from asserting themselves in the classroom is not students' but teachers' 'own negative expectations about her [or his] ability to deal with disruptive student behavior' (ibid., p. 17).

Canter and Canter characterise between three common types of teacher 'response styles' to disruptive behaviour:

- 'wishy-washy', non-assertive, inconsistent responses which convey to students a sense of the teacher's insecurity and lack of confidence, and invite a constant testing of wills between the 'powerless' teacher and the students;
- 'hostile', rigid authoritarian responses, creating a battleground in the classroom, undermining students' self-esteem;
- confident and consistent assertive responses with positive expectations for setting boundaries, reorganising students' need for encouragement and learning 'no room for confusion' about the result of both acceptable and unacceptable behaviour.

Canter and Canter advocate setting up a classroom discipline plan with three parts: rules, positive recognition, and consequences. Rules should be limited in number, focus on observable events, be applicable throughout the time period, apply to behaviour only, and may involve students in their compilation. Key to motivating students to choose appropriate behaviour are 'positive reinforcers' which include teacher praise, rewards of various sorts and positive communications with parents. An example that Canter and Canter (ibid., p. 45) set out at secondary level is shown in the box on p. 164.

During independent work time, teachers should circulate around the classroom looking for opportunities to recognise and reinforce desired behaviour. Where students display behaviour that breaks any of the rules, teachers should apply the specified consequences. If these consequences are to be effective, they 'must be something that students do not like, but they must never be physically or psychologically harmful' and 'do not have to be severe to be effective' (ibid., p. 80). Consequences should be clearly laid out and arranged in a hierarchy of severity, as in the sample discipline plan.

Students should be explicitly taught the classroom discipline plan (ibid., p. 115) and teachers should:

- Create lessons to teach your students your classroom discipline plan.
- Explain to students why you need rules.
- Teach the rules.
- Explain how you will positively recognise students who follow the rules.

Sample Discipline Plan for Secondary Students

Classroom Rules

Follow directions
Be in the classroom and seated when the bell rings
Do not swear

Positive Recognition

Praise
Positive notes sent home to parents
Privilege pass

Consequences

First time a student breaks a rule:	Warning
Second time:	Stay in class 1 minute after the bell
Third time:	Stay in class 2 minutes after the bell
Fourth time:	Call parents
Fifth time:	Send to principal
Severe Clause:	Send to principal

- Explain why you have consequences.
- Teach the consequences.
- As soon as you've taught the lesson, immediately begin reinforcing students who follow the rules.
- Review rules frequently at the start of the year. Review as needed as the year progresses.
- Post your discipline plan in the classroom.
- Send a copy of your classroom discipline plan home to parents.

Canter and Canter recommend that, at the beginning of every year, teachers should take the time to 'identify the academic activities, routine procedures and special procedures for which [he or she needs to determine] specific directions' (ibid., p. 123). They list specific directions (ibid., p. 139):

- Don't assume that students know how you want them to behave in all the situations that occur during a normal school day. These expectations must be taught.
- Identify the classroom situations where specific directions are needed. Then determine those directions.

- Teach your specific directions immediately prior to the first time the activity takes place.
- Teach the lesson with the same care you would any academic lesson.
- Explain your rationale for teaching the direction.
- Explain the directions.
- Check for understanding.
- Review the specific directions for each activity as long as is necessary.
- Post visual clues (charts, posters, illustrations) around the classroom to help remind students of appropriate behaviour during different activities and procedures.

Off-task, low-level behaviour should not be ignored. 'It's not in your students' best interest' (ibid., p. 169). Instead, the behaviour should be re-directed. However:

> When you find yourself having to redirect a student three times a day (elementary) or two times a class period (secondary), you can assume that the student is not receiving enough structure to help him control his behavior. In these situations, turn to your disciplinary hierarchy and issue a warning.
>
> (ibid., p. 167)

After implementing the stated consequences of a rule-breaking misde-meanour, teachers should look for every opportunity to recognise appropriate behaviour. Providing escape mechanisms for students, such as allowing them to write the teacher a note to explain the incident after class may help to diffuse anger.

Student behaviour experienced as confrontational and challenging the teacher's authority (tears, tantrums and displays of anger for example) can seem very undermining to teachers in classrooms. Canter and Canter's advice (ibid., pp. 177–8) is:

- Stay calm.
- State what you want: 'I want you to sit down and complete your assignment'.
- Preface your statement of want with understanding for the child.
- Repeat your statement of want a maximum of three times. If the student still argues, let him know that he may be choosing to receive a consequence.

This focusing technique should only be used to diffuse a student's anger when a student is trying to manipulate a situation in a way that is not in his best interest. This technique is not meant to be used as a means to cut off communication.

Canter and Canter's solution to the behaviour of students who constantly disrupt class is the one-to-one problem-solving conference between teacher and student to discuss a specific issue. The aim of this conference is, ultimately, to support the student to choose more appropriate ways of behaving. Following such a meeting, for those students who continue to behave inappropriately in class, Canter and Canter (ibid., p. 237) advocate developing an individualised behaviour plan which should very clearly prioritise 'one or two of the difficult student's most critical problem behaviors', establish 'firmer, more meaningful consequences' for the student's behaviour, and make provision for positive recognition of improvement.

Ten behavioural principles

A number of other researchers have spent a great deal of time considering issues of classroom management from a behavioural perspective. Glynn *et al.* (1997), for example, generated the following ten principles for understanding and changing students' behaviour within the context of a school and community behaviour management initiative in a New Zealand mainstream, then Māori medium, school setting. This section draws on material included in a report to the New Zealand Ministry of Education Glynn *et al.* (1997) and on material included in Berryman and Glynn (2001).

Underlying all the ten principles which follow is a basic concern with what people say and what they do, and not on assumptions about what they are doing or what their intentions may be. Attention is focused on people's actions, and on the contexts and outcomes of their actions. Behaviour statements are based on observed events. There is an avoidance of emotional statements about behaviour and its effects. Judgemental statements in assessment and evaluation of someone else's behaviour are also avoided. Any emotional and judgemental statements about behaviour made by other people are refocused back to the actual behaviours and events which occurred.

Four of these ten principles are aimed at changing behaviour through altering the *antecedents* (contextual or setting events) that precede or accompany it. The remaining six principles are aimed at changing behaviours through altering the *contingencies* of reinforcement (rewarding or punishing) that follow it.

Antecedent principle 1: Take time to plan ahead

Careful thinking and planning ahead can help avoid having to deal with challenging or undesirable behaviours. Teachers and parents need to think ahead and foresee possible behaviour difficulties likely to arise in their day, and plan their strategies and responses ahead of time, rather than relying on finding a quick solution in the heat of the moment.

Antecedent principle 2: Change the setting

One way to alter behaviour is to change the consequences which follow it. This usually involves increasing the positive consequences for appropriate behaviour or introducing new positive consequences. Another way is to change or alter aspects of the setting or context in which the behaviour occurs. For example, a classroom task requiring students to learn a list of vocabulary or spelling items can be an activity in which many students soon become bored and disengaged. However, this task can be turned into a more enjoyable and engaging activity by forming students into groups of three and requiring them each to teach some of the words to their partners and to be taught some of the words by each of their partners. Not only is this strategy likely to result in a higher level of student engagement with the task, but it also is likely to result in more successful learning of the required items. This strategy typically requires planning ahead and is usually more powerful than introducing consequences for off-task or non-engaged behaviour in the heat of the moment.

Antecedent principle 3: Give clear instructions

One way to ensure that children and students learn to do as they are told without undue resistance or delay is consistently to give instructions that are polite, clear and concise. An instruction is usually a direction to do something. The instruction functions as an antecedent condition for the behaviour of compliance. Sometimes it is necessary to give a 'reprimand' or a clear instruction to stop some undesirable or potentially harmful behaviour.

Before an instruction is given, it is important first to gain the child's or student's full attention. This avoids unnecessary repeating of instructions which can undermine their effectiveness. The instruction should next specify exactly what action is required, and should not contain additional distracting emotional statements, 'put down' comments or verbal abuse.

Example:

'Thomas, put away those scissors and bring your work over here please.'

Not: 'Thomas, if you don't put away those scissors you'll get into big trouble. I loathe people who don't do as they are told. Bring you work here, you little time waster.'

Antecedent principle 4: Model what you want

Modelling is a powerful form of learning. When one person 'models' or demonstrates specific ways of behaving in particular situations, other people who observe this behaviour may learn to imitate that behaviour in similar situations. Of course, people may imitate more than the 'model' intended

– students imitate our poorest as well as our best performances! Also, our modelling may have even stronger effects if the observer sees the modeller being rewarded. Observers may also learn not to perform behaviour they have already learned if they see it bringing unpleasant consequences for the 'model'. Modelling can also have long-term and far-reaching effects. Children may not have an opportunity to imitate a behaviour they have observed until a similar situation arises for them. What they learn may not be performed until much later. Modelling of behaviour is well understood and well used by the advertising industry, and in the teaching of sports and leisure skills. It is also a principle of learning that is preferred by some cultural groups, for example, by Māori. Its use is evident in cultural settings such as *pōwhiri* (traditional ceremony of welcome) and *whakatau* (informal greeting) and is regularly employed in teaching new skills within *kapahaka* (cultural song and dance group). Modelling is a principle that is insufficiently used by teachers in many classroom learning contexts.

Examples:

Children watch a fitness training video in which a model demonstrates complex stepping routines. Children learn to imitate these routines along with the model and soon learn to perform the routines without the model.

Young children observe their teacher using abusive language when responding to disruptive behaviour in the classroom, and then reproduce this language with each other when they encounter challenging behaviour in the playground.

Contingent principle 1: Contingent positive consequences

The behaviour learnt readily and performed most often is behaviour that usually has positive consequences. These positive consequences include social attention, praise, recognition, access to favourite activities with our favourite people, and so on. They are most effective when they regularly and reliably accompany or 'reinforce' desirable or preferred behaviour in particular contexts. But, just as importantly, these same positive consequences should not also reinforce undesirable behaviour This can often happen accidentally, as when a child learns to get parent attention by whining or grizzling.

Examples:

A teacher thanks a child for starting to clear away materials after an art lesson.

A teacher converses with a child who has asked a question.

A teacher quietly praises a student for working well.

Contingent principle 2: Get in early

When someone's behaviour is getting out of line or beginning to cause concern it is best to step in as early as possible to deal with it effectively. Ignoring the first few undesirable incidents may allow these behaviours to be reinforced by positive consequences outside of our control. The earlier a teacher intervenes in a 'behaviour chain', the easier it is to prevent behaviour from escalating into a major problem.

Examples:

Instead of getting increasingly bothered as two children begin arguing about who found a play item first, a teacher selects a game that two can play and takes a moment to get them started.

The first time a student calls out an abusive remark in class the teacher enters a mark beside the student's name. From the classroom behaviour plan, this student knows that when there are five such marks, s/he will be placed on detention.

Contingent principle 3: Accept gradual improvement

Changing behaviour from undesirable or inappropriate to desirable or appropriate, or from non-engaged to engaged, may be a gradual process. It is important for parents and teachers to provide positive consequences for quite small gains at first. It may be necessary to reinforce children for at least starting when instructed, even if they do not finish everything. It may be necessary to acknowledge that a child is shouting out or interrupting less often than previously, even if sometimes that behaviour still appears.

Contingent principle 4: A little and often

What really counts is not the amount or the intensity of the consequences which reinforce or punish behaviour, but the number of opportunities a person has to experience the consequences of his behaviour. A pre-school child may learn after five separate experiences of having to 'sit and watch' for one minute that smashing someone else's block tower leads to time out from block play. The same student would not learn this nearly as effectively if the first four instances had been ignored and the fifth instance followed by five minutes of 'sit and watch', Thus in the context of behaviour change, '5 x 1 does not always equal 5!'

Examples:

Every time a child snatches a toy from the hands of another child, the teacher draws her aside and has her sit and watch for one minute while other children play appropriately. After five or six instances, she no longer snatches toys.

A teacher quietly praises a student who has a low attention span every five or six minutes throughout the lesson, provided she finds him still actively engaged with the work set.

In a primary classroom, students all have points cards on their desks so that the teacher can award points for attending well, for good work and for cooperative behaviour throughout the lesson. When one student starts a loud argument with another student, the teacher removes his points card and sends the card to 'time out' by pinning it 'in jail' on the classroom notice-board. After the student has been behaving appropriately for five minutes, his card is returned. This sequence may be repeated several times over two days, and the student no longer provokes arguments in class.

Contingent principle 5: Positive ways to reduce unacceptable behaviour

There are positive alternatives to introducing unpleasant or punishing consequences in order to reduce undesirable or unacceptable behaviour. One way is to define and select another behaviour the child or student can perform that is incompatible with (i.e. that cannot go on at the same time as) the undesirable or unacceptable behaviour. This alternative behaviour is then reinforced by following it with positive consequences, instead of providing negative consequences for the original behaviour. Note that this is not just 'ignoring the unwanted behaviour and it will go away' but actively reinforcing a more appropriate and desirable alternative.

Example:

Fred spends a great deal of his classroom time out of his seat and wandering about the room distracting other students. His teacher selects an alternative (and incompatible) behaviour, namely working at his desk. She regularly and consistently reinforces this by positive comments to Fred and by adding points to his individual points card whenever her spot checking finds him working in his seat. Fred now spends more and more time working as this seat and, as a result, he engages in less and less wandering about and distracting others.

Contingent principle 6: Effective sanctions for unacceptable behaviour

The principles introduced so far offer a wide range of positive strategies for responding to unacceptable behaviour. However, there needs to be a 'bottom line' a clearly stated sanction which is reliably applied to behaviours which are potentially harmful to the children engaging in them or to their classroom peers. This 'bottom line' is reached only after teachers have first carefully tried to implement several possible alternative strategies. The 'bottom line' strategy is basically the worst thing that we will allow to happen to children in our care if they persist with harmful and unacceptable behaviour following several attempts to change it using any of the previous principles. Hence these sanctions must be clearly defined, explained to children, and very carefully implemented. Implementing these sanctions should not in itself either model or provoke further physical or verbal abuse and so should never be accompanied by emotional or angry 'put down' and abusive comments. Sanctions should be imposed for a specified length of time, and removed when specific behaviour change criteria have been met. At these times it is most important that children continue to receive positive attention for any desirable and appropriate behaviours which occur during the time when unacceptable behaviours are being responded to with sanctions.

A behavioural approach to avoiding 'extreme' behaviour

Sometimes, for a variety of reasons that may be associated with, for example, abuse of a physical or sexual nature, difficulty in relating to peers, pressures at home, school or in the community, students may develop 'extreme behaviours', that is 'those that significantly and seriously disrupt the functioning and well-being of the student' (Dunckley, 1999, p. 12).

Preventing this kind of behaviour from developing is far preferable than intervening later on. Dealing with severe behaviour incidents is far more challenging and stressful than dealing with mildly disruptive incidents, however, the behavioural principles involved are the same. Hence, it makes good sense, even when considering severe behaviour incidents to first implement a range of preventive strategies to construct a context in which severe behaviour incidents are less likely to appear. Effective prevention strategies that all schools can adopt (ibid., p. 13) may include:

- Policies and practices that promote non-violence, mutual respect and respect for property.
- Interesting programmes that are achievable for all. Students who experience success are less likely to engage in negative behaviour.
- Praise and positive reinforcement for effort.
- Stable, predictable environments with familiar routines and consistent limits. Students benefit from knowing what is acceptable behaviour, what is required and what will happen if transgressions occur.
- Positive environments. Create situations where students will value praise and comments (from teachers or others).

- Teaching that reinforces acceptable behaviour. Do not assume that this will be learned incidentally. For example, teach students to put their hands up to gain attention and praise them for following instruction and taking turns. Reinforce students for following the rules of games and activities, and help them cope with both winning and losing.
- Defusing incidents through positive comments. Friendly positive direction will encourage co-operation (for example, *When you have removed your hat, you can come and join us*). Give choices. Choices reduce the likelihood of outright refusal (for example, *You can finish this work now or at lunchtime*).
- Being aware of events that may be stressful for students and teachers. These situations cannot always be avoided, but careful management can reduce the risk of extreme behaviour.
- Avoiding situations known to lead to extreme behaviour for individual students. Know the circumstances under which a behaviour is likely to occur and make changes accordingly.
- Early intervention. Don't ignore behaviours that are likely to become extreme.

Dunckley (ibid., p. 14) offers the following checklist for the classroom in order to minimise the risk of 'extreme behaviour' among students:

1 The majority of the teacher's statements are positive.
2 Students are getting clear direction and know what is expected of them.
3 Students know the timetable and have the equipment they need to participate in the classroom programme.
4 The work is achievable.
5 There are clear routines.
6 The rules are understood.
7 There are choices and consequences and these are known by the students.
8 The teacher is consistent and fair.
9 The teacher avoids creating conflict and dissension.
10 The teacher uses management techniques that avoid the need for compulsion.

Dunckley notes that, on occasion, students may be aggressive, out of control and a danger to themselves and others. Her advice to teachers in this situation is to do the following:

> assist the student to regain control. Safety is a priority and the goal is to defuse the situation. . . .
>
> Staff members will need to follow the school policy. Where the aggressive act has been completed and it is unlikely that further aggression will follow, there is no need to intervene, the violence has stopped. Certainly,

the matter needs to be dealt with, for example the victim is attended to, and there are consequences for the perpetrator.

Where the perpetrator is in a highly anxious, or agitated state, have another staff member attend to the victim and get the perpetrator to sit quietly until they are calm enough to talk about what has happened. When they do talk, it is important to be non-judgemental and not to lecture, remind the student of the rules and follow through with consequences.

If the behaviour continues to be threatening and disruptive, isolate the student from the others. Ask for their co-operation in doing this: *Come outside for a minute just until things have settled . . .*

The purpose is to assist rather than to punish the student. Irrational and abusive language should not be taken personally. If they are being physically aggressive then it may be necessary to restrain them, in accordance with safe practice.

(ibid., p. 17)

The issue of physical handling and restraint of students in schools

Dunckley (1999) refers to physical restraint as a last resort that should only be used to manage a dangerous situation. It should be employed carefully and in accordance with school policies, that should indicate when restraint can be used. It may be necessary to remove a student from a group of peers. This can be achieved 'by asking the other students to leave. It may be more appropriate, and safer, to bring other staff to the place where the student is, rather than the other way around' (ibid., p. 10).

It is important for those associated with schools to check school, local area and/or national policies on physical restraint of students in schools. Some national education departments have issued guidance to schools on this question. In England guidelines are available in Circular 10/98 (DfEE, 1998a). In Wales guidelines are available in Circular 37/98, *The Use of Reasonable Force to Control or Restrain Pupils*, obtainable from the National Assembly for Wales (NAW, 1998). In Northern Ireland the Department for Education Northern Ireland (DENI) has a guidance document entitled *Towards a Model Policy in Schools on the Use of Reasonable Force* (DENI, 2002).

Various training packages in restraint techniques are available for teachers to ensure that, as far as possible, no one is harmed during the process of restraining individuals. Training for Team Teach, a training course commonly available to teachers in UK schools, is advertised as emphasising:

• Positive handling as but *one part of a whole setting approach to behaviour management*. Physical techniques should not be taught in isolation. In T.E.A.M.- T.E.A.C.H. training, they account for only two out [of] eight modules.

- The training has evolved from a residential care and educational background. It continually *emphasises positive relationships* as being the key element in our working. The physical techniques help to protect and maintain these relationships.
- The physical techniques have sufficient *range and robustness* to be appropriate across the age and development range, for both the intentional and non-intentional 'challenging' individual.
- The physical techniques provide *a gradual, graded system of response* commensurate with the situation, task and individuals involved, allowing for phasing up or down as dictated to by the circumstances at the time.
- The stress is always, where possible, on the *'last resort'* option when using 'reasonable' force.
- There is an emphasis on appropriate and *targeted verbal and non-verbal communication*. Paraverbal skills matter at all times, during a restraint, however, it is what you say and how you say it that is important.
- The aim is for the person to calm down sufficiently so *that staff can return the physical control* and help find a better way.
- A *C.A.L.M.* (Communication, Awareness/Assessment Listening/Looking and Making safe skills) approach is expected at all times when managing such situations.

(http://www.team-teach.co.uk/keypoints_page1.html)

However, 'safe practice' is not the only issue to be considered here. A number of writers (Bowers, 1996; Cooper, 1999; Cornwall, 2000) have expressed disquiet about the apparent lack of concern for ethical issues surrounding the restraint of students against their will. It is important to note there is a difference between physical restraint, to hold a student still until aggression (hitting, kicking, punching others) subsides, and punitive incarcerations such as locking the student away for extended periods of time, as can occur when the principles of 'time out' are misunderstood, or misapplied, often in the heat of the moment.

Cornwall (2004) notes the confusion between the right to protection of the 'Self' and others and restraint as coercion; between restraint as discipline and self-restraint; and between the ethical and commercial bases of the systems that staff might use to control student behaviour. He feels that the 'control' ethic stems from the individualisation of behavioural 'problems', that is, deficit theorising, rather than an understanding of the creation of violent conduct, particularly the influence of the environment, and the design of sufficient opportunities for students' personal and social development.

Writing from a New Zealand perspective, Dunckley comments that students 'in an agitated state require guidance and direction to increase their sense of security . . . where possible and appropriate give a choice, time for the student to respond, then, after an appropriate time, follow through with consequences' (1999, p. 16).

When restraint is used, it is easy to violate the cultural values of students. Some of the cultural constructs for Māori which might be violated in this context include *mana* (personal autonomy, self-esteem), *whakamā* (a feeling of shame from having one's *mana* belittled in front of others) and *wairuatanga* (a sense of loss or threat to one's spiritual connectedness with other people and with one's ancestors). Understanding how culture impacts on any actions you might take and how these actions impact on the self-esteem and well-being of students is very important. Within a Māori world-view, the most important issue is to restore calm and order, to assist the student to 'put things right' and not simply to punish:

> Teachers have a responsibility to know how to handle difficult behaviour safely. They should work within their levels of competence and seek further training and guidance if necessary. This includes extending their understanding of cultures other than their own and using this knowledge to prevent incidents, defuse potentially violent situations and deal with behaviour without causing unnecessary distress and loss of mana to the student and their whānau [extended family, or peers and others working in a relationship similar to that of an extended family].
>
> (ibid., pp. 11–12)

Smith (2004) takes a view that it is very important to minimise the risk of physical confrontation in the first instance, rather than having to take action after the event and offers guidelines for doing so:

> On the whole it is wise for teachers to avoid confrontations with students when these can be avoided, but there are occasions when they cannot be, and there are circumstances when a confrontation is beneficial. You cannot always avoid a confrontation, for instance, if you are summoned by a colleague to help in some crisis. The angry student may turn on you and continue with you what began with your colleague. There are some circumstances when you may decide that you are not going to put up with a student's provocative or stupid behaviour any longer, or decide to demonstrate to a student who continually bullies or teases others that he or she has met their match. A confrontation could then be beneficial to the student concerned, to other students who witnessed it, and to your classroom management.
>
> If convinced that confrontation will be beneficial, you have next to be sure that you can manage it. If, once it has started, the student continues to be defiant or provocative, and, if the worst comes to the worst, you

have to be sure that you can manage the situation should the student attempt a physical challenge. Once started, confrontations sometimes develop very quickly and unpredictably, so that it is foolish to initiate one and then find that it has gone out of control and escalated into a situation which cannot be managed successfully, becoming demeaning and undignified.

Useful ground rules for both avoiding and managing confrontations are to take care about language, consider whether to respond at all to minor irritations, reflect on non-verbal cues and signals you may be giving, refrain from physical intervention and plan responses which lower rather than raise the temperature of the classroom climate.

(Smith, 2004, pp. 261–2)

Constructivist approaches

On the surface, behavioural approaches appear to offer clear frameworks for managing student behaviour in a very positive way. However, considered in isolation, they tend to beg a number of very important questions, particularly in the area of ethics and culture. First, there is an assumption that the school curriculum to which students are expected to comply is appropriate and relevant and that school and teacher processes and practices are equitable and reasonable for all students. Second, there is an assumption that teachers, from a behavioural view, will necessarily know which types of rewards and sanctions will be 'meaningful' to individual students and will therefore function as positive or negative reinforcers. In addition, there may be cultural differences in values, preferences and interaction styles between students and between students and teachers which need to be taken carefully into account in constructing even quite straightforward behaviour management programmes.

Glynn and Berryman (2003, personal communication) make the important point that not all effective approaches to classroom management are based on behavioural principles: 'For example, some inclusive education practices are driven by a belief that inclusion in the classroom community of practice will improve a student's self-efficacy and hence behaviour in class.' Providing opportunities for students to bring their own experiences and means of sense-making into class and curriculum activities is one way that teachers can encourage inclusion. Opportunities to do this are especially important in mainstream contexts when the culture of the school can marginalise or make invisible the culture of minority groups.

Beginning with a focus on the learning process, Bruner (1996, p. 84) notes that human learning is 'best' when it is 'participatory, proactive, communal, collaborative and given over to constructing meanings rather than receiving them'. A corollary of Bruner's view is, as noted by Bishop and Glynn that educationalists need to work out ways to 'create learning environments within classrooms wherein learners' sense-making processes are used and developed in order that they may successfully participate' (1999, p. 165). Teachers need to 'interact with students in such a way that knowledge is co-created' (ibid.). According to this view, learners can be 'co-enquirers and take part in the whole process of learning from goal-setting to assessment and evaluation' (ibid.).

Two examples of how students have taken the role of 'co-enquirers' and have assumed 'the power to determine which learning styles they need to use' (ibid.) come from the authors' own direct experiences in classrooms. In one, students were informed of the learning outcomes of the unit of work that derived from the relevant national curriculum document. They were then invited to contribute their own views and questions that might best achieve the particular outcomes. After considerable group and class discussion of these student contributions the teacher negotiated the form and structure for the series of lessons. In the other example, a group of secondary-aged students who had experienced considerable difficulties in mathematical learning were asked to negotiate a group decision about the overall aim of their mathematics lessons during the final stages of their compulsory school-ing. They were asked whether they wished to follow the formal external examination syllabus like all other students, or a less demanding one. Having made their choice, the more academic option, their lessons then took the form of a learning co-operative, each member encouraging the others to reach greater depths of mathematical understanding.

Where there is an acknowledgement of students as active agents in their own learning, constructing and co-constructing meanings in a social context, in the classroom, there is no need for the teacher to expect to be 'the foun-tain of all knowledge'. The Māori context of *ako* emphasises reciprocity in learning and teaching, as *ako* is a common root word used for both 'teach' and 'learn'. Implicit in this model of the teaching and learning process is an understanding of the kind of relationship that needs to exist between teacher and learner where there is a shared responsibility for learning, respect for each other and a fundamental belief that each has something to learn from the other (Bishop *et al.*, 2003).

Conclusion

Individual strategies are not applied within a vacuum but within specific classroom contexts. Teachers' perceptions about students and their families impact upon how teachers relate to their students and what the class-room climate and experiences are like for those students (Bishop *et al.*, 2003). In a New Zealand context, Bishop *et al.*'s (2003) research showed that when teachers' understandings of their Māori students changed, their relationships and interactions with these students also changed in a number of important ways:

They [teachers] increased caring, raised their expectations, improved the classroom management, changed the classroom interactions from traditional to discursive, interacted meaningfully with more students and [as a result of these changes] overall focussed less on student behaviour and more on student learning and their learning how to learn. As a result of these changes, Maori students became more academically engaged, completed more work in class, attended class more regularly and saw their summative assessment scores improve.

(ibid., p. 198)

Another recent research report on teacher effectiveness in the UK concludes that students look to the teacher for a sense of security and order, an opportunity to participate actively in the class and for it to be an interesting and exciting place (Hobby and Smith, 2002).

Such conditions are most easily realised where teachers follow what have been characterised as the 'four rules' of classroom management:

1   Get them in, by starting lessons smoothly and promptly.
2   Get them out, by arranging an orderly conclusion to lessons.
3   Get on with it, by selecting suitable content with appropriate methods and materials.
4   Get on with them, by awareness of each student as an individual.

(Smith and Laslett, 1993, pp. 3–13)

Closely akin to notions of teachers as needing to be good classroom 'managers' in order to create an environment that supports positive student learning are views of student behaviour as closely attuned to contextual factors. Watkins and Wagner (2000) refer to 'inside the person' thinking (by many professionals) characterised by an assumption that difficult behaviour is the result of deficits within students. They claim that understanding behaviours needs to break out of the limitations of within-student explanations to consider within-class and within-school explanations: the teacher and the classroom. Watkins and Wagner refer to this as 'outside the walls (of within student explanations) thinking'. Hobby and Smith (2002), in discussing classroom learning environments, claim that whole-school 'culture' influences teachers' behaviour and values and that it is only through changes in teachers' behaviour and values that significant lasting changes can take place in students' behaviour in classrooms.

In understanding the impact of the whole-school culture on teachers' behaviour and values, it is also important to understand that this culture is all too frequently defined and determined by members of dominant majority groups. Consequently, it is highly likely that there will be negative impacts on the cultures of minority groups with the school. One key step towards effective behaviour management in classrooms is for teachers who are members of dominant cultural majorities to reflect and explore the ways in which their values, beliefs and preferred ways of behaving might be impacting on those of minority cultural groups in their schools.

Chapter 10

Addressing behaviour at school-wide level

Introduction

Inclusive schools respond to increasing student diversity through their curriculum policies, their pastoral systems and in their classroom practices. A key feature of inclusive schools for children and young people with emotional and behavioural difficulties is related to what a number of researchers refer to as 'ethos'. However, the use of the term ethos, like special needs, inclusion, behaviour difficulties, disaffection, and so on, is problematic. There is no common agreement on what the term means but it is used in discourse on the assumption that there is a common understanding (Norwich, 1999). However, some features of what is meant by a school 'ethos' conducive to the inclusion of disaffected and challenging children can be discerned from research. Daniels *et al.* (1998) and Visser *et al.* (2002) perceive ethos as a calm atmosphere which is orderly. Carrington and Elkins refer to an 'inclusive school culture' described as a philosophy of acceptance where all people are valued and treated with respect' (2002, p. 51) which is indicated in the inclusive language used in the school prospectus and expressed school policies (Radford, 2000).

Richards (1999) identifies positive relationships in which adults are supportive, non-judgemental, and non-threatening as indicators of inclusion. Wright *et al.* (2004) in discussing features of inclusive schools for 'disruptive minorities' refer to the influence of positive inclusive attitudes by senior staff on a set of complex interactions. These include teacher and parent relations, and teacher expectations and perceptions accompanied by structural processes working at the policy level. They point out that these characteristics have the potential for reducing exclusion rates.

Individual student behaviour may be indicative of a range of contextual issues that need to be addressed at whole-school level. Sometimes individual student behaviour can be addressed through attention to school-wide practices that affect all students. Sometimes it requires decisions at whole-school level to introduce a new initiative or form of provision that will support individual students more appropriately. In this chapter we look at practices that impinge on the whole student population as well as those that are intended to support individuals more specifically.

Working from cultural understandings

We have already discussed in previous chapters the importance of family and culture in shaping the thinking and behaviour of young people and their teachers in schools. In some parts of the world there is an increasing interest in exploring how to support students from different cultures whose behaviour is considered unacceptable at school. This approach aims to establish or strengthen links with students' home communities so that those community norms and values might help to encourage more socially appropriate behaviour. There is an implicit acknowledgement here both of the fundamental human need for a sense of belonging and acceptance in a social group and of young people's thinking and behaviour being shaped by the social context (Bruner, 1996). However, in some parts of the world, there is an increasing interest also in exploring ways in which schools might change their pedagogical practices and behaviour management strategies to better accommodate the aspirations and preferences of minority communities.

A whole-school, bicultural approach: the 'Hikairo Rationale'

One of the criticisms of behaviour management techniques in many schools is that they tend to silence the cultural and community contexts, together with the traditional values, in which student behaviour is defined and understood (Glynn and Bishop, 1995; Macfarlane, 2000c). One behavioural intervention approach which is based on the values of the local community is Macfarlane's 'Hikairo Rationale' (Macfarlane, 1997). Macfarlane has described an approach to 'managing' challenging student behaviour developed for students identified as experiencing 'profound' emotional and behavioural difficulties in a school in Rotorua, New Zealand. This bicultural approach was designed within a framework of traditional concepts and values of the local Māori community, but also in relation to concepts of human development and behaviour management from a Western European worldview.

The rationale emphasises:

- the traditional Māori value of 'aroha', connoting, in the context of school discipline, 'co-operation, support, understanding, reciprocity and warmth' (ibid., p. 88);
- a sense of opening doorways by creating meaningful relationships, destroying unhelpful, negative myths associated with students' previous reputations and establishing clear, fair boundaries for behaviour;

- teachers' assertive communication which is 'part of an established order of Māori protocol' in speaking on the *marae* (traditional community meeting place);
- respect for all students and an awareness of the need to build students' self-respect;
- an awareness of the reality of the situation of each of them;
- a secure and nurturing environment where students can taste success, feel valued as community members and be encouraged to take responsibility for the choices they make;
- shared ownership of the situation of the student by the student, the teacher and the *whānau* (familial and/or extended family).

Bishop *et al.* (2003), working with teachers in New Zealand mainstream classrooms found that cultural responsiveness was what made teaching practices effective for Māori students. This meant Māori students were able to bring their experiences and sense making processes into the classroom in order to engage more fully with the curriculum.

Both Macfarlane and Bishop *et al.* comment from a Māori context which, on the face of it, is very different from that of many other cultures. The views expressed by many teachers in the UK (Open University, 2004) and their ways of working are closely compatible with the teaching approaches described by Macfarlane in the Hikairo rationale and by Bishop *et al.* (2003). It would be easy to conclude that good teaching for one set of students automatically is good teaching for all. However, compatibility of pedagogic approaches does not imply that the cultural underpinnings and under-standings of Macfarlane's 'Hikairo Rationale', and, therefore, the differences between the cultural contexts of students in the UK and the cultural contexts of Māori students in New Zealand, should be ignored. Each culture has its own world-view and its ways of constructing meanings, or understandings about behaviour and how to go about changing it. Among the Māori people of New Zealand, for example, the concept of restorative justice is built on the concept of always maintaining personal *mana* (an individual's autonomy, integrity, self-esteem and standing within the group). Resolution of conflict between individuals must be achieved in ways which respect and restore the *mana* of all parties, including victims and aggressors. Following from this principle will be attempts to repair any damage and hurt to those involved.

Introducing 'restorative justice'

Restorative justice also draws upon community values and is becoming increasingly common in many countries as an alternative to a retributive justice approach which is characterised by sanctions, discipline and punish-ment as the means of preventing, managing and controlling behaviour. Restorative justice is concerned to move away from the primacy of assigning blame and punishment to finding a mutually agreeable way forward by negotiation. The prime focus is on 'putting things right' between all those involved or affected by wrong-doing.

The process of restorative justice has been introduced into a number of schools, in New Zealand and in the UK, where it can be seen as embodying a set of important skills required by mediators and facilitators but under-pinned by a third view as an ethos or philosophy:

> that encompasses the values of respect, openness, empowerment, inclu-sion, tolerance, integrity and congruence . . . everything we do here at this school [is] informed by this ethos, these values and a philosophy which gives central importance to building, maintaining and when necessary, repairing relationships and community.
>
> (Hopkins, 2004, p. 20)

Initiatives such as 'restorative justice' have been designed to address prob-lematic individual behaviour from a focus on traditional community values. Such initiatives have shifted the focus on to whole communities and away from a focus only on the victim or the perpetrator in order to harness the necessary resources to address the problems that have resulted in unacceptable, unsociable behaviours (Schweigert, 1999).

One important aspect of the restorative justice process within the context of Māori students in New Zealand schools is that the *hui whakatika* (restora-tive justice meeting) is particularly effective when conducted according to Māori protocol. This meeting will be conducted by Māori elders, or by a Māori professional, with elders present, and will focus on reaching a consensus position on what should be done to 'put things right'. By following Māori protocol (rather than the protocol of the school), this process can help address issues of power imbalances between school authorities and the individual student and their community. School personnel, including any senior management involved, as well as professionals and *whānau* members must listen respectfully, not interrupt others, speak only when 'given the floor' and follow the advice and guidance of the elders. In this way solutions can be reached that do not automatically lead to 'stand downs', 'suspensions', or expulsions of students, but nevertheless acknowledge that harm or hurt has been caused which must be repaired. The school, however, does not own, and so cannot completely control or manage the process. It has to be responsive to community-preferred ways of dealing with challenging behav-iour. On their part, the elders responsible ensure the process is respectful of all individuals and is positively affirming of their positions. We discuss restorative justice in more detail in Chapter 11.

Another initiative associated with the resolution of students' disputes at primary school level in schools in the UK that has some elements in common with restorative justice, in that it depends on harnessing the support of the school community for both victim and perpetrator, is that of 'Circle Time' (Mosley, 1996). As Tew (1998, p. 20) comments, in many traditional communities the circle is a symbol of 'unity, healing and power'. Using circles for members of a group to exchange views is 'ancient' and can be found in the traditions of groups as diverse 'as the North American Indians and Anglo-Saxon monks'. As used in schools, 'Circle Time' refers to a meeting, following the traditional protocols of involving all participants in discussion where all are bound by strict rules for both teachers and students:

- No one may put anyone down.
- No one may use any name negatively (creating 'safety' for all individuals including teachers and parents).
- When they speak, everyone must listen.
- Everyone has a turn and a chance to speak.
- All views are taken seriously.
- Members of the class team suggest ways of solving problems.
- Individuals can accept the help or politely refuse it.

Considerable skill is needed for a 'Circle Time' programme to run effectively (Mosley, 1996, p. 36):

- the ability to listen well;
- the ability to be honest sometimes about your own feelings and thoughts;
- the ability to use good eye contact and show emotional warmth and empathy;
- the ability to recap what pupils have said and reflect it back to them to show you have understood;
- the ability to notice and thank pupils for the skills focused on in Circle Time: i.e. thinking, looking, listening, speaking and concentrating.

'Circle Time' is probably best known for its use with younger children. The model developed by Jenny Mosley follows a given structure:

- warm up and fun;
- a round where all students have the opportunity to speak;
- 'open forum' where individual issues and problems can be raised;
- negotiation of group action plan to address the issues raised, if necessary;
- celebration of success;
- closure, ending on fun.

The rules must be followed strictly. If a student breaks a rule, a visual warning is given. If this persists, time away from the circle follows. In recent years the use of 'Circle Time' has also been extended into the secondary sector (Tew, 1998).

While there are clearly some functional similarities with the Māori 'hui whakatika' process, there are also some important differences, particularly that the conducting of Circle Time is very much according to school protocols and under school control.

Application of an ecosystemic approach

As we have already commented in Chapter 6, educationists have begun to understand some of the behaviour problems that arise for individual students from dysfunctions in the family system, in the school system, or in the family–school relationship system (Campion, 1985; Dowling and Osbourne, 1985). Difficulties for individuals arise when they become caught up in patterns of interactions between or within parts of the system which serve the needs of the system as a whole but are personally detrimental to those individuals.

Cooper and Upton outline how an ecosystemic approach can be applied within the school context. They describe how, invariably

> sustained conflict, whether it be between teacher and student, student and student or teacher and teacher, can be seen in terms of individuals or groups pursuing different goals, and ignoring, denying or opposing the validity of their opponents' goals, with a result that opposition leads to entrenchment and continually escalating conflict.
>
> (1991, p. 25)

From an ecosystemic viewpoint, the solution to this type of conflict 'is to seek an understanding of the conflict situation which does not apportion blame or guilt, and which, if adhered to, leads to the development of cooperative relationships between the individuals concerned'.

As Cooper and Upton (ibid.) note, the typical ecosystemic intervention strategy is 're-framing':

> To reframe . . . means to change the conceptual and/or emotional setting or viewpoint in relation to which a situation is experienced and to ['re-theorise' or] place it in another frame which fits the 'facts' of the same concrete situation equally well or even better, and thereby changes its entire meaning'
>
> (Watzlawick *et al.*, 1974, p. 95)

Cooper and Upton cite an example of re-framing from Molnar and Lindquist (1989):

> Rick was belligerent towards his teacher and domineering toward his 12-year-old classmates, using his superior physical development to reinforce this. The teacher attempted to enlist Rick's co-operation in a

number of ways, using praise for positive behaviour, and giving him special responsibilities to encourage positive leadership. Rick's behaviour did not improve, however; he continued to bully his classmates and publicly flaunt the teacher's authority. This angered the teacher, and a number of confrontations took place, which, in the teacher's words 'only strengthened his [Rick's] image'.

Key factors in maintaining the existing patterns of behaviour interactions are the different perceptions held by participants. The teacher then decided to re-frame the situation:

> An opportunity arose for this when Rick started to act silly and be disruptive during a drama session. Instead of challenging Rick for his misbehaviour, the teacher reframed his view of the situation, choosing to see Rick's behaviour as a rational means of dealing with the embarrassment he felt at being the largest boy in the class, and so appearing conspicuous in these activities. The teacher states:
>
>> During a rehearsal in which the students were practising hand movements to a song and Rick was acting silly, I walked over to him and told him that I could appreciate his discomfort in participating. As an adult, about his size, I, too, felt awkward in trying to do the activities. I invited him to feel free to step aside and just watch, as I was doing.
>
> Rick's initial reaction was one of surprise. At the next rehearsal, however, the teacher noted that Rick's involvement became more serious, and, in the long term, Rick's behaviour toward the teacher started to improve greatly, to the extent that their relationship is generally more positive and co-operative.
>
> An essential preparatory stage in the process of performing such an intervention is that of sleuthing, in which the teacher attempts to discover as much as possible about the perception of the problem situation held by the pupil(s) involved. This also involves the teacher in clearly defining her own perception of the situation . . . It is only on the basis of accurate sleuthing that an intervention which is equally meaningful and credible to all parties can be achieved.
>
> (Cooper and Upton, 1991, p. 25)

One initiative that can be viewed as 'ecosystemic' in the way in which it permeates the whole school system and influences every level is the 'Quality Circle Time Model' mentioned earlier (Mosley and Tew, 1999). Mosley (undated) demonstrates how the school as a whole can be conceptualised as a fully functioning system comprising a set of interlinking subsystems in her illustration of how the whole school needs to be implicated in efforts to address behavioural concerns. Mosley notes a number of key elements in the model:

> The Quality Circle Time Model involves a commitment from schools to set up an ongoing process of Circle Meetings for adults and children, at which the key interpersonal and organisational issues that affect school development can be addressed.

According to Mosley, there are eight key elements involved: *N.B*

1 Improving the Morale of Staff

If staff in a school are to respond in a positive and warm manner to children, they need to have the ability to support each other as members of a team . . .

Adults commit themselves to working on their personal and professional development by engaging in regular Circle Times . . . The aim is to work on maintaining emotional safety, and to promote specific relationship skills.

2 Three Listening Systems

Quality Circle Time sets up three systems within which children can speak with themselves and each other. These are:

(a) *Circle Time* provides children with a weekly opportunity to experience positive relationships with other people. The games and exercises used are designed to foster a sense of the class as a community, and to establish a safe boundary within which other activities can take place.
(b) *Bubble Time and Talk Time* are one-to-one listening systems, respectively for primary schools and for secondary schools.
(c) *Think Books* are offered as a daily non-verbal communication system.

3 Golden Rules

Golden Rules are the means by which the values of Circle Time are extended into every area of school life . . .

All members of a school are involved in the discussion and establishment of Golden Rules. Once agreed, they are displayed in every area of the school.

4 Incentives

The reward system is structured to reinforce the Golden Rules. Stickers and certificates are given to those who observe the rules.

They are given by the whole school community – including lunchtime supervisors, caretakers and children.

In structuring an incentive system like this, schools appear more likely to focus staff attention on observing students who are keeping to the levels, rather than becoming preoccupied with instances of rule breaking. Mosley (ibid., pp. 7–9) regards the system of sanctions which is set up to be meaningful to students as 'the key' to Circle Time operating well.

5   Golden Time/Privilege Time

A regular half-hour slot of free time is given over to educational activities chosen by the children. This is a reward for their observing the Golden Rules, and acts as a major incentive to keeping them in mind. It means that children who are always good are rewarded, and the idea of fun is bound up in the whole policy. It involves offering people privileges that are individual, highly motivational and community-based, but which can be withdrawn in the event that the Golden Rules are broken:

(a)   Visual warnings are placed beside children's names if they break a Golden Rule.
(b)   If they choose to break another rule while the warning is out, they lose a part of their Golden Time. Their privileges are withdrawn.
(c)   For children who are close to losing all Golden Time, *Earning Back Contracts* are on offer.

These 'Golden Rule' procedures can be seen to also exemplify the principles of contingent positive reinforcement, frequency rather than intensity (a little bit often) and positive approaches for reducing inappropriate behaviour as described by Glynn *et al.* (1997) in Chapter 9.

6   Lunchtime Policy

Good practice means creating possibilities for all kids to join in a range of different activities. It also means providing quiet places for them to go. The model does not prescribe how children play, but it does encourage children to find activities that they enjoy, and to find ways of relating to each other in caring and inclusive ways. That is why the Quality Circle Time model insists that schools teach playground games, and why it 'zones' the playground into activity areas that can be supervised by older children who have been appointed as *Playground Patrols*.

A community service-type *Task Force* is formed for all children who need to be constructively occupied.

This strategy appears to be grounded on the principle that engaging in behaviour and attracting reinforcement for behaviour that is incompatible with, or alternative to inappropriate or disruptive behaviour provides a positive approach to reducing disruptive behaviour.

> Football *Parliaments* are held in order to ensure that football contributes to the positive ethos of a school and does not pull against it.
>
> Lunchtime supervisors are given the same rights as teachers, and are encouraged to use the same incentive and sanction system, whilst also being invited to regular Circle Time meetings with children and with members of staff.

Mosley accepts that there will be a few children – 'children beyond' – who need other approaches. For them, teachers are introduced to a range of programmes that incorporate behavioural, therapeutic and peer support:

7   Children Beyond

> Tiny achievable tickable target systems are drawn up from within the support of class Circle Times.

(a)   Children are offered the opportunity to attend smaller therapeutic Circle Times.

(b)   If other children see troubled children being offered this sort of support, they come to see the school as a moral community that is prepared to support and help its more disadvantaged members.

8   Containment

> If all the methods outlined above fail to help the 'child beyond', then there is probably no more that an ordinary mainstream school can offer. The focus of attention needs to shift to preserving the emotional health of class teachers, through regular Circle Times.

Teacher support teams

As Mosley has commented in the context of 'Quality Circle Time', one way in which schools can support teachers to share a common understanding of, and competence in dealing with, problematic and challenging behaviour in classrooms is through the establishment of teacher self-support groups. In Mosley's model these groups meet to discuss important issues and concerns in Circle Time sessions. Other researchers have adopted an approach based on mutual support groups, for example Daniels *et al.*'s (1993) work on teacher support teams (TSTs). These are embedded into the system of the school staffing structure. Daniels *et al.* describe their aims and functions:

teacher support teams (TSTs) . . . offer a forum for collective analysis of teaching problems by classroom teachers, some of which may otherwise involve expensive special educational provision in special schools and units. TSTs . . . are an example of a school-based development designed to give support and assistance to individual *teachers* who voluntarily seek help in solving, or at least easing, teaching problems. . . . TSTs put teachers in the foreground. . . . TSTs offer the possibility of intervention that is distinctive by dint of the focus on teachers rather than children or school policy. They utilise . . . the potential support that consultation and collective problem solving can offer teachers. Staff approach TSTs for collaborative support in understanding problems and designing appropriate forms of intervention related to learning and behaviour difficulties and/or more general matters. These teams aim to enable staff to develop their confidence and competence in making provision for children with SEN in mainstream classes.

(ibid., p. 169)

Key to the success of TSTs in schools is a consideration of the composition of the team. In the pilot study in the UK, for example:

The TSTs comprised a deputy headteacher, a special needs co-ordinator and a class teacher. The teams were selected on the principle of having teachers not solely identified with SEN and teachers able to command the respect of their peers. The school was given the task of identifying and agreeing on a regular and committed time (usually between ½ hour and 1 hour) during which the TST could meet and operate.

(ibid., p. 170)

Key, also, in the pilot was a recognition that each school must tailor the role and process to its own context and requirements:

A key premise was that each school was to develop its own particular style of TST operation within very broad guidelines. Each TST, in consultation with their colleagues in school, designed and developed procedures for how to request assistance and respond to requests for support. This involved the consideration of questions such as:

- Who can request – only teachers, teachers and classroom assistants etc.?
- Who serves on a TST team; should membership rotate and if so how often?
- Who should chair and minute meetings?
- Who should have access to records and where should they be stored?
- How should issues of publicity and confidentiality be handled?
- How should follow-up meetings to initial consultations be arranged and managed?

- How should external agents (support services, welfare officers, parents) be involved?
- How should the team be evaluated for future team development?

(ibid.)

Useful strategies emerged from the pilot studies:

Most requesting teachers saw the strategies and approaches suggested by the TST as workable and useful, even if not especially novel.

Strategies suggested to referring teachers by TSTs may be grouped as follows:

1 Use of extra staff – including the SEN co-ordinator.
2 Strategies for use within class, such as charts, contracts and report books as well as individual programmes and group management approaches.
3 Lunchtime management strategies such as the deployment of toys and games.
4 Involvement of parents in planning and managing specific support for learning and behaviour.
5 Use of external support of educational psychologists.

Rather than receiving suggestions alone, many teachers reported that it was the opportunity to discuss and reflect on their own concerns with the support of colleagues that they particularly welcomed. The act of framing and defining the concern appeared to be an important function of TST sessions for requesting teachers.

(ibid., p. 172)

Values permeating the system

Mosley's work and that of Daniels *et al.* clearly focus on school core aims and values. This is also a feature of a study by Richards (1999) into the characteristics of schools which are successful in including students whose behaviour is difficult to manage. Factors identified in Richards' study were:

Adult–student relationships (which are) . . . supportive, non-judgemental and non-threatening.

Curriculum content (process), accreditation . . . developed to supply meaningful and relevant knowledge and skills at a level that provides challenge and achievement. Credible yet achievable accreditation.

Record keeping and communication . . . with parents . . . to support parents with issues relating to the emotional and behavioural difficulties of the children. . . . Where it is felt it may assist in either avoiding difficulties or solving problems.

This is an extremely important function in managing behaviour at school. There can be few situations more stressful and belittling to parents than to find that the school is holding them accountable for the behaviour of their children at school, while at the same time, affording them neither the means nor the power to intervene. According to Richards,

> careful but flexible planning of . . . timetabling and staff allocation;
>
> flexible behaviour and discipline policies . . . avoiding unrealistic expectations.
>
> (ibid., pp. 100–1)

Richards concludes that the interactions and outcomes characteristic of successful work with students whose behaviour is identified as a focus of concern by teachers involves: 'Students, parents, staff, management and governors' who perceive they have 'dialogue, participation, supportive relationships, ownership and voice' (ibid., p. 99) to achieve consensus and ownership of:

- appropriate curriculum;
- shared concept of EBD;
- incorporated pastoral system;
- flexible policies;
- problem-solving approaches;
- shared responsibility.

Local support for systems change in schools

One way in which schools may be able to harness support for change and development in their own systems and practices is by enlisting the advice, guidance and, sometimes, practical help from external agencies or services at local level. Engaging effectively with the views and concerns of those working inside schools is not always straightforward or easy, however.

In a number of countries, including the UK and New Zealand, the role of external support services, their relationship with schools and, often, their funding bases have also changed in recent years. In New Zealand, for example, one component of the government's policy initiative, Special Education 2000 is the establishment of Resource Teachers Learning and Behaviour (RTLBs). This programme provides post-graduate professional development for experienced teachers. RTLB work closely with regular class teachers in introducing a wide range of inclusive teaching strategies to fully include students experiencing behaviour and learning difficulties (Thomson *et al.*, 2001). These strategies include cooperative learning (Johnson and Johnson, 1989), strategic teaching (Brown, 1992), reciprocal teaching (Westera and Moore, 1995), the Hikairo Rationale (Macfarlane, 1997) and peer tutoring (Cameron and Walker, 1994; Greenwood *et al.*, 1985; Medcalf, 1992).

The role of the RTLB calls for:

> a transformation or paradigm shift in the way in which schools meet the learning and behavioural needs of all their students. The RTLB has the challenging task of supporting all those 'other' teachers [not just those with particular responsibilities for students with special needs] to take up their individual and collective responsibility for the learning and behaviour of all the students in their classes and school (Glynn *et al.*, 1992)

> A high level of consultative and collaborative skills will be essential if RTLBs are to assist colleagues to vary the way they present the curriculum in their classes and to vary their preferred teaching and assessment practices. These changes are necessary so that classroom lessons are more accessible to students with learning and behavioural difficulties.

> The new role also requires RTLBs to negotiate, facilitate and co-ordinate changes in schools systems and routines, such as playground supervision and school rules. RTLBs need to consult and collaborate widely within their school. They also need to consult and collaborate with professionals and agencies outside the school, such as psychologists, visiting teachers, and the Children and Young Persons Service.

> . . . Within an educational perspective, assisting students experiencing learning and behaviour difficulties is seen essentially as a teaching and learning issue for the whole school and the community. It is no longer a case of assessing to establish profiles of deficit which justify excluding students from access to learning in regular classrooms (Ysseldyke and Thurlow, 1994).
>
> (Glynn, 1998a)

Reflecting on the tensions facing support teachers in assuming a similar role in a UK context, Sproson (2004) comments:

- Theory suggests that their job is to create 'self-managing schools' but the end product is unreachable within short time limits, possibly within longer ones.
- Theory suggests consultancy – schools whether rightly or wrongly often want 'hands on' help.
- Effective support teaching is viewed very differently by individual staff members – it is also viewed differently by different stakeholders e.g. parents, students, teachers, governors, LEA officials.
- Many teachers hold seemingly unchangeable beliefs about responses to 'bad' behaviour which make it almost impossible for them to modify their practice.

The professional practice of RTLBs in New Zealand is also seriously challenged by different views held by stakeholders. The collaborative problem-solving ecological model they try to work with can be thwarted and undermined in schools where senior management and teaching staff reject the model and insist that the RTLB provide one-on-one support for individual students.

This can be especially problematic where some teachers hold beliefs that automatically associate behaviour patterns and characteristics with particular ethnic groups while at the same time having minimal authentic knowledge or contact with these groups.

Working from attachment theory

System-wide strategies and initiatives for all young children with special educational needs typically exhort health and social services staff to be vigilant in identifying children under 5 years old who might be at a disadvantage. This is a plea for multi-professional working, for innovative partnerships between voluntary and statutory agencies working with children in their early years, creating development plans to show that appropriate provision is available for children with special education needs. It is also important that there is multi-professional contribution to baseline assessment of these students on entry to school and of course within system-wide programmes such as the national literacy strategy. However, rarely are links made between these general strategies and assisting young children with behaviour difficulties. Nor is reference made to any specific strategies and initiatives for young children who exhibit, or are likely to exhibit behaviour difficulties.

Nurture groups

Early childhood nurture groups (Bennathan and Boxall, 2000) were first established in the 1970s in the Inner London Education Authority (ILEA). One example of an approach, which is derived from the theory of attachment is that of 'nurture groups'. Bennathan (2000) describes the growth of nurture groups as a response to a perceived rise in the numbers of young children arriving at school from backgrounds of social deprivation. The first experimental groups were established in 1970–1 by Marjorie Boxall, an educational psychologist employed by the ILEA in Hackney, an area of North London ranking high on all indices of social deprivation. One was based in an infant school and one in a junior school.

> Nurture groups were special classes of some 12 children in primary schools run by a teacher and a helper. They were for children already in the school who were showing signs of severely deprived early childhoods,

unable to learn because of extreme withdrawal or disruptiveness. For some children, 'everything that could go wrong had gone wrong', and it seemed that the only thing to do with them was to start again. This meant recreating in school the total experience of a normally developing child from babyhood onwards. The routine of the nurture group day was planned to provide a predictable, reliable structure in which the children would come to feel safe and cared for, so that they began to trust the adults, to explore and to learn. The structure combined the nurturing of an adequate family with the control required to manage in a group, taking turns, waiting, making choices, carrying tasks through to completion and clearing away. The children then began to make sense of their experiences, to be able to ask questions, to discuss, to feel some control over their environment and to internalize some control over their behaviour.

(Bennathan, 2000, pp. 8–9)

Underlying the organisation of the groups is the principle that responses to individual children's behaviour should be appropriate to the developmental stage she or he may have reached (that is, start where the child is at). The child may need comfort like a baby, control like a 2-year-old in a tantrum or attention like a 3-year-old asking endless questions. Nurture groups operate on the assumption that, as the children's emotional needs are met consistently rather than responded to as they may have been in a normal class (either by ignoring or attempts to suppress the behaviour), children will develop greater trust, self-confidence, and personal self-organisation and will be more ready for formal learning. In some local education authorities nurture groups have been integrated into the organisation of mainstream infant schools.

In the London area in the 1970s and 1980s there was considerable support for the establishment of nurture groups in mainstream infant schools as a whole-school response to the emotional needs of some young children (ILEA, 1985). However, in some quarters this approach was heavily criticised as discriminatory against particular groups of children.

Bennathan (2000, pp. 14–16) recalls charges of racism, for example:

On this point, it is true that there were many black children in the early groups. One reason for this is that the groups were in areas with large black populations. Also, black immigrants to London in the 1960s and '70s faced extremely harsh social conditions. There was the loss of extended family support; the loss of safe play space; poor housing conditions; the necessity for mothers to work long hours, often at the hardest and worst paid jobs; and a serious lack of good child care facilities. Not surprisingly, many children came into school showing the effects of this stress.

In defence of nurture groups, Bennathan quotes a recent book *Black in White* (1995), by Jean Harris-Hendriks, an English child psychiatrist, and John Figueroa, a Caribbean academic:

> In the late 1960s a phrase, 'West Indian autism' had brief currency. It was racist, since it attributed to a particular culture a problem common to all children who are under stimulated; that they are expressionless, unresponsive even when attempts are made to stimulate them, delayed in speech and motor skills and may end up stimulating themselves by repetitive behaviours such as rocking.
>
> In the early seventies many Inner London schools started 'nurture groups'. These were invaluable and deceptively simple arrangements whereby young children who for whatever reason, and irrespective of their nationality or skin colour, were unprepared to cope with pre-school and primary school, were lovingly and systematically taught the skills to care for themselves, the language to communicate with other children and enabled to play. The results were invaluable to the children, their teachers and their parents and it is sad to record that, because so many small black children joined these groups, the provision in the end was labelled as racist. This was the view of some educationists, including those of the same skin colour as the children, but not of the parents who valued what was being offered and could see how their children benefited. The children lost out, whatever their skin colour.
>
> (Bennathan, 2000, pp. 14–16)

O'Connor and Colwell (2002) caution against accepting attachment theory uncritically as an explanation of children's difficulties. The nurture group aims to provide the experience of positive relationships in a secure environment through a trusting relationship with the teacher developing age-appropriate personal, emotional and social skills through membership of a small group within the mainstream school. Also, it appears that these groups were creating culturally safe environments in which the values and experiences of black families are legitimised and accepted.

It is interesting to observe that initiatives by New Zealand Māori to establish pre-school contexts (*kōhanga reo*) and later primary schools (*kura kaupapa Māori*) in which a holistic approach towards meeting children's physical, social, emotional, intellectual and spiritual needs was taken were labelled as separatist and racist by letter writers and commentators in the media.

Cooper *et al.* (2001) claim that children who demonstrate emotional and behavioural difficulties are experiencing emotions and demonstrating behaviours more appropriate to younger children. Briefly, it is argued, age-appropriate behaviour results from experiences of early caring which move the child from almost wholly egocentric concerns and almost total dependence on adult attention to an awareness of themselves as individuals in relation to other people. Difficulties of achieving safety, trust and security limit the development of awareness of higher-level needs concerned with socialisation such as affiliation, self-esteem and self-actualisation.

The emphasis of nurture group work is on supporting social, emotional and cognitive development. The nurture group work is integrated into the work of mainstream schools and is aimed at the return of children to full-time classes. Entry to the group, progress within the group and departure from the group are determined by diagnosis and evaluation using accepted measures. Doyle (2001) describes a readiness scale for reintegrating students into their mainstream classroom which assess self-control and management of behaviour; social skills; self-awareness and confidence and skills for learning.

Nurture groups appear to have had a positive effect on whole-school practices in changes to the way teachers think and talk about children (Cooper, 2004). They have led to an increased confidence (empowerment) with 'difficult' students and to a growing awareness of the social-emotional factors in learning. Doyle (2001) comments that the experience of a nurture group and the use of a nurture group reintegration scale have helped to generalise the application of principles of nurture throughout the school so that the school becomes a more inclusive and nurturing environment. Toothill and Spalding (2000), discussing the reintegration of children from a special school for children with emotional and behavioural difficulties back into mainstream schools, comment that the younger students who returned to the more supportive, familiar class-based environment of the primary school with an ethos of nurturing based on a nurture group were the least problematic transfers.

The 'Quiet Room'

The provision of space conceptualised as a sanctuary within the mainstream school for students who are troubled or stressed in some way is becoming more common in some parts of the UK (Renwick and Spalding, 2002; Spalding, 2000). The theoretical rationale for this can be seen in part as paralleling the function of nurture groups (Bennathan and Boxall, 1996). King and Chantler illustrate this notion of sanctuary provision in their description of the introduction of a 'Quiet Room' into a primary school in the north of England. Some students came from families under considerable stress for a number of reasons:

> The catchment area also includes a Women's Aid refuge, a local authority hostel for homeless families, and sheltered housing for the disabled and their families. Over the last six years . . . there has been an unusually high incidence of serious illness and bereavement among students and

their families. These features are having a considerable effect on the organisation and effective running of the school.

(2002, p. 183)

The authors elaborate on the kind of stress that, in turn, is experienced by the students from these families:

The . . . Women's Aid Refuge was established . . . for women and their children fleeing violent situations. The number of children attending from the refuge is variable as is the length of their stay . . . Arrivals and departures tend to be sudden and are principally due to the family being found by the 'violent partner'. As their stay in any one school is often short it is not unusual for the needs of children from these families to go unassessed. A consequence of this is that no provision is in place for these children. Children from the local authority hostel for homeless families are often also traumatised by the moves they have been forced to make; the situation that led to the move; and the severe disruption to their lives caused by their homeless situation.

The sheltered housing for disabled people in the catchment area of the school includes housing for families with young children. In some cases, a child is acting as the primary carer for a parent. These children often do not receive support from any other agencies.

Over the past five years, there has been an unusually high incidence of serious illnesses and deaths among the school community. Six parents and two teenage siblings have died and two students have died of cancers; there have also been three other students who have received long-term treatment for cancer. There is no apparent explanation for this high incidence of serious illness and death. The deaths and illnesses have considerable effect on the pupils and staff. In all of these circumstances, the school works closely with the children, their families, agencies such as Cruse Bereavement Care and the hospitals and hospices. . . .

All of the children affected by these factors need special support.

(ibid., p. 183)

A dedicated space named the 'Quiet Room' with a friendly adult available was set up to provide:

- someone for the children to talk to when required;
- assistance with personal care and physical support (for example, for those children who have experienced incontinence in class on a regular basis);
- small-scale support programmes to address a specific issue or to help a child through a difficult period (for example, to support a child in the period around a custody hearing);

- opportunities for small discussion groups, in which children feel able to talk about the issues that are troubling them.

(ibid., p. 184)

The 'Quiet Room' was staffed on a permanent basis because demand was unpredictable and might be urgent. Pragmatically, however, the staff had to be prepared to work flexibly in other areas of the school also:

> The 'Quiet Room' is staffed by a half-time support assistant, who was appointed because of her past experience of working with children in the health services. She is not a counsellor, but spends the majority of her time talking to the children and creating situations in which they feel able to express themselves. When not in the Quiet Room, she works in class supporting or observing an individual child. She works with the children on Monday, Tuesday, Thursday and Friday mornings. Wednesday afternoons are given over primarily to planning and reviewing in association with the school's Special Educational Needs Co-ordinator (SENCo).

(ibid., p. 185)

The students referred to the 'Quiet Room' were identified by teachers as experiencing difficulties that included 'behaviour problems', both withdrawn behaviour and disruptive activities, poor self-esteem, difficulty in socialising with peers and relating to adults, fear and an inability to concentrate in class. Each session in the room began and ended with the student being collected from, and returned to, the mainstream class. During these sessions, various activities:

> take place according to age and circumstances for the visit. The activities are used as a vehicle to help the children relax, express themselves, chat and work through different issues. Many of these planned, educational activities are similar to and based on those used in nurture groups (Bennathan & Boxall, 1996).
>
> Relaxing music is played and the children are provided with a snack (drink and toast). General story books are available relating to different problems and situations. These are often used as a stimulus for conversation about different areas. For example, the 'Mr Men' stories by Roger Hargreaves can provide a useful starting point for discussion. The story of 'Mr Happy' can encourage children to talk about things that make them happy and sad.
>
> Art equipment is provided so that the children can paint, draw, cut and stick, or make models out of Playdoh. The decoration of the room encourages interaction with the children, and the children's artwork is displayed, if they so wish, in the room.

Construction toys designed for varying ages and general games such as skittles, board games, large snakes and ladders, Jenga and puzzles are available. A doll's house has just been introduced to accompany the puppets and teddies.

Dressing-up clothes are provided and those children attending in a group enjoy these. The clothes and the doll's house allow the children to role-play different situations.

For those children who want to write and practise different skills, a large whiteboard is available. One child who was trying to improve his handwriting found the whiteboard very useful. He was able to practise with support, in a different environment from the classroom, a skill he was finding difficult.

Worksheets are also used to promote discussions. They can be about both specific (divorce or bereavement, for example) and non-specific (such as self, family, friends, school or feelings) situations.

(ibid., p. 187)

It is clear that such 'Quiet Rooms' provide attractive, safe and enjoyable environments for students who are stressed and anxious. In terms of the principles of applied behaviour analysis, they can be seen as powerful 'setting events' (antecedents) for calm and relaxed behaviours. There is also a risk that access to such positively reinforcing contexts could come to act as a reinforcer for avoidance and escape behaviours. However, given the extremely aversive and punitive environments that many of these students come from, access to 'Quiet Rooms' may be both helpful and necessary for reasons of safety.

Addressing bullying behaviour in schools

In Chapter 2 we examined bullying as an example of challenging behaviour that can be understood from a variety of different perspectives, which suggest a range of different approaches to intervention. One of the problems in evaluating interventions that target bullying is that there is no agreed definition of 'bullying'. Different viewpoints imply different assumptions about the nature of the problem, and, therefore, also imply different, sometimes contradictory, solutions. Three common explanations for bullying behaviour attribute it to the influence of supernatural forces, biological inheritance and situational influences (Rigby, 2002).

To be effective, a school's behaviour policy needs to contain not simply a statement of principles for responding to behaviour regarded as acceptable, but also, in the case of an anti-bullying policy, a clear set of procedures about what should happen in the case of a bullying incident.

Responses to bullying behaviour often fall into one of two categories: those that assume bullying is an anti-social act which needs to be reduced through various types of punishment contingencies, and those that focus on establishing respectful behaviour between people so as to minimise bullying through the abuse of power in personal relationships. These two views are, essentially, a debate about means and ends. One sees the desirable end 'as the elimination of hostile, aggressive behaviour between people' (ibid., p. 463), the other 'as achieving constructive, respectful behaviour between people' (ibid.). From one view 'we can best proceed by identifying and punishing behaviour we wish to stop' (ibid.). Typically any violation of rules is treated similarly, whether major or minor. Policies may rely completely on 'rules and sanctions and zero tolerance for rule infractions' (ibid., p. 238). From the other view, 'positive improvement in behaviour between people can be brought about through instruction, persuasion and modelling of respectful behaviour' (ibid.).

Differences in responses to bullying behaviour may also arise because of issues with ownership and understanding of anti-bullying policies. Deficit theorising may simply seek to blame the home circumstances of the bully and even those of the victim for not equipping them with more pro-social behaviours, on the one hand, or more effective coping strategies, on the other. In some instances the school hierarchy may try to take sole responsibility. At other times a more broad-based anti-bullying policy might be negotiated with all members of the school community. Rigby lists suggested elements in such a policy:

1 A strong statement of the school's stand against bullying.
2 A succinct definition of bullying.
3 A declaration of the rights of individuals in the school community – students, teachers, other workers and parents – to be free of bullying and (if bullied) to be provided with help and support.
4 A statement of the responsibilities of members of the school community: to abstain personally from bullying others in any way; to actively discourage bullying when it occurs; and to give support to those who are victimised.
5 A general description of what the school will do to deal with incidents of bullying. (For example: the severity and seriousness of the bullying will be assessed and appropriate action taken. This may include the use of counselling practices, the imposition of sanctions, interviews with parents, and, in extreme cases, suspension from school.)
6 An undertaking to evaluate the policy in the near and specified future.

(2002, p. 239)

One important element in considering how to respond to bullying is the recognition of an imbalance of power between victim and bully. Redressing this imbalance, therefore, may well require the intervention of some kind of authority. An initiative that follows the view of bullying as an anti-social act is the so-called 'bully courts' (Elliott, 1991). Here, the victim writes down the details of the incident(s), and victim, bully and any witnesses are invited to a meeting of the court. Each individual is questioned by a panel consisting of students and teachers. This panel then discusses the case in private, makes its decision about consequences. The head teacher has the right of veto in the case of an appeal. Records are kept for future reference.

The opposing view, that bullying can be addressed by encouraging and modelling socially acceptable behaviour, is reflected in Pikas's (1989) 'Method of Shared Concern' which has been put into practice by schools both in Europe and Australia. This involves working with members of bullying groups individually before involving the victim. In the individual meetings, the teacher expresses concern for the victim, finds out from the bullies what they know about the situation and then invites these individuals to offer a solution. Pikas takes the view that using punishment is often ineffective. Changing group behaviour towards the victim is the most important issue. The victim may not always be totally innocent of drawing the bullying on him/herself. Once the victim is involved, the teacher can then mediate between him/her and the group.

Another initiative that assumes the allocation of blame is inappropriate and counter-productive is the so-called 'No Blame approach' (Maines and Robinson, 1991). This involves seven steps to be taken by the teacher:

1 Take an account from the victim, allowing the victim to express feelings as well as details about the circumstances.
2 Hold a meeting of all those involved except the victim. This meeting should include bystanders and those who failed to intervene.
3 Explain the distress felt by the victim.
4 Inform those present that they can do something to overcome the problem.
5 Take suggestions from group members about what they can do to help the situation and put some or all of these suggestions into practice.
6 Check the progress of the group one week later.
7 Convey to the group a sense of their potential for kindness and support for the victim.

In an evaluation of a project to pilot this approach in an independent boys' school, Demko (2004, p. 29) concluded that if this approach is to be success-ful 'the whole school must be committed to it'. In other words, the whole school must share an understanding of what it is all about. 'Before teachers, or anyone else, can understand the effects of bullying, they need first to understand the pain and suffering to enable them to empathise with the victim' (ibid., p. 30).

Harnessing community support

In 1993 a programme was developed to address bullying and other disruptive and violent behaviours in New Zealand schools. This programme, which became known as Eliminating Violence (EV) (Special Education Services, undated), offered a clear and coherent framework to people in schools and communities to collaborate and implement procedures aimed at bringing about positive change. Overall, the programme aimed to develop peaceful, safe schools by ensuring that the environmental systems and structures were consistent and supportive of pro-social behaviours and with systematic consequences for anti-social behaviours. For the purposes of this programme, bullying (violence) is defined as: 'The control of others' behaviour by fear, force, intimidation or manipulation and always involves an abuse of power' (Special Education Services, undated, p. 1). The programme is embedded in two series of values and beliefs. The first set of values and beliefs is to do with violence, society's responsibilities and the rights of the child. They included:

> We work to eliminate violence and manage anger. Violence is a behaviour. Anger is an emotion.
>   Violence is learned and can be unlearned.
>   Violence is always an abuse of power in unequal relationships.
>   Anger and conflict are aspects of everyday life.
>   Anger can be managed effectively and channelled positively.
>   It is an individual's responsibility to eliminate their own violence and manage their own anger.
>   It is society's responsibility to provide structures that support non-violence; feedback and other consequences of behaviour; assertion so that violence is not rewarded (explicitly or implicitly) and support so that people who are marginalised have others standing with them where abuses of power are possible.
>   Children are persons in their own right.
>   Every child has the right to be treated respectfully, made welcome and included, and to be safe in schools and homes.
>   (Special Education Services, undated, p. 2)

The second set of values and beliefs is to do with how participants should respond when confronted by violent behaviours. According to the Special Education Services (ibid., p. 3) these included:

- Participative decision-making.
- Sharing information.
- Open expression and acceptance of feelings.
- Checking things out without making assumptions or judgements.
- Being open about what you want from a person or situation.

- Personal responsibility and working together to find solutions to problems.
- Being able to assert yourself about your views.
- Sharing responsibility, including others, and giving others the opportunity to take the initiative.
- Participating as an equal and having fair expectations of others.
- Seeing an action which does not have the desired effect as a learning and growth experience and not as a failure.
- Consideration of others' needs.
- Sharing speaking time.
- Active involvement.

The programme, which has been implemented in New Zealand schools by educational psychologists and other special educators, begins by schools recognising that they need additional support in the area of managing student behaviour, and applying to participate. Trainers then observe the extent to which acts of violence (as defined using the definition above) are seen within the school environment. The observation data identify the extent to which violence is of concern and also help to identify parts of the school's system that needs to change. Trainers then feed this information back at staff and community meetings. A majority buy-in to train in the programme must occur before the next phase of the programme begins. The next phase includes the theme week at which the school, again using collaborative decision making, renames the programme and thus metaphorically continues to eliminate violence from their school. During this week students participate in adapted learning experiences similar to those that have been undertaken by staff.

The Eliminating Violence programme involves all members of the school staff, all students, and the wider home community. Each group becomes actively involved in developing their own understandings about violence, then learning skills and strategies to identify a range of violent behaviours in order to respond effectively if or when confronted by these behaviours. Boards of Trustees are charged with the task of rewriting policies to reflect the programme's philosophy while school staff members work to develop school-wide practices that not only integrate the programme across the curriculum but also review the school structures so that they reflect the second set of EV values and beliefs. Parents are encouraged to work with the school to support the programme but also to learn the strategies and internalise the values to use in the home.

The Eliminating Violence programme has been adapted and reconstructed by members of the Pasifika community for use in schools with high numbers of Pasifika students. The Eliminating Violence programme has also been adapted and reconstructed by members of the Māori community for use in schools with high numbers of Māori students.

Practical issues in reintegrating students from special provision for 'emotional and behavioural difficulties' (EBD) to mainstream schools

MacLeod (2001) describes a project designed to support the integration of students from the special sector to mainstream schools at the point of transfer between primary and secondary schools. She notes that government targets for reducing the numbers of students excluded from mainstream schools and the development of local education authority policies on inclusion indicate that the political agenda favours this change. However, in practice there are a number of barriers to such inclusion:

> Identified barriers to effective integration include, firstly, responses demonstrating a lack of conviction within special schools about the suitability of such change: parental reluctance to forsake the protective environment of a special school is frequently mirrored by a possessive attitude towards students by the schools themselves. Secondly, it can be suggested that, although committed in policy terms, LEA practice is not always geared towards inclusive priorities: the complexities of funding arrangements; LEA boundaries; the inconsistency of Statementing procedures; the lack of an ethos promoting the removal of Statements; and the lack of multi-agency collaboration support this contention. Finally, some mainstream schools can appear to have an anti-inclusive agenda: a reluctance to accept any students with SEN other than those who score highly in emotively sympathetic terms, for example students with physical disabilities, is most strongly evident in an unwillingness to accept students with EBD. The effect of performance table results and the lack of teachers with specialist training are cited as reasons justifying this attitude.
>
> (MacLeod, 2001, p. 191)

Among the factors that MacLeod (ibid., p. 192) identified as crucial to the success of reintegration are:

- Students who achieve well academically within the overall range of achievement of the mainstream students, have the greatest likelihood of success in the mainstream school.
- An awareness among the students of the consequences of their behaviour and an acceptance of the mainstream school's sanctions.
- Parental support for the mainstream placement.
- The existence within the mainstream school of a comprehensive set of support strategies for students, including the use of multi-agency support and support from the referring special school.

There are some countries where, legally, mainstream education is the norm for all students. In England, for example, the Department for Education and

Skills (DfES) document *Inclusive Schooling: Children with Special Educational Needs* (DfES, 2001c) notes that, under English law, 'mainstream education' can only be refused on the grounds that a student's inclusion would be incompatible with the efficient education of others where there are no reasonable steps maintained schools or local education authorities could take to prevent the incompatibility. Education law does not set out what should be taken into account when deciding if a step is 'reasonable' (ibid., para 45), however.

In the UK, the DfES (2001c) has listed a number of steps that it is reasonable to expect schools to take to include students. For primary-aged students with severe temper tantrums, the reasonable steps to ensure inclusion which are not incompatible with the efficient education of other children may include:

- addressing factors within the *class* that may be contributing to the problem – e.g. addressing teasing by using circle time as a forum for discussing teasing and how to respond to it;
- teaching the child alternative behaviours – i.e. taking quiet time in a specially designated area at times of stress;
- providing the child with a channel of communication other than tantrums – i.e. fetching another child identified as their 'listening partner', or completing a 'think bubble sheet' to identify the stressor, the accompanying feelings and his or her possible courses of action;
- using a carefully designed system of behaviour targets, drawn up together with the child, and linked to an effective reward system which, wherever possible, involves parents/carers;
- ensuring that all staff who deal with the child have been briefed on potential triggers for outbursts, and effective ways of heading off trouble at an early stage – i.e. an agreed school-wide system where the child is asked to take a colour-coded object to another member of staff as soon as the emotional temperature is rising;
- drawing up a contingency plan for what will happen if there is a confrontation in class: in conjunction with the child, identifying a key helper who will be summoned to remove the child or the rest of the class from the situation, identifying how they will know the need is urgent, and setting out what the later consequences will be for the child if this system has to be used;
- ensuring that if there is any possibility that positive handling may need to be used to prevent injury to others or damage to property, that relevant staff have had training in appropriate techniques, that these have been carefully explained to the child, and that the circumstances under which they may be used have been recorded on a written plan agreed with and signed by the child and his or her parents/carers.

(ibid., para 46, p. 16)

For a secondary-aged student with emotional and behavioural difficulties, the reasonable steps to ensure inclusion which are not incompatible with the efficient education of other children may include:

- identifying a key worker in school whose role is to meet regularly with the student to build the relationship, monitor progress, pull together multi-agency support, pass on relevant information to staff, and mediate between student and teacher where relationships are strained;
- ensuring close home–school links so that the school are immediately aware of changes to the home situation which may impact on the child's behaviour and can make special arrangements where this occurs;
- providing for the student to attend an in-school support centre either full time during periods of stress, or on the basis of withdrawal from lessons which are particular trouble-spots;
- providing the student with a carefully structured and monitored way of withdrawing him or herself from difficult situations for example, use of a sanctuary card for access to an in-school centre or quiet '*cool-off*' area;
- arranging one-to-one or group work where conflict resolution strategies can be discussed and role-played;
- involving the student in a planned programme to build self-esteem, such as tutoring younger students or being part of a group that counsels or supports students who are experiencing friendship problems;
- ensuring that all staff who teach the student have shared, and are briefed on, effective strategies to deal with overt challenge, for example phrasing instructions as choices ('*put the magazine on my desk or in your bag*'), avoiding language which might make the student feel publicly shamed, constructing face-saving ways out for a student who has backed him or herself into a corner;
- ensuring that all staff have had training in de-escalation techniques for dealing with parents or students;
- ensuring that an emergency plan is in place through which all staff can summon assistance if needed.

(ibid., para 46)

Teaching strategies that support the inclusion of students

Corbett has reported on a case study researching the characteristics of successful pedagogy to support inclusion in a primary school in the London Borough of Tower Hamlets. Her conclusions indicate that the school's system is permeated by a sense that all learners and the entire staff are included in curriculum decision-making:

There is a real effort made to involve the learners, to create situations in which they can meet with success and to build on their existing level of knowledge. Learning Support Assistants (LSAs) are well briefed by teachers and work co-operatively to ensure that there are no individuals who are isolated from the group and not participating in any meaningful way. So many skilful strategies have been learnt and adapted by the teaching team that it is hard to say where mainstream teaching ends and specialist teaching begins. I felt that they had skilled themselves up to be able to accommodate the needs of children with Asperger's syndrome, autism, Down's syndrome, Williams syndrome and Attention Deficit Hyperactivity Disorder, who were included within their school population. There is a will to learn and a capacity to be highly flexible.

(2001, p. 58)

Corbett outlines findings as they reflect three key elements of the *Index for Inclusion* (Booth *et al.*, 2000): school culture, policy and practice:

School culture

There is a culture of open co-operation in the school. Every morning, the staff team meet before school starts in order to go through the key events of the day and to share any particular issues or problems. There is no stigma attached to being unable to cope with a child who is behaving in a way which is disruptive to the class. As the headteacher says 'We have informal support structures where everybody knows that a difficult child is not your fault. You don't have to take on the guilt for that. We have very good communication with our educational psychologist who will always come up with strategies if we ask her. Our SENCO has regular meetings for all children at any stage of the *Code of Practice* and we share our IEPs and our different ways of doing them. Teachers feel less threatened when they share problems. It's always been a culture of this school that you don't take on someone's behaviour as our problem. It's a whole school problem and the whole school has to work at it. . . . In most cases, we have very good relationships with parents. Teachers go to their homes. They seem very willing to come to school to discuss things.'

. . . There is a culture of reasoned dialogue, rather than confrontation. Children are listened to with respect. This overtly child-centred approach does not make this an anarchic school but one which feels safe, comfortable and confident.

(Corbett, 2001)

The school structure, elements of staff cooperation, the provision of informal support structures for teachers facing disruptive students, the emphasis on people and relationships and the commitment to reasoned dialogue all point to a school that would be culturally safe for students from different cultural backgrounds.

School policy

School policy to support effective inclusion operates at two key levels: in the use of funding for personnel; in the use of learning support assistants (LSAs). One of the members of the senior management team describes the approach:

> '. . . nearly all the school's disposable income is put into people – learning support assistants, primary helpers, not including LEA-funded LSAs. This really helps if you are trying to meet individual needs. . . . You see that when you go into classrooms. There are lots of adults around.'

Among the adult resources the school has access to are specialists in specific learning difficulties and autism and a counsellor, who works in the school three days a week. This greatly assists children experiencing emotional difficulties and their teachers and support staff.

School practice

[D]ifferentiation means using many teaching styles and sharing specialist skills. There is a real commitment to including all learners which involves using diverse strategies and working at many different levels on whole-class tasks. Staff recognise that children learn in many different ways and that some prefer visual rather than oral stimulus. Individual achievement is the goal. As the SENCO says:

> 'This means ensuring that children are all working on something at which they can gain success and move forward at their own level so that they can take the next step.'

By utilising a range of different learning strategies, and by working at different levels, this school is equipping its teachers to cater more appropriately for increasing diversity among its students. The following case provides a specific example:

> 'A four year-old blind boy, with his LSA, is participating in the Numeracy Hour. The teacher is working with six children on the carpet to do a session on "Recognising Shapes". She holds up a picture which has raised spongy shapes of triangles, squares and circles which the boy can feel. It is a feely-shaped, large book (an inclusive resource). The teacher gets the other children to interact with him (e.g. passing around a penny when they are exploring

round shapes). The group were helped to see the shape by the teacher drawing it on his hand.' (field notes)

Through considering ways in which resources and teaching approaches can include learners with disabilities, all the group can benefit, as what works well for this child may also be very helpful to others who find the interactive learning is reinforcing.

(ibid., pp. 56–7)

Strategies for change

In order to understand and appreciate behaviour as a function of both person and context, a school as a whole has to move from a simple focus on the student with behaviour difficulties to a focus on the behaviour incidents, through consideration of patterns of disruption. Watkins and Wagner assert that this can result in a decision to implement whole-school strategies such as 'Assertive Discipline' (Canter and Canter, 1992) in eliminating violence. As we have already discussed, a 'multi-level view' of behaviour, postulated by Watkins and Wagner, takes into account the effect of contexts in which it occurs and refers to three levels of patterns in school behaviour: the individual level, the classroom level and the organisation level. Each level is nested inside another because, they argue, each level also has its own context. Behaviour improvement policies aimed at change at all those levels: the individual, the classroom and the school levels are therefore most likely to be effective.

In the successful schools visited by Visser *et al.* 'misbehaviour was confronted but it was the "deed" which was condemned not the person' (2002, p. 25). This position provides a more positive basis for generating collaborative solutions, rather than simply punishment and/or personal humiliation and takes into account the cultural contexts of behaviour. For example when resolving behavioural issues, Māori educators will often refer to the concept of *mana*. This concept refers to an individual's personal autonomy, integrity, self-esteem and standing within the group. Solutions to conflict between individuals need to ensure that everyone's *mana* remains safe and intact, and that balance and harmony is restored. *Mana tangata* is the personal authority and respect one gains, according to one's ability to develop and maintain skills. Sometimes these skills are learned through personal motivation and achievement and sometimes skills are 'handed down' by elders or by older siblings.

Watkins and Wagner outline a school-wide strategy for improving school behaviour:

> *Check your assumptions . . .*
>
> - developing methods for gaining compliance [that is, methods about how best to gain compliance]?

- developing methods for maintaining classrooms in some teacher-centred form [that is, about how to maintain teacher-centred classrooms]?
- developing methods for learning about behaviour and thereby improving our schools and the learning in them [that is about ways to understand and improve the school's role in producing and changing behaviour]?

Map the difficulties . . . attempting to adopt a multi-level view . . . to obtain a picture of the real pattern of difficulties in the school [that is, analyse and prioritise behaviours arising at individual, class-wide and school-wide levels].

Devise the intervention . . . a team of insiders . . . supported through appropriate frameworks for thinking and action, will be best placed to devise and implement the intervention.

Review the impact [the effectiveness of the intervention] . . . review is a key to learning, and needs to be planned in so that the effectiveness of the intervention can be evaluated.

(2000, pp. 19–20)

Collecting evidence about behaviour at school level might include, for example, occasional informal surveys, reviews of school behaviour at staff meetings to identify locations, contexts and situations where difficult behaviour does, and does not, occur. At classroom level, information on behaviour patterns might be collected, for example, through tracking individual students and observing class activities through the eyes of students as closely as possible and/or through reciprocal classroom observation by peers on the staff. It may well be important to structure the content of the classroom observation with an agreed list of areas to be observed.

A whole-school approach involves all those who have to operate or are affected by a behaviour policy and is likely to be most effective in creating and maintaining the necessary ethos and associated practice. Watkins and Wagner (2000) describe how staff can work cooperatively in improvement teams to create a behaviour policy and with the support of peers to develop practice. As a consequence, the school ethos can become more caring and supportive and the use of sanctions is reduced. The notion of students, parents, staff, management and governors having a stake in the school behaviour management through dialogue, participation and supportive relationships is recognised by Richards (1999), which Radford (2000) claims results in a sense of ownership and empowerment through the willingness to work and act in cooperation and alongside others. We have already seen how the involvement of the community can help to reduce the exclusion of Afro-Caribbean students in schools in Enfield (Grant and Brooks, 2000) and improving the classroom and playground behaviour in New Zealand schools (Glynn *et al.*, 1997). Similarly, McPherson (1999) points not only to involving parents and students but also to the benefit of consultation and dialogue beyond the school with community groups and youth workers.

In a recent evaluation of an initiative to improve the level of behaviour across the whole school at Tennyson High School in England, McCall concludes that the most important lessons learned from this school's experience are:

- Any behaviour that is challenging or disruptive involves attributes of the individual, the operation of peer norms and the influences of home, the school, and the wider social context. It is important to see both the whole perspective and the distinctions between these interacting elements.
- Invariably the school's response has to be a range of interventions. Whilst these have to be appropriate to the way in which the nature of the difficult behaviour is conceptualised, they may also need to be 'best fit' trial and error procedures as the school better understands and utilises pupils' responsiveness.
- It is as important to reflect upon and modify deficiencies in the management of behaviour in the school's environment and systems, as it is to clarify and understand the fuelling effect of any child's difficult or distressing circumstances.
- A central underpinning is to work towards a whole school environment that is conducive to good ethos and discipline.
- Attention must be paid to positive behaviours and to mechanisms that enable students to visualise the nature of their unacceptable behaviour and its short-term and longer-term consequences.
- Despite the potential for recurring difficulties and setbacks, it is important for the school to work towards stronger than average ties with other neighbouring schools, parents and local community agencies.
- The value of internal and external review is that is can show the progress that has been made as well as highlighting the continuing challenges and needs.

(2004, pp. 65–6)

Developing new school initiatives

Fullan (2001) notes a number of very important issues to be taken into account when new initiatives are introduced into schools, for example, to address student behaviour seen as challenging or troubling to peers, teachers and others. Some of these issues are:

- Identifying the characteristics of the change in a school that a new initiative might require. These might be, for example, establishing clearly the need for such an initiative, being very clear about what it will entail and having an understanding of the complexity and practicality of the implementation process.

- Being aware of the 'local characteristics' of the district, community, principal/head teacher and teachers, for example the extent to which there is community pressure/support/apathy, and the extent to which the community comprises people from different ethnic and cultural backgrounds. It is also important to understand that the community contains key human resources, people from different ethnic backgrounds who have a good understanding of how challenging behaviour is generated by problematic school contexts and interactions. These same people are likely to generate more appropriate and adaptive solutions than schools can generate on their own.
- Being aware of 'external factors' associated with government and other agencies. For example, there might be funds for new policies and initiatives at central, local, or school level.

Leadership is clearly very important in developing new initiatives. In the literature associated with the influence of leadership on implementing new initiatives, Goleman (2000) notes the following kinds of leadership styles: *authoritative*, where the leader mobilises support for change, *affiliative*, where s/he builds relationships and/or affiliations, *democratic*, where consensus is reached through participation, *coaching* where the leader demonstrates and exemplifies aspects of the proposed intervention, *coercive* where s/he demands compliance, and *pacesetting* where s/he leads by example. Goleman (2000) concludes that authoritative and coaching styles positively influence the culture of the organisation. A coercive style may lead to resentment and resistance whilst pacesetting may lead to burn-out.

Fullan (2001) outlines three concerns in relation to maintaining new developments in schools:

1   There is often a tendency to oversimplify the initiative itself and also its implications in the short and long term. Decision-making is never based totally on rational models and evidence. It may involve intuition and immediate action as well.
2   Change takes time. The '25%–75% rule' of ideas – time suggests that it takes three times as long to put something into practice as it does to generate the ideas. Progress is incremental. Sometimes people need pressure to change. It may be necessary to plan for evolutionary change and problem-solving. It may also be possible to use the opportunity to change the school's infrastructure to accommodate change.
3   Passion and commitment are often identified with a sense of ownership. It is unwise for any individual, whether school leader or support person,

to assume that their version is what the change should be. Successful innovation needs individual implementers to own it. Individuals must work out their own understanding of the change process. Conflict and disagreement are inevitable and fundamental. Lack of implementation may not imply outright rejection. Apart from the rejection of basic values, possible reasons for this may include, insufficient time, inadequate resources. Those resisting may be justified in doing so for reasons not fully taken into account in the initial stages.

One response to mobilising more people and resources to support students whose behaviour is seen as troubling to teachers in schools is to acknowledge that teachers cannot do it alone (Fullan, 2001). One possible solution might be to attempt to involve the families and community members more in the education of young people. However, whenever a school commits to adopt this approach, Coleman (1998) advises that teachers must do the following:

- Realise that effectiveness of parental input and collaboration with schools is dependent on invitation from teachers, rather than on parents meeting requirements imposed by the school.
- Make parent–teacher collaboration legitimate by asserting the rights of parents to collaborate with teachers. It is also important for teachers to acknowledge that they have much to learn from collaborating with parents, rather than simply having much to impart to parents.
- Facilitate collaboration by arranging meetings and discussion of various sorts and by providing information about the curriculum and teaching methods.
- Encourage collaboration by suggesting learning activities that parents/carers and their offspring can do together. Examples of these sorts of activities include 'Pause, Prompt, Praise' (Glynn, 1995), responsive writing (Jerram et al., 1988; Glynn et al., 2003).
- Provide feedback on student's achievements.

As collaborative partners, parents are entitled to receive focused feedback on their children's performance (McKinley and Else, 2002). However, with regard to schools inviting community participation, parents and communities should not have to wait for such an invitation. Parents clearly have the right to initiate changes that will address behavioural difficulties their children encounter at school. Nevertheless having an invitation from the school makes it far easier and less stressful for parents to collaborate with teachers.

If we take the example of community involvement in schools to address issues of catering for student diversity and facilitating the educational and social inclusion of those who otherwise might be marginalised, Fullan (2001) advises setting up what he terms 'Action Teams' for school, family and community partnerships. Epstein *et al.* (1997) propose five steps in creating such partnerships:

Step 1   Create an action team: at least three teachers, three parents and an administrator.

Step 2   Obtain funds and other support: LEA funds, local businesses, school discretionary funds, separate fund-raising?

Step 3   Identify starting points: collect information about the school's current practices of partnerships – strengths, needed changes, expectations, sense of community, links to students' achievement.

Step 4   Develop a three-year outline plan, and a one-year detailed starting plan.

Step 5   Continue planning and working: annual presentation and discussion of progress and future developments.

Conclusion

Features of the teaching and learning practices of schools which are more successful in including children and young people with emotional and behavioural difficulties appear to be those features associated with successful schools for all students (Hobby and Smith, 2002). We have already seen how low academic achievement is associated with behavioural difficulties. Hobby (Hobby and Smith, 2002), in a summary report of research into the expressed perceptions of classroom learning in 15,000 classes of some 8,000 students, argues that: 'pupils' motivation and desire to learn will significantly affect their academic progress (as well as promoting more rounded, social development)' (ibid., 2002, p. 8).

Hobby argues that teachers create learning environments, which he calls the classroom climate, and which are defined as:

> The collective perception of pupils of what it feels like, in intellectual, motivational and emotional terms, to be a pupil in any particular teacher's classroom; where those perceptions influence every pupil's motivation to learn and perform to the best of his or her ability.
>
> (ibid., p. 9)

Government strategies for emotional and behavioural difficulties in mainstream schools also appear to have moved beyond a preoccupation with the behaviour of individual students to professional practice as the means of reducing and preventing difficult behaviour, for example the nation-wide programmes for training Resource Teachers of Learning and Behaviour in New Zealand (Thomson *et al.*, 2001). Also, in recent work by Bishop, Berryman, Richardson and Tiakiwai (2001, 2003), Bishop addresses the issue of challenging behaviour and low achievement of Māori students in Years 9 and 10 in inclusive teaching strategies, such as discursive teaching and co-construction of learning tasks, that successfully engage Māori students in classroom learning.

In the UK, the Green Paper (DfEE, 1997) and the Programme for Action (DfEE, 1998b) referred to strengthening staff skills for managing students and young people with emotional and behavioural difficulties. The Teacher Training Agency (TTA), a government agency, has established standards (TTA, 2002a) for newly qualified teachers which make it clear that all teachers should be able to deal effectively with basic classroom management and behavioural issues. For example, teachers should be able to do the following:

> demonstrate and promote the positive values, attitudes and behaviour that they expect from their students. . . .
> . . . they understand how students' learning can be affected by their physical, . . . cultural and emotional development.
>
> (ibid., pp. 7, 29)

Students from cultural backgrounds different from their teachers may often be placed at a disadvantage in that teachers may have inadequate understandings of students' behaviour and how to go about changing it in ways that do not threaten students' self-esteem or cultural safety. According to the TTA, teachers should:

> know a range of strategies to promote good behaviour and establish a purposeful learning environment.
> . . . identify and support more able students, those who are working below age-related expectations, those who are failing to achieve their potential in learning, and those who experience behavioural, emotional and social difficulties.
> . . . differentiate their teaching to meet the needs of students, including the more able and those with special educational needs.
>
> (ibid., pp. 34, 46, 59)

Also:

> Those awarded Qualified Teacher Status must demonstrate that they set high expectations for students' behaviour and establish a clear framework for classroom discipline to anticipate and manage students' behaviour constructively, and promote self-control and independence
>
> (ibid., p. 66)

It is not only the findings of the research by Hobby and Smith (2002) that is of direct interest here but also the definition and descriptors of the constituent features of classroom climate which is derived from student–teacher relationships and the teacher's teaching skills, as divided into the following nine measures:

1 Clarity – the transparency and explicit relevance of what goes on in class.
2 Environment – the comfort and attractiveness of the physical environment.
3 Fairness – justice and equality within the classroom.
4 Interest – stimulation and fascination in class.
5 Order – discipline and structure in the classroom.
6 Participation – student involvement and influence in the running of the class.
7 Safety – absence of threat or fear.
8 Standards – expectations of achievement and encouragement to improve.
9 Support – encouragement to try new things and learn from mistakes.

(adapted from Hobby and Smith, 2002, p. 9)

To these measures it is crucial to add the need for schools to respond to students' challenging behaviour in ways that acknowledge and affirm their cultural beliefs, values and preferred ways of learning and interacting.

Hobby and Smith claim that teachers can directly influence classroom climate by their behaviour and skills. Carpenter and McKee-Higgins (1996) are critical of control and sanctions as a means of managing behaviour difficulties in classrooms and propose an instructional or teaching and learning approach to behaviour management aimed at creating a positive learning climate in classrooms. Briefly, a positive learning climate involves teachers in providing appropriate learning tasks, rewarding positive responses and developing positive interactions with students. Assessment of the effectiveness of interventions in response to problem behaviour should be sensitive to gradual improvement in students' behaviour.

Chapter 11

School, home and community working together

Introduction

Many governments, such as those in the UK and New Zealand, are recognising that schools on their own may not be able to provide a sufficient response to the learning and behavioural needs of students from increasingly diverse cultural and community groups. They envisage a role for external groups in liaising with schools to prevent social exclusion and in reintegrating those already socially excluded into mainstream society (Tett *et al.*, 2001). This process of liaison is sometimes driven by professionals, and sometimes by parents, carers and/or the local school community. In New Zealand, for example, the Ministry of Education is concerned to reduce the number of students being excluded, stood down or suspended from schools, especially those from cultural groups whose students are over-represented in these statistics. It requires schools to consult with their local communities, particularly their Māori community. This is expressed in key education policy documents such as the *National Administration Guidelines* (NAG) (Ministry of Education, 2001b), and the Special Education 2000 policy document (Ministry of Education, 1997, 1998a). NAG 1 (v), for example, states that schools' Boards of Trustees are required: 'in consultation with the school's Māori community, [to] develop and make known to the school's community policies, plans and targets for improving the achievement of Māori students' (Ministry of Education, 2001b).

In this chapter we address major issues in establishing effective working relationship between schools and students' homes and local communities, and between schools and external agencies.

Collaboration with families and community groups

A culture is sometimes defined in terms of activities shared and enjoyed by specific groups of people. On the one level people who participate in these cultures may simply share common interests and preferences, and may meet together occasionally to share activities and experiences. However, on another level, culture has a deeper and more pervasive meaning. The cultural context in which a young person is reared has a very important role in influencing both thinking and behaviour. It can involve a close and enduring interconnectedness with family and other group members, and an on-going sharing of values, beliefs, lifestyles, and ways of knowing and of understanding the world. In this deeper sense, culture is often linked with membership of ethnic groups (Glynn and Bishop, 1995) or class.

The concept of culture is used also by various groups to identify and define themselves, and to differentiate themselves from others. The Waitangi consultancy group (Quest Rapuara, 1992) considers that:

- Culture holds communities together and provides common frameworks of meaning to their members.
- Culture includes the processes of decision-making and communication, the way families are structured and whom we regard as important.
- Culture expresses community values in relation to land, time, work and play, reward and punishment, good and evil.
- Culture comprising the collective memory and heritage finds expression in art, music, drama, literature, religion, and social events.

This definition makes it clear that culture involves collectively held values, beliefs and practices (ways of living and working together) that provide a basis of shared meaning and understanding for members of a group or community. These collective values, beliefs and practices are learned from living within a particular group or community for a long time. The values, beliefs, practices, and world-views of people from these cultures may first have been acquired in geographic locations very different from where they are now living. They are considered important enough for the group to value as a heritage to be passed down to their children. Culture is an essential dimension of personal identity and well-being, as individuals and as communities. Culture also strongly influences how individuals see, interact with and make sense of the world around them.

Working with groups of Māori Year 9 and 10 students in mainstream New Zealand schools, Bishop et al. (2003) found that these students understood culture as comprising two main components. The first component was made up of the visible signs, images and icons immediately recognisable as being from a particular culture. Schools often work to include the visible iconography of minority cultures (cultural performance groups, bilingual signs, art work) in their school environments (Bishop et al., 2003). According to the students participating in Bishop et al.'s research, this component comprises a responsive context in which minority cultural students can safely bring their own experiences into the classroom. The alternatives are to leave cultural experiences and identity at the school gate and behave according to the constraints set by the majority culture or to resist teachers and have their behaviour judged as challenging or resistant. At the level of learning and teaching in the classroom, the non-visible component of culture could involve students being encouraged to use their prior experiences as the basis for engaging with classroom tasks or for co-constructing learning tasks. The most effective teachers utilise both the 'visible and non-visible' components of culture. In Bishop *et al.*'s research, effective teachers were described as being interested enough in Māori students, and their culture to learn something about it from the students themselves or from their families and then to adapt their curriculum tasks and teaching interactions accordingly. Providing culturally responsive learning contexts generally resulted in improved relationships between the students and their teachers. At the beginning of the study, researchers found, as these students had indicated, there was little evidence from their teachers' interactions with them that their cultural experiences were called upon to assist their learning in the classroom. The study then moved on to address ways of increasing cultural responsiveness and discursive teaching in the classroom through targeted professional development for classroom teachers.

Culture should not be something that is put aside while the 'real' educational issues are addressed (Bishop *et al.*, 2001, 2003). It should not be something that hinders learning at school, and it should not be left at home, although, in the case of New Zealand, this is what has happened to Māori culture in many mainstream schools (Glynn, 1998; Glynn and Macfarlane, 1999). Sometimes behaviour that is worrying in some respect can arise as a result of conflicting values, preferences and practices that occur when students' home cultures differ from the culture of their teachers or their schools. It is important therefore, that both the visible and non-visible components of culture begin to occupy a more prominent space in the minds of teachers and other education professionals in their efforts to understand and improve student behaviour.

Families and local voluntary community groups are, potentially, an important source of additional support for schools in developing initiatives to address problematic student behaviour. Embedded within different home–school partnership arrangements are presuppositions about the ability and right of families and/or local community groups from a diversity of backgrounds and cultures to support their children at school. These presuppositions can serve to include or alienate both parents and their children. Wearmouth (2004a) draws on Dale (1996, Chapter 1) to discuss four common partnership arrangements between schools and parents/carers which clearly reflect different kinds of power relationships in supporting students who experience difficulties of various sorts in schools:

1   The traditional 'Expert Model' which is similar to the doctor–patient relationship. The professional is assumed to have expertise with which

to decide what needs to be done. Parental involvement is not of prime importance except to provide information.

2 The 'Transplant Model' where parents are viewed as an untapped resource for helping to teach of the child. The role of professionals is to transplant their skills and expertise to the parents to help the parents to become teachers. Professionals maintain control over decision-making.

3 The 'Consumer Model' in which power is shifted from the professional-as-service-provider, to the parent-as-consumer. As consumers, parents have the power to draw upon their own expertise and knowledge about their children in deciding what services they need for their child.

4 The 'Empowerment Model' where the right of the parent-as-consumer is combined with a professional recognition that the family incorporates a social system. Families rely as much on informal networks of support – neighbours, other family members, friends – as on the formal network of professionals. Under the Empowerment Model the role of the professional is to recognise the family's own support network and empower family members to meet their own needs, with professional support.

Many parents may welcome strong directives from teachers at least in the initial stages of discussing and negotiating ways to support the improvement of the child's learning and behaviour. However, others may be very concerned about involving themselves in initiatives where the intention is to 'engineer in' behaviour seen as 'desirable' by those who may understand little of the child's background.

In some schools the consumer model of parent–school partnership might be experienced as uncomfortable for a number of reasons. Parents might be felt to usurp some of the power and control more usually owned by professionals inside educational institutions. Also, there is an inherent inequality in a market system which ensures that children whose parents are the most literate, persistent and articulate are advantaged (Audit Commission, 1992; Gross, 1996). There may therefore be a very real concern about the way in which, as Gewirtz *et al.* (1995) comment, in the UK, education is viewed as a commodity, a position which is becoming increasingly common in New Zealand also.

Entitlement to resources

In the context of student behaviour seen as challenging or worrying, there have been many debates on the cause of the difficulty and appropriate forms of curriculum differentiation or intervention which have involved parents and carers. In the UK, throughout the 1980s and 1990s there was a series of initiatives designed to support parents in exercising their rights. However, exercising rights requires a high level of motivation and determination as well as, sometimes, access to legal representation and financial resources. The inevitable consequence of this is that some parents are better able to exercise their rights than others. Across the UK providing for 'special educational needs' implies meeting individual needs that have been assessed, not with providing what local authorities decide they can afford or what they or schools think is desirable. The basis of special education legislation is that of entitlement for individual learners. Gross (1996) concludes that resources are unfairly allocated to children whose parents are more literate, persistent and articulate and supports the notion of formula funding in the interests of 'fairness' for all children. This is an important criticism of the 'market-model' applied to special education. Making the same point about unfairness, the Audit Commission observed:

> LEAs admitted that factors which had no bearing on the level of need of a child were influential in the decision to issue a statement. The most significant factors were the level of determination of the school or the parent and whether the parent was represented by a lawyer or voluntary organisation.
>
> (1992, in Open University, 2001a, p. 101)

However, as Simmons points out:

> Those who support the case for formula funding in the interests of 'fairness' must be prepared to acknowledge that they support the dismantling of entitlement. Seen in that light, how many professionals or voluntary agencies would say publicly that they were in favour of removing entitlement from the most vulnerable sector of the educational community? ... Are they really willing to support restructuring which would give disabled children only what local politicians had determined was available rather than what was needed?
>
> (1996, in Open University, 2001a, p. 101)

Simmons concludes that the solution to the problem is not to remove entitlement from learners, but to persuade local authorities to fulfil their obligations towards every child. Even if the local authority does meet its resource obligations, however, there is still no guarantee that the child will be accepted by the school as a fully participant member and that his or her needs will be met appropriately across the curriculum.

Effective practice in supporting students with behavioural needs

A review of literature on students from minority cultures who have learning and behavioural needs provides clear indicators of effective practice. (Berryman *et al.*, 2002). Cultural groups included in this report were indigenous North Americans (both Indians and Alaskans), African-Americans, Mexican-Americans, American born Chinese, Portuguese-speaking Americans and Australian Aboriginals. Despite the distinct cultural differences between these groups, there were a surprising number of problems and solutions in common, often due to these groups' common experiences of colonisation, particularly within education. This literature was compared with New Zealand literature on meeting the needs of Māori children in order to gain insight into the most effective interventions.

Common indicators of effectiveness identified overall included the importance of a team approach in which students, parents, cultural experts, and professionals all work together. These teams were more effective when they were built on a basis of collaboration, where the parents/caregivers and family members used their expertise to inform the professionals involved as well as receiving information from the professionals.

Common problems encountered by these groups were remoteness from resources, conflict between national and local perspectives, lack of appropriate assessment and lack of appropriate training for indigenous groups and for their local professionals. A common strategy for overcoming problems involved developing a clear understanding of what models of excellence in these contexts might look like.

In the context of family literacy and improving learning outcomes for students from cultural backgrounds different from the school, McNaughton and Glynn (1998), Glynn *et al.* (2000a, 2000b) and Tellier-Robinson (1999) all point out that parents need to be viewed as an immensely rich resource. These writers identify the importance of teachers collaborating with parents in order to work more effectively with their children. Collaboration, however, implies interdependence between parents and teachers. For example, specific guidance for families on how to carry out reading activities at home can contribute to children's progress at school (McNaughton and Glynn, 1998). The effectiveness of this guidance depends on the degree to which families feel instrumental in influencing school processes and goals (Delgado-Gaitan, 1990). Families are likely to feel instrumental when well-written narrative texts in the students' home language that deal with topics of concern and interest to the home culture are developed and utilised for families to read to their children. Families can then contribute not only to their children's reading at home, but also to their reading at school. However, effectiveness of the pedagogies which families practise at home also depends on the specific literacy goals and actions shared between home and school (Gallimore and Goldenberg, 1993) and on the availability of culturally and linguistically appropriate resources.

Tellier-Robinson (1999) interviewed nine Portuguese-speaking parents of children with special needs. Almost all the parents she interviewed believed that the most important aspects of education take place in the home. There was a general feeling among parents interviewed by Tellier-Robinson that professionals were not fully aware of the daily demands on parents of children with severe physical needs, and that schools did not really appreciate the achievements of parents in teaching daily tasks to their children. Parents perceived that feeding and clothing, as well as other informal aspects, were an important part of education, and that the parents had a primary role in the education of children such as these. The general consensus was that what the children could do was immensely more important than what they could not do.

Several parents in this study considered that their children were not being sufficiently challenged in their educational programme. Surprisingly, many of these children were bilingual, and some of them were more fluent in English than their siblings, perhaps because they were 'taken everywhere' by their parents, and also perhaps because they had regular contact with English-speaking professionals. Only by speaking with the parents themselves was this important finding revealed. Parents also had other very good ideas. One parent suggested that schools did a lot to support and involve parents of special-needs children, but that the parents themselves had ideas about how they could do even better (Tellier-Robinson, 1999). Bronfenbrenner (1978) proposed that the groups who most needed parent education were all those who were not parents, that is, all those who did not, no longer, or never would have children. Government policy-makers in health education and welfare authority agencies are located at the macro-systemic level in Bronfenbrenner's model of human development. He argues that some of these people and agencies may actually be part of the problem for contemporary parents, rather than part of the solution. Ladson-Billings (1995) sees parents as the experts who are best able to identify effective teachers. Ladson-Billings used parent and community information as the basis for teacher selection in her research on the qualities of effective teachers.

Parents and educational professionals tend to hold values and set behavioural standards and expectations that are consistent with, and affirming of, those of the culture in which they live and work while children's attitudes and behaviour may gravitate towards the cultural norms of their families, peers and communities (Kauffman, 1997). Educational professionals from the majority or dominant culture are in danger of seeing their own culture as 'normal' or the 'default setting' against which other cultures are viewed as deviant, or deficient. Where there is conflict between the culture of the child and the culture of the classroom, barriers to learning can be created, often unintentionally. For those who want to understand the child, it is necessary to understand the culture (values, beliefs, practices and preferred ways of knowing and learning) of the child and the parents.

There is evidence that, very often, educational professionals still operate from the position that minority ethnic students are welcome to participate fully in the services provided in the mainstream education system, so long as their language and culture remain at home (Glynn et al., 2001). This may be so even where minority ethnic people's rights to define aspects of their children's education are underpinned by law. In New Zealand, for example, over many years, Māori people have continually asserted their rights under the Treaty of Waitangi to define and promote Māori knowledge and pedagogy. However, the frequently cited words of Governor Hobson who signed the Treaty of Waitangi on behalf of the British Crown, 'He iwi kotahi tātou' (We are one people) represent a continuing colonising position taken by many professionals and policy-makers. This position fails to acknowledge the integrity of Māori ethnicity and culture within the context of the curriculum and pedagogy in mainstream schools and strongly parallels findings in the evaluation of the Special Education 2000 policy (Bevan-Brown *et al.*, 1999; Bevan-Brown and Bevan-Brown, 1999). Timutimu-Thorpe (1994) cites specific examples in her research involving Māori families coping with children who have disabilities, where difficulties have arisen from a failure to acknowledge Māori ethnicity and culture in providing health, education and community services.

For members of the dominant culture to assert that 'we are all one people', is to assert that 'we are all the same'. Such a position runs the risk of marginalising or trivialising minority languages, cultural practices and identity. A more respectful way to begin a relationship is to acknowledge and appreciate differences. There is a Māori whakatauki (proverb):

He tangata kē koutou,
He tangata kē matou,
Engari i tēnei wa,
Tātou, tatou e.

Freely translated, this means: 'You are a different people from us, we are a different people from you, but in this context we can live and work together.' Recognising and appreciating the differences between majority and minority cultures is a more appropriate place to start and a stronger basis for building a relationship than asserting sameness (Glynn *et al.*, 2001).

Sharing expertise

This section reports on the way in which the shared expertise of families, community members and professionals can result in positive outcomes for minority ethnic students with learning and behaviour needs. We draw on a research report to the New Zealand Ministry of Education on five different sites of effective practice with Māori students (Berryman *et al.*, 2002). This study describes five special education interventions in the form of collaborative stories. Each collaborative story is located in a site of practice judged, by local Māori communities as well as by the local SES (formerly Specialist Education Services), and now Ministry of Education (Group Special Education) and by other educational professionals, as demonstrating effective outcomes for Māori. These five collaborative stories provided details of shared interventions involving SES staff, by Māori students, their families and other educational professionals.

Collaborative Story 1 involved a *whānau* in which three pre-school children were identified with severe hearing and language needs. Each child was fitted with hearing aids. At the time of the interviews all three children were working through education development plans (EDPs) with SES support. This team of Māori and Pākehā (non-Māori) SES workers, together with other service providers and educators worked collaboratively with the whānau to support the children within an inclusive educational context.

Collaborative Story 2 involved two Māori boys in a *whānau* in a provincial city who lived with their grandmother. Both boys experienced traumatic incidents in their life that resulted in severe behaviour and learning needs. Using an ecological approach, the Māori special education advisor supported this grandmother to work with both schools to ensure that the boys' education would lead to more successful outcomes. The special education advisor provided hands-on support to each of the boys, to the grandmother as well as to school staff.

Collaborative Story 3 involved a partnership between an *iwi* (tribal) Trust and an SES District Office. This partnership funded and delivered *wānanga taiaha* (live-in martial arts education programmes in the traditional use of the *taiaha*) for young Māori and Pākehā male students. The programmes addressed students' learning of Māori language and culture as well as building social skills and self-esteem. Students were carefully selected to ensure a balance between high achieving role models and students with severe and challenging behaviour. *Wānanga* were held approximately every six months and students were able to attend more than one.

Collaborative Story 4 involved the Eliminating Violence programme implemented by the Board of Trustees, principal, staff, parents, *whānau* and students of a small inner city school as a school-wide behaviour intervention. The Eliminating Violence programme in this school, where 97 per cent of the students were Māori, became known as SWEET AS! This collaborative story describes the changes that took place in the school following a change of principal and the implementation of the Eliminating Violence programme with the assistance of an SES co-ordinator. Apart from one Māori member of the school Board of Trustees, all the key participants at this site were Pakeha, but all were committed to working in ways that were culturally appropriate and safe for Māori students and families.

Collaborative Story 5 involved a community-wide implementation of Kawea Te Rongo (an early childhood Māori language and communication programme). This programme provides screening tools and training resources to assist the teachers and families of these students to identify the individual child's learning needs in Māori language, and to assist them with planning collaborative interactive language programmes for implementation at home and at school. Following training by a national training team, local teams offered training in Kawea Te Rongo to teachers of Year 1 and 2 students in Māori language immersion classrooms. The collaborative story from this site describes how one group responded to this challenge in the Wellington and Hutt areas.

Results from these five effective practice sites share a number of common features, namely:

1 The achievement of effective and balanced working partnerships between parents/*whānau* and educational professionals, in which each party acknowledged and supported the expertise of the other.
2 The negotiation of collaborative and culturally competent approaches to understanding and resolving problems.
3 The demonstration of willingness, by both professionals and parents, to listen to new ideas, and to work beyond their experience and/or their cultural comfort zones.

In addition to these common features, three senior Māori women who were also fluent native speakers of Māori, identified twelve core Māori cultural concepts that they judged as being practised at each site. These core concepts were:

- *ngā tūranga takitahi me ngā mana whakahaere* (recognition of the position and contribution of each individual and their particular responsibilities);
- *kanohi ki te kanohi* (acknowledgement of the importance of people meeting face to face, and being seen to be fully involved in the work);
- *wairuatanga* (acknowledgement of the dimension of spirituality as a key element of individual well-being and wholeness);
- *whānaungatanga* (embodiment of the principle of interconnectness and interdependence among all members of a working group, with responsibilities and commitments to each other, as in an extended family);
- *kotahitanga* (the type of unity of purpose and commitment that arises from sharing a common goals and understandings);
- *manaakitanga* (the duty of care that leaders or hosts have to nurture and provide for all the needs of their colleagues and visitors);
- *mahi tahi* (working together in a group in a direct 'hands-on' manner);
- *mana tangata* (recognition of the autonomy, status and self-esteem of every individual whether child or adult);
- *ako* (an understanding of teaching and learning that blurs the distinction between teacher and learner and emphasises the balance of power and reciprocity in effective teaching and learning interactions);
- *wānanga* (a traditional and contemporary forum for advanced learning, involving a rich and dynamic sharing of knowledge and expertise, and

an exchanging of views. Within a *wananga*, ideas are given life and spirit through dialogue, debate and lengthy deliberation);

- *aroha ki te tangata* (the love one shows for others, involving sharing, caring and showing unconditional support and generosity towards others, irrespective of culture or ethnicity);
- *mana motuhake* (the qualities of autonomy, status and self-esteem that illustrate the uniqueness and independence of Māori as a people).

Berryman *et al.* (2002) conclude that these twelve cultural concepts provided the *whariki* (mat or foundation) upon which effective school, home and community partnerships were constructed at each of the five sites. They note that it was the understanding of, and commitment to, the cultural values and practices, associated with these concepts by Pākehā teachers and professionals that made for effective collaborative work with Māori.

The findings from the five New Zealand case studies correspond closely to the findings from international literature. They suggest clear parameters for an effective model of collaborative school, home and community partnerships to meet the needs of students with special education needs from diverse cultural groups.

Collaboration between schools and professional groups

As a result of experience with a wide variety of children, and working intimately with these students, the teacher may be the first one who identifies a child with learning and behavioural needs. Assessment is a key task within special education. Even where the parent makes the first approach, it is often the teacher who is responsible for the first set of assessments and for referring the child to the appropriate specialist. Parents (and students) may need information on special needs and educational principles and resources, while professionals may need information on individual life histories and their cultural significance. Thousand *et al.* (1997) extend Faircloth and Tippeconnic III's (2000) list of team members (students, parents and educators), and suggest that there should be a collaborative team consisting of teachers, specialists, paraprofessionals, the student and his or her peers, members of the family and administrators. These authors advocate that all team members should work together to identify the support needed to meet the student's educational needs.

Collaboration with external agencies is integral to the work of many schools in supporting students whose behaviour is viewed as difficult or challenging. External agencies include social welfare, health and community education services, housing agencies and local community groups. This collaboration is not straightforward, however:

We already know a great deal about the problems and pitfalls of schools' work with other agencies (see Dyson and Robson, 1999; Lloyd, 1997; Kendrick, 1995; Armstrong and Galloway, 1994). These include territorial battles over budgets, different professional ideologies and structural barriers in terms of line management and reporting as well as the rather different legislative frameworks which impact on professionals. The Children Acts of 1989 and 1995 in England and Scotland respectively, for instance, explicitly adopt a children's rights philosophy which is markedly absent from education legislation in both countries.

(Tett *et al.*, 2001, p. 7)

In a study of the nature, extent and effectiveness of links between schools and local agencies and communities in Scotland, Tett *et al.* concluded that 'most schools did not have strong links with their communities' (ibid., p. 7). Most schools reported very little collaborative practice and what there was 'tended to centre around the formal curriculum and take place with other schools' (ibid., p. 7). Control of schools' activities was dominated by professional community groups and customer ? consumer? groups were less common in schools leading to a speculation that 'most schools defined their communities primarily in terms of their student constituency rather than their locales' (ibid.). This practice runs the risk of disconnecting the school from its historical, social and cultural contexts, such that the school may no longer 'belong' to the community in which it is located. This would seem to minimise the chances of the school playing an active role in community development. Where collaboration was identified as effective, different notions of the purposes of education and the structures needed to meet these purposes had led to two fundamental dimensions of practice: 'institutional boundaries' and 'pedagogic purpose' (ibid., p. 13). The relationship between them can be modelled on four quadrants of a matrix (Figure 11.1).

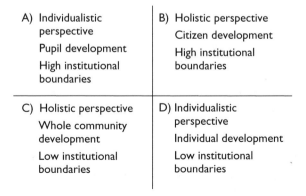

Figure 11.1 Matrix of relationship between institutional boundaries and pedagogic purpose

Quadrant A Individualistic perspective/high institutional boundaries (*pupil development*). The purpose of education is to support the work of schools and focuses upon addressing the problems that frustrate progress in the learning of pupils. Institutions define roles and rules in ways which can create a boundary between the school and other professionals, and between the school and community education professionals and the community.

Quadrant B Holistic perspective/high institutional boundaries (*citizen development*). In this category the education system recognizes the challenges of social and economic regeneration: it is involved in education and training to enable members of the community not only to gain employment but also to improve the quality of individual lives. Yet professional and institutional traditions can still frustrate collaborative working.

Quadrant C Holistic perspective/low institutional boundaries (*whole community development*). In this perspective the local authority, the institutions and agencies recognize the importance of community developments as well as lifelong learning. They form collaborative partnerships to ensure effective provision of education to enable members of the community to participate as citizens in the practice of local democracy.

Quadrant D Individualistic perspective/low institutional boundaries (*individual development*). Education seeks to support the learning needs of all individuals in the community: students; young people outside school; their parents; and the lifelong learning needs of adults in the community. To support these needs institutions strive to become responsive to the expressed needs of the community and to establish collaborative patterns of working with other organizations and agencies. ... The data suggest that the distribution of interests and power in a locality will determine which model predominates.

(Tett *et al.*, 2001, pp. 14–15)

The different institutional boundary positions in Tett *et al.*'s model appear to allow for two-way partnerships between school and community. A high boundary position suggests a partnership initiative that is largely school-driven, while a low boundary position suggests a partnership that is largely community-driven.

Tett *et al.* illustrate differences in underlying values, purposes, delivery of the programmes and resourcing in collaborative work to support 'troubled' young people in two cases studies, the first in a secondary school and the second in a primary school. The first case study focused on student development (Quadrant A) in an urban secondary school, with a community wing attached. The second focused on whole community development (Quadrant C) in a rural community primary school. In both case studies, the collaboration was with a voluntary sector agency that specialised in working with a small group of troubled and/or troubling young people to develop individually focused programmes.

In case study one, the collaboration was the result of the personal concern and contacts of the deputy principal at the school and the co-ordinator of the voluntary agency. The staff of the voluntary sector agency came from a variety of professional backgrounds, mainly social work and community education. They aimed to develop individually negotiated and targeted support for individual students whose behaviour and/or attendance were considered problematic in order to establish or maintain school attendance. The agency's core funding was external to the school.

The intervention described in case study two focused on primary-aged students who were in difficulty in school or with the police. The collaboration originated with the headteacher who collaborated with the senior voluntary sector agency worker on a programme of group work. The sessions of group work ran for two hours a week in the school, with various games and activities delivered jointly by the agency worker and the primary 1 teacher. These activities were designed to discover issues important to the students that needed to be addressed and to build trust and confidence between students and between adults and students. Group members were selected from a list of students referred to the agency by teachers, social workers, educational psychologists.

Tett *et al.* (2001, p. 17) note that, in terms of values: 'In case-study one the over-riding priorities of the school were about the effective academic education of the majority of its students.'

Tailor-made contracts were negotiated in which students and families agreed patterns of attendance/behaviour 'rewarded' by periods of withdrawal from school which varied from non-attendance at lessons to complete withdrawal for a limited time. Individuals were supervised by agency staff. Time out of school might be spent on a range of 'alternative' curriculum activities to what the school provided. This alternative curriculum included woodwork and motor cycle riding and maintenance.

In contrast, case study two 'saw the school as being there for the whole community and for the whole child and there was as much emphasis on social, as on academic, development' (ibid.) In the secondary school the educational outcomes were viewed as most appropriately achievable by working with the small number of troubled young people separately. The result of this was that the school was enabled to continue operating in the same traditional way:

> In case-study one the priority was the protection of the development of the academic potential of its other students and this was seen as best achieved through using the voluntary agency to provide expertise that the school did not itself have in order to work effectively with troublesome students.
>
> (ibid.)

The intervention in the primary school reflected a view that the school should be proactive in creating time to work with all children. It was anticipated that a reasonably high proportion of students, not merely the few, might be involved in some work of this nature:

> Case-study two had an overall orientation to the community which was seen as including parents, adults participating in the school's community programme and the geographical community and a headteacher who was committed to giving 'ownership to the community'.
>
> (ibid.)

With regard to purposes:

> Because the case studies were dealing with different age groups – 12–16 compared with 9–12 – there was a stronger focus on attendance and employment in the former and on disruptive or withdrawn behaviour in the latter. There were differing views in the case studies about how this purpose was best achieved with case-study two viewing the key issue as involving young people in making decisions and thinking about what they are doing, with case-study one more concerned about dealing with problematic behaviour and minimizing its effect on the rest of the school. In case-study two, the active involvement of the well-regarded primary 1 teacher in the group work was designed to embed it in the everyday work of the school and to extend her repertoire of pedagogic skills.
>
> (ibid., pp. 17–18)

Programme delivery was also very different:

> In case-study one, while the school was fully committed to the comprehensive principle [this school was a regular mainstream community school], . . . the form of the collaboration in essence was a subcontracting arrangement whereby the school temporarily handed over responsibility for particular young people to a specialist agency since there was no joint development or delivery of the programme . . . This reflected a view that the school was not particularly well equipped in terms of either expertise or inclination to deal with exceptionally difficult pupils. In contrast, case-study two provided an example of joint participation in decision making at all levels from planning through to delivery and evaluation which had resulted from an approach to young people that saw the school as doing something to develop children socially as well as academically. The joint working, therefore, was seen as giving opportunities for both the school and the agency to provide a better programme than either could do on their own.
>
> (ibid., p. 18)

Finally, with regard to resources:

> [I]n the primary school case study the school input was 'funded' by the headteacher teaching the primary 1 class of the teacher taking the group. She was officially designated as a non-teaching head in the staffing allocation so this allowed her to take the class . . . In the other case study funds were available to refer disruptive pupils and the current arrangements were therefore seen as cost effective in ensuring that the smooth running of the school was not disrupted. . . .
>
> In terms of professional expertise, the head teacher in case-study two saw the voluntary agency as having the skills that the school did not yet have but, by releasing a teacher, a staff development opportunity was provided that enabled the acquisition of some of these skills for the school. In the other case study it was assumed that the professional expertise held by the voluntary organizations' workers was so different that it was neither possible nor necessary for this to be shared with the school's teaching staff.
>
> (ibid., pp. 18–19)

Tett *et al.* (ibid., p. 19) summarise the differences between the interventions in the two schools as:

Values	social and academic education for all
	vs
Purposes	academic education for majority involving young people in decision-making
	vs
Tasks	developing all students socially and academically
	vs
Conditions	sub-contracting out of difficult students collaborative sharing of expertise
	vs
	complementarity of expertise

Community interests and the principle of 'restorative justice'

In this section we explore concepts and practices of restorative justice as a positive and constructive approach schools might use in responding to challenging student behaviour and the harm that this behaviour does to others. However, understandings of restorative justice, of the causes of problematic behaviours and of what behaviours are important for maintaining the well-being of individuals and the community vary widely across different cultures. Hence, the use of restorative justice by schools to deal with challenging behaviours of students from minority cultural groups may be problematic when authority and power in the school are held mainly within a dominant cultural group. There is a danger that the school will exert control over the location and timing of the process, the protocol to be followed, and over what restorative actions need to be taken, and by whom. Where the behaviour or decisions of powerful members of school staff may be part of the problem to be addressed (as in decisions to stand down, suspend, or exclude students), students from minority cultural groups, their parents and community members may have little power to suggest and initiate solutions. A more balanced and equitable protocol for restorative justice procedures may involve locating the process outside of the school, in a community context, by following protocols and procedures that are understandable by members of those cultural communities, and led by appropriate community members. Macfarlane (2000c, 2000b) describes how such an approach has been developed to restore equity and well-being among Māori students, both transgressors and victims, and their whānau (extended family).

One of the issues to be addressed in the area of partnerships between home, community, schools and other professionals to establish and maintain student behaviour that predisposes to positive learning is the question of what constitutes the common good to which all should aspire. A number of researchers have expressed concerns about 'adults and institutions no longer setting clear standards for behaviour or articulating their values, youth socially segregated from adults, institutions such as schools and churches becoming isolated from each other' (Schweigert, 1999, p. 165). No longer, in this view, is there any sense of working towards the 'common good'. Crime, violence, antisocial acts and depression among young people appear to be associated with lack of boundaries and community support, and the break-up of families (Bronfenbrenner *et al.*, 1996; Benson, 1997). Urbanisation, industrialisation and assimilation have contributed to the destruction of community values as well as oral, traditional, kinship, controlling influences, as is particularly seen in contemporary New Zealand Māori society where many young parents have been disconnected from the support of their wider families and tribal groupings.

There is no one agreed view about what might constitute 'the common good', however. Schweigert (1999) notes Seligman's (1995/1996, p. 35) views on differences between two different traditions in definitions of what constitutes the 'common good': 'civic virtue' and 'civil society':

> In the *civic virtue* tradition, morality and virtue are a public enterprise; the moral sense is located in the community and the practice of membership forms each citizen in a life of virtue in pursuit of the good of the community . . . Citizens achieve the public good in the civic virtue

tradition by overcoming self-interest, as a moral community pursuing the common good.

Citizens in the *civil society* tradition, on the other hand, are encouraged to pursue their self-interests in free and fair exchange, the cumulative result of which will benefit the whole. The civil society tradition locates the moral sense in human nature, as a capacity of each individual. The individual conscience is the seat of virtue and moral education is the cultivation of the virtues as private attributes. Civil society is thus understood as 'an assortment of morally autonomous individuals, each with his or her own concept of the good life, with the function of society being limited to ensuring the legal equality of these individuals' (Seligman, 1995/1996, p. 35).

(Schweigert, 1999, p. 166)

One way of bringing together in practice notions of the 'common good' is through the process of 'restorative justice'. In an article which examines the process of restorative justice, Schweigert (1999, p. 163) makes clear three educational characteristics of restorative justice. Restorative justice does the following:

- brings together the 'moral authority in personal communal traditions' and the 'moral authority in impersonal universal norms' in ways which reinforce each other;
- focuses not on individuals, families or institutions, but on the ways and spaces where they interact and intersect;
- moves the focus on to whole communities and away from the victim or the individual who has committed the crime in order to harness community resources to 'make the changes that can successfully address the problems that emerge as crime'.

Community-based restorative justice

In a number of areas around the world, for example in North America, Europe, Australia and New Zealand, restorative practices in the form of highly structured processes of victim–offender conferencing are being, or have already been, developed. Schweigert (1999, pp. 168–70) describes how, around the world, practice has led the theory:

Frustrated with the shortcomings of the criminal justice system, practitioners are experimenting with various alternatives that might be more successful in assisting victims, reducing crime, reforming offenders and resolving conflicts. As restorative practices are initiated and developed, reformers tap into a rich variety of social and philosophical sources: mediation and non-violent conflict resolution processes, community development and empowerment strategies, European traditions of direct victim restitution, biblical notions of justice, theories of crime as addiction, affect theory, the theory of reintegrative shaming and traditions of community justice in non-European culture – African village moots, Native American peacemaking circles and Māori family conflict resolution rituals. These efforts are also fuelled by a continual critical dialogue regarding the shortcomings of the retributive theory of justice and a search for a philosophy of criminal justice that honours the norms of procedural justice yet incorporates substantive values and pursues distributive justice. The articulation of theory, in turn, has fostered a growing [US] national movement that is inspiring new practices, promoting legislative reforms and funding for pilot programme providing frameworks for evaluating results and encouraging a growing body of research.

Schweigert sees restorative justice as most clearly and simply defined as repairing the harm done to all who have been hurt by particular offensive behaviour. Restorative justice comprises five aspects:

- a redefinition of crime;
- a refocus on the victims of crime;
- redirection of the accountability of the offender;
- reinvestment in social control by the community;
- redesign of the judicial process.

Schweigert redefines crime as:

> an injury to another individual or individuals or to the collectivity of individuals, rather than merely as an offence against the state. This reorientates the moral obligations of crime around personal harm and interpersonal relationships, and it subordinates the legal power of the state in controlling crime to informal social controls and processes of conflict resolution in communities.

The prime concern of restorative justice reform is to refocus on the victim:

> The victim takes an active role in the process, articulating harms done and fears caused, expressing these directly to the offender if he or she desires to do so and helping to determine what should be done to repair the damage done by the offence. Restorative justice seeks to empower the victim more than punish the offender, even empowering the victim to recognise that the offender is not all bad.
>
> (M. S. Umbreit, Director, Center for Restorative Justice and Mediation, University of Minnesota, personal communication, August 1996)

Schweigert notes an obligation on the part of the offender to restore what he or she has harmed as a result of the crime, to the fullest possible extent:

> Justice requires that the offender be held accountable primarily to the victim or victims rather than the state, which means the offender takes an active part in repairing damage done. Restorative justice is therefore empowering and constructive for the offender as well as the victim, since the offender is called upon to give of his or her self to help determine how the harm can be repaired and then to complete the restitution. The offender must earn his or her way back into the trust of the community (Pranis, 1996).

The local community in which the offence or crime occurred plays a dual role:

> The community is often harmed by the offence and thus in need of restoration as a victim; and the community is also accountable to the offender and victim with an obligation to control misbehaviour. Crime calls attention to social problems or harmful social conditions, provides an opportunity for the community to affirm its values and behavioural norms and requires the community or state to provide a process through which this conflict can be resolved.

A structured process of participation by victims, offenders and community establishes a network of responsibilities:

> The process of justice is redesigned to increase interpersonal account-ability without sacrificing due process protections . . . With restoration of the victim at the centre, several restorative practices have been imple-mented as part of the justice process: victim restitution, community policing, community prosecution, sentence to service, community probation, victim–offender mediation and various forms of victim–offender conferencing.

Restorative justice therefore takes an active, problem-solving and balanced approach to restoring the victim, offender and the community (Bazemore, 1992). It opens the criminal justice process to the wider and deeper issues involved in any crime. Success is judged as the extent to which individual and community well-being is restored.

Various writers have described how victim–offender conferencing is a problem-solving process which is geared toward future solutions rather than an attribution of blame for past actions (Umbreit and Coates, 1992; Carey, 1996). Traditional community conflict resolution processes can employ culturally appropriate mechanisms to address and resolve tension and make justice visible and more productive (Anderson *et al.*, 1996). The process must ensure that all participants are respected and permitted to contribute to the solution. Individuals are trained as mediators to hold the space in which injury can be converted into personal healing and community development. Schweigert (1999) observes that victim–offender conferencing often includes the following:

> (a) the facilitator opens the session with introductions of participants and of the process; (b) the victim and offender describe the incident from their points of view; (c) together, the parties identify the issues and interests at stake; (d) participants explore possible ways to solve the problems that have been raised; (e) the victim and offender agree to a settlement, which may include financial reparation, personal service, community service, education or training or counselling for either party, or other possible actions jointly agreed-upon; and (f) the facilitator closes the session by summarising what has occurred in the process and the terms of the settlement.
>
> (Schweigert, 1999, p. 171)

Powerful mechanisms of situated learning (Lave and Wenger, 1991) are brought into play in a process that empowers community members to experience reciprocal accountability, respect and support.

The concerns of social disintegration are addressed by harnessing a community to respond to the wrongdoing, and by empowering that community to cooperate in solving the problem. Individual freedom and equal participation are combined with a communitarian preference for defining moral expectations and reparation at the level of the local community:

> The notion of crime as 'personal injury' establishes moral accountability among people in a social network, evoking the moral authority of communal traditions embedded in affective bonds of caring and mutual responsibility and exercised in caring, shaming, repenting and forgiving. The offence creates a new relationship or alters an existing relationship, within which the offender is directly accountable to the victim to repair harm done and the victim is accountable in some sense to the offender to receive his or her reparation and repentance.
>
> The injury also generates moral accountability on the part of the social networks of the victim and offender, to hold the offender accountable, to support the victim and offender, to resolve the conflict through emotional and reparative solutions and to reintegrate the victim and offender into their respective networks as valued and respected participants . . . restorative practices strengthen the moral authority of communal traditions by overcoming the exclusion (due to crime) of the offender (and often the victim) from social networks. The moral authority of these

traditions is demonstrated in the actions of members of the communities involved, when they effect the reintegration of offenders and victims through receiving them with empathic listening, confronting wrong-doing, accepting repentance and restitution, actively supporting the healing of offenders and victims and forgiving offenders.

(ibid., p. 175)

Braithwaite (1997) claims that many responses to young people with problems fail because they treat young people as isolated individuals and do not operate in the context of the community of people who know and care about a person. The associated problems of disadvantage are based on the inadequacy of families and associates emphasising the importance of caring and unconditional love for young people to value and nurture learning and develop social responsibility. Usually this social and human capital is provided by a caring loving family, but for many young people the immediate family does not or cannot always provide this. However, the wider community circle of people who know, care about and are respected by a young person could provide this loving care.

Braithwaite proposes a 'family group circles' model which draws on the experience of restorative justice within the criminal justice system to reduce criminal offending. 'Family group circles' involve victims and offenders meeting with people from the community whom the offender respects and trusts, and who care about the offender, to discuss what needs to be done to help the victim and the offender to right the wrongs and restore their lives.

In some schools and local education authorities particular programmes which are based on general terms on the principles of 'restorative justice' have been devised to address issues of problematic behaviour. Braithwaite discusses ways to adapt the 'family group circles' for educational settings in the UK context. Informal social support with education, relationships and employment from people trusted by the young person would be provided by 'youth development circles'. All members of the circles would be chosen by the young person involved and could include trusted peer friends, and the circles would remain in place for the whole period of secondary schooling through to post-school placement and replace parent–teacher consultations.

A number of benefits of this approach are postulated by Braithwaite, in particular, the emergence of an expectation to support young people in difficulties by the wider community when immediate families fail to do this and to enable children in their turn to become caring, responsible, democratic citizens. By incorporating restorative justice strategies in their behaviour management strategies, schools do not just assist individual students or families, but also help to restore the integrity of their communities.

In New Zealand, the Restorative Practices Development Team at the University of Waikato has set out a number of guidelines for restorative practices in schools based on the outcomes of research projects intended to reduce student suspensions (Restorative Practices Development Team, 2003). The aims of restorative practice in schools are to do the following:

- Address the problem.
- Encourage understanding of the effects of the offence on all individuals involved and on the school community.
- Invite the taking up of responsibility (not necessarily all by the offender).
- Avoid creating shame and blame.
- Promote the healing of hurt.
- Open up avenues of redress.
- Restore working relationship between those involved.
- Include everyone (including offenders) in the community envisioned by the process rather than divide people into insider and outsider groups.

According to the Restorative Practices Development Team (ibid., p. 11):

> Restoration requires that harm done to a relationship is understood and acknowledged and that effort is made to repair that harm. In order for that restoration to happen, the voices of those affected by the offence need to be heard in the process of seeking redress.

On the basis of their experience, the Restorative Practices Development Team advise that a restorative conference will need to include the senior administrators of a school, usually the head teacher/principal and deputy head/deputy principal and a trained facilitator. A very important preliminary task is to 'identify the appropriate community of care around the young person on whom the conference will focus' (ibid., p. 28). This decision should not be made structurally in terms of the family or the school. 'There needs to be some contextual relationship to the person that defines them as part of the community of care' (ibid.). Key questions to ask include:

Is there a victim?

Who has a stake in addressing this issue?

To whom does resolving this issue matter?

(ibid.)

If there is a victim, the restorative process will not succeed as well as it might do without his/her participation. However, no attempts should be made to persuade an unwilling victim to attend. A prime consideration is safety for all involved. If key people cannot or will not attend, or it is clear during the conference that the perpetrator is not willing to accept any responsibility for his/her actions 'then the facilitator should consider abandoning the process' (ibid.).

The Restorative Practices Development Team (ibid., p. 20) outline the process of a restorative conference as follows:

1 As appropriate, a conference will begin with *karakia* [prayers] and *mihimihi*/greetings.
2 'The problem is the problem, the person is not the problem' goes on the board or is spoken about.
3 What are you hoping to see happen in this *hui* [meeting]? Each person has a chance to speak.
4 What is the problem that has brought us here? People tell their own versions.
5 What are the effects of that problem on all present (and others)?
6 What times, places and relationships do we know of where the problem is not present?
7 What new description of the people involved becomes clear as we look at the times and places where the problem is not present?
8 If there have been people/things harmed by the problem, what is it that you need to happen to see amends being made?
9 How does what we have spoken about and seen in the alternative descriptions help us plan to overcome the problem? People contribute ideas and offers of resources that help overcome the problem.
10 Does that plan meet the needs of anyone harmed by the problem?
11 People are given responsibility to carry each part of the plan forward. Any follow up is planned for.
12 *Karakia* [prayers] and thanks. Perhaps offer hospitality.

Introducing restorative practices in schools requires considerable forethought and prior planning, negotiation and deliberation. The Team at the University of Waikato suggest that:

1 The support of the management, staff and community of the school is an essential ingredient for the success of restorative conferencing. We therefore recommend that all schools undertake a detailed consultation process prior to initiating any project.
2 Schools that wish to consider establishing Restorative Conferencing need to analyse carefully whether the process fits within the culture of the school. The restorative ideals, as opposed to a punishment focus, have to be deeply embedded in the school's culture for the project to be successful.
3 The relationship between the disciplinary role of the Boards of Trustees [Boards of Governors] and the conferencing processes should be clarified from the outset. At times the demarcation lines between these linked roles can create problems. Clear policies need to be established between these two disciplinary processes. This is particularly important

in determining responsibility for reporting to disciplinary committees or the board and the extent to which completion of agreed outcomes will remove the risk of suspension.

4   We recommend the use of a community support person to complete the community liaison and administrative work that is vital to the conducting of conferences. The use of the support worker appears to enhance the participation of all groups in the process.

5   In high schools the deans [heads of year] should be trained as convenors to assist in the referrals of students to conferences. As the staff members who hold an overview of the issues in their area of responsibility, they have greater potential to ensure pro-active steps are taken to address disciplinary issues as they arise. Deans should therefore be one of the staff members primarily responsible for recommending conferences.

6   The conferencing process can be used for a range of different types of problems: including continual disobedience, assault, vandalism, alcohol and drugs.

7   The process has the potential to be extended into other contexts within the schools as a model of handling contentious issues. This could include developing processes to address classroom conflicts, bullying, peer mediation, staff conflicts and issues within Boards of Trustees.

(Restorative Practices Development Team, 2003, p. 46)

It is important to note, however, that understandings of restorative justice, of the causes of problematic behaviours and of what behaviours are important for maintaining the well-being of individuals and their communities vary widely across different cultures.

Conclusion

Recent special educational developments across the world have seen a shift to working within an inclusive paradigm. Teachers and other educators are therefore now required to deal with greater cultural, physical and intellectual diversity. This is a challenge in terms of programme development, class structures, time-management and service delivery. Teachers are pivotal members of the team for they are the link between the specialist expertise of parents and community, on the one hand, and the specialist professional support team, on the other. With these additional responsibilities, the task of the teacher can be considerably challenging but also increasingly satisfying and rewarding.

Effective teamwork does not just happen. Daniels *et al.* (1998), in a study in England funded by the DfEE into mainstream school responses to students with emotional and behavioural difficulties, found an absence of coordinated multi-agency approaches to the needs of children. Difficulties can be created by the fact that different agencies work for different statutory bodies.

Resources can be tied to different departments, priorities, projects and pro-grammes. An effective team approach requires collaboration. Collaboration works best when the parties recognise each other as more or less equal partners. The best support for the child who has special needs is where specialists work together as a team and where that team includes parents, family and community members. Teams can consist of those concerned with the child's medical needs or those concerned with the child's learning and behavioural needs. The most effective team will be a combined team that caters for all aspects of a child's needs.

Proper consideration of the location of power and its significance is therefore very important in conceptualising ways in which families might support their children. Families have the potential to make a major impact on children's learning and, as a number of researchers have indicated, can support the learning of those who experience difficulties (Glynn *et al.*, 1979; Heaton, 1996; Ostler, 1991; Riddick, 1996). The corollary of recognising this potential impact is a need to accord respect both to the role of families and to the families themselves by sharing information about children's progress and acknowledging that families also have expertise that should be harnessed to support children's learning.

In New Zealand, the Special Education 2000 (SE2000) policy guidelines (Ministry of Education, 1997, 1998b) state that educators should have the skills and confidence to assist young children and students who have a broad range of needs and abilities. However, in the education of children such as these, the teacher or other educator, who may have undergone several years of specialist training, should be seen as only one of the 'experts'. New struc-tures for the delivery of special education that have begun to emerge in some countries indicate that local teams made up of specialists, teachers, parents and family and community members can be more effective. This shift poses challenges for educators. Two important challenges are the desire of parents and family members and their ability to operate as members of such teams. This involves recognising that the students themselves have areas of expertise and that others involved with the students including parents and family members also have different areas of expertise (Glynn *et al.*, 1997), and that effective solutions will draw on all appropriate sources.

Students who experience learning and behaviour difficulties at school have expertise with respect to their own education, because they have lifelong experience of what their own needs are, and the problems they engender, as well as what factors influence their behaviour at home and at school. However, parents, too, have the same number of years of experience in understanding and coping with the challenges faced by their child. Parents are experts in meeting the day-to-day needs of their child, supporting their educational achievements and aspirations, and helping them to overcome the many problems they encounter. The expertise of parents and students should be seen as complementary to that of education professionals.

Potentially, therefore, parents and carers are an important resource in supporting the learning of all children, and may be the only additional resource for those who experience difficulties (Wearmouth, 2004a). The attitude of any educational institution to the role of families as prime educators of children is of great significance. The kind of home–school partnership arrangements that exist between school and parents or carers and the way in which schools respond to family culture and background can serve to include or alienate both parents and their children. Particular approaches and strategies convey various preconceptions about the ability of families and/or carers from a diversity of backgrounds to support the learning development of their children. Educators need to acknowledge and respect cultural differences and values, and to incorporate the advice of community members in developing strategies for responding to challenging behaviour. This might involve developing relationships with their community members in order to allow them to determine who should have access to their homes and families and how this should be done. Professional training also needs to include strategies to ensure educators develop an ability to work within a team approach, and alongside people from other cultures, to ensure issues are handled with safety and respect.

Glynn et al. (1992) identify the intersecting responsibilities for the same children that are shared between home and school, but also point out how surprisingly few educators utilise the combined strengths and knowledge of home and school to the benefit of these children. They propose the development of partnerships between parents and professionals that are equitable in order to provide a worthwhile context for locating intervention approaches. In addition, the writers warn that the process of enskilling parents in teaching roles, must not deskill them in their parenting and family roles. This means that training activities initiated by educational professionals must be compatible with the continued maintenance of the home language and culture (Karetu, 1990a; Wong-Fillmore, 1991). Glynn et al. describe a five-dimension, parent–professional relationship continuum designed by Pugh (1987, cited in Glynn et al., 1992, p. 180). The continuum ranges from level 1: non-participation of parents in the intervention, through level 2: external support to the professionals, level 3: participation in interventions; level 4: partnership in interventions, to level 5: control over the professionals' input in interventions. As they explain, partnership in this continuum is about equity in sharing knowledge, resources, power and decision-making while control is about self-determination and the taking of personal responsibility.

Chapter 12

Developing school policy

Introduction

A policy can be conceptualised as a document providing an overall direction or strategy that can guide the development of a specific plan of action. Policies can have expressed or implied aims which are generalised statements or actions of intent. Policies can include targets, expressed or implied, and which are capable of being measured. However, not all plans of actions are expressed in writing in the form of policy documents. Sometimes, a strategy or plan of action may be expressed orally or indeed be implied by the actions, conduct or practices of individuals and groups of people.

One crucial area of school policy should be the school behaviour policy. Watkins and Wagner (1995) note that addressing behavioural issues in schools should not focus solely on individual students and their perceived inadequacies (that is, embody deficit theorising), but should include the contexts of school, classroom, teacher and peer group within the frame of reference. While the position we have taken throughout this book supports the views of Watkins and Wagner, we would also include in this frame of reference families, communities and ethnic groups. Policies addressing behaviour in schools should therefore:

> involve thinking about and intervening on almost every aspect of the way the school is run. This may include:
>
> - pupil behaviour (that is learning and social behaviour, individually and in groups);
> - teacher behaviour (such as approaches to managing classrooms, styles of responding to difficulties, and so on);
> - school behaviour (such as the style of the organisation and how it typically responds when difficulties or concerns are raised).
>
> (Watkins and Wagner, 1995, p. 55)

Watkins and Wagner conclude that effective approaches to addressing issues of school behaviour take into account the extent to which a school has practices and methodsprocedures which can:

- identify behaviour patterns at the level of individual students, classrooms and the whole school;
- facilitate problem-solving through exploring the problem situation, reaching new understandings by reflecting on findings and re-framing the problem so that effective action can be taken.

In this chapter we are concerned with school behaviour policies that aim to encourage and maintain appropriate learning and behaviour interactions conducive to self-discipline within a calm and purposeful learning contexts. At the same time we are concerned with policies which take into account the importance of students' needs to belong to, and participate safely in their school community and to be respected as individual human beings who are members of ethnic and cultural groups. We do not think students should have to leave their ethnic and cultural experiences at home. We reflect on the aim of developing a school behaviour policy grounded in a philosophy of inclusive education practice that respects the need for ownership by all members of the school community itself, and by members of the various communities in which the school is situated.

In Chapter 1 we described the importance of schools understanding the national and international educational policy contexts and legislation on human rights, social inclusion, and equity of participation. It is clear that these macro-level policies should guide and inform policy-making and imple-mentation plans at school-wide level. School policies that are inconsistent with or contradict national and international policy priorities may receive little support from government, or from many local communities. Sometimes, however, national level policies are not readily endorsed and embraced at local level, presenting school policy-makers with some strong challenges. For example, in New Zealand, the Treaty of Waitangi defines the relation-ship between Māori and non-Māori, which arises from their status as joint partners in founding the nation in 1840. While many non-Māori New Zealanders have come to regard the Treaty of Waitangi as an expression of principles such as partnership and equity, Māori have long regarded it differently. Māori have regarded the Treaty as a charter for power sharing in the decision-making processes of government, for self-determination as an indigenous people and as a guide to intercultural relations in New Zealand (Durie 1998). The Treaty of Waitangi now occupies an important position by providing guiding principles for subsequent legislation, government policy and administrative practices. These principles, which can be summarised in terms of partnership, protection and participation are being increasingly addressed within school policy documents. They provide both motivation and direction for the state school system to redress the damage to Māori people, their language and culture in over a century of state education. Policy-makers at school level have found these principles particularly challenging since they go to the heart of school governance as well as the ownership and control of both curriculum and pedagogy.

Addressing these principles at school level for Māori students experiencing behaviour and learning difficulties requires schools to identify their Māori communities, and consult with them to ensure that Māori language, cultural values and preferred ways of learning and teaching are reflected in the school's curriculum delivery and management processes. Further, Bishop and Glynn (1999) argue that the Treaty of Waitangi also provides a sound model of partnership and interaction to guide the relationships between schools and all of their migrant and refugee communities. One major policy implica-tion of aligning school policies with the Treaty of Waitangi principles is that a monolingual and monocultural approach to meeting the needs of students with behaviour and learning difficulties is no longer acceptable.

Purpose

The Elton Report (DES, 1989, pp. 97–8) described the purpose of drawing up school behaviour policies as establishing:

- *The reasons for rules*. It may be clear to teachers why particular rules are necessary. It is not always clear to pupils or parents. Rational authority depends on understanding. Any rule for which no rational explanation can be provided is suspect.
- *The affective curriculum*. Schools teach values as well as knowledge and skills. Some of this teaching is done in lessons. Most is through the way in which teachers and pupils behave to each other, including how rules are applied. A set of written rules does not mean that they will always be applied by all teachers in the same way. There must be a consensus among staff on the aims of the affective curriculum.
- *Models of behaviour*. Most sets of rules are written for pupils. The behaviour of teachers must be consistent with them. If pupils are told, for example, to be polite and respectful to others, teachers must provide good examples of such behaviour in their dealings with adults and children.
- *Consistency with religious education and personal and social education*. Tolerance and self-discipline are common themes in these areas. The values which underlie the rules must be consistent with them.

School policies can be framed to specify and support positive means of responding to difficult patterns of behaviour. They may outline (Watkins and Wagner, 1995, p. 57):

- ways for staff to review how the school organisation affects behaviour;
- ways of improving school facilities and environment to increase student involvement;
- developing statements of expectations in school and classroom;
- clarifying how the curriculum addresses behaviour and helps students learn;
- methods of reviewing classrooms and their management;
- systems for all staff learning/developing (including mid-day supervision team);
- improving the reward climate of the school.

School policies can be framed also to ensure the cultural safety and well-being of students from diverse ethnicities and cultural backgrounds and to promote their full inclusion in learning activities in the classroom and school.

Aims and values

In order to facilitate behaviour management practices which are compatible with each other, policy frameworks need to flow from a coherent set of beliefs and values which are shared across an organisation (Palmer *et al.*, 1994). As the report of the Discipline Task Group, *Better Behaviour – Better Learning*, notes:

> A shared value base is an important prerequisite in promoting positive behaviour and in reacting to discipline problems when they occur; values underpin practices. For example, a range of studies has revealed the close connection between the beliefs of the senior management team in a school and its exclusion rates. Schools where senior staff had a strong commitment to the social as well as the academic purposes of education tended to have lower exclusion rates'
>
> (Scottish Executive, 2001, p. 7)

In the late 1980s in the UK, a government committee under Lord Elton was commissioned to enquire into discipline in schools. On the basis of its findings a report was drawn up (DES, 1989) which contains a set of suggested principles (ibid., pp. 100–3) on which to build schools' behaviour policies. These principles are relevant not only to schools in the UK but also to schools in other parts of the world.

The Elton Report suggests 'mutual respect' as a useful starting point for building policy, with the head teacher taking the lead role in proposing principles and standards and the whole teaching and non-teaching staff, including school governors, involved in working it out.

The Department of Education, Northern Ireland document *Promoting Positive Behaviour* (DENI, 2001) also suggests that the values of the school and staff and a sense of collective responsibility are important factors evident in schools where student behaviour is not seen as inevitably problematic. The report suggests that the following factors are important:

a positive atmosphere based on a sense of community within the school and values which all of its members share;

a sense of collective responsibility among staff, and a commitment to the school by the students and their parents.

(DENI, 2001, p. 8)

A number of reports and studies refer to the influence of the beliefs of the leaders and managers of a school in sustaining appropriate values, attitude and beliefs (DES, 1989; DfE, 1994b; OFSTED, 2001; Richards, 1999; Visser et al., 2002, for example). Visser et al. (2002) comment on the importance of the values, attitudes and beliefs of a school as a whole in which staff cared about students and recognised and valued diversity. They noted the importance of having the support of a 'critical mass' of influential staff (but not necessarily a majority) who are key players in the school.

Richards (1999) found that, in schools which were inclusive, adults perceived student emotional and behavioural difficulties as a special educational need and not just as behaviour to be controlled. This shared view was reflected in school policy documents. However, Watkins and Wagner (2000) claim that it is not only a matter of achieving a common understanding of emotional and behavioural difficulties, but also it is the open discussion of, and sharing of, different perspectives that are important.

It is this cooperative recognition of diversity of views, and the subsequent reflection on them that deepen understanding and inform the development of effective inclusive school policy and practice. The process of encouraging all who have to operate the policy to reflect on their own beliefs and values and come to an agreed position is a challenge for schools. Radford claims: 'Behaviour, however, is an emotional topic (Hanko, 1995). Staff may be reluctant to participate in conscious reflection on their feelings, beliefs and attitudes about behaviour' (2000, p. 86).

As we have already discussed, this kind of deep reflection and discussion may be particularly difficult or challenging when teachers come from a cultural background that is different from that of their students. Nevertheless, the development and implementation of effective school behaviour policy do not depend on teachers who come from the same cultural backgrounds as their students, although this may be a distinct advantage. Rather, when teachers are prepared to listen to the beliefs, values and practices of their school's cultural communities, and seek to form partnerships with them, effective policies can be developed and implemented. This was evidenced in one of the sites of effective special education practice for Māori students in the study of Berryman et al. (2002), described in Chapter 10.

Policy content

In order to put principles into practice and achieve its policy objectives the Elton Report (1989) advises schools to do the following:

- keep the number of rules to an essential minimum, making obvious the reasons for each rule and avoiding 'obscure, arbitrary or petty rules;
- wherever possible express rules in positive terms: for example 'take care of the building' rather than 'don't write graffiti';
- derive the rules from the principles underlying the school behaviour policies;
- strike a balance between rewards and punishments and clearly specify both;
- apply punishment consistently and differentiate clearly between serious and minor offences;
- make clear to students when a rule has been broken but make fair allowances for difficult home circumstances, for example, in the case of lateness where a student is responsible for younger siblings;
- avoid punishing the innocent with the guilty as with the punishment of whole groups because students' resulting 'sense of grievance damages the school's atmosphere';
- avoid humiliating students in front of peers because 'public ridicule makes good relationships impossible' and 'breeds deep resentments which can poison the school's atmosphere';
- aim to succeed rather than win when dealing with conflict situations because de-escalation is more likely to result in success than confrontation;
- recognise all non-teaching staff, in particular, midday supervisors, as integral to the school community and as needing to be aware of the school's behaviour policy and their role in applying it consistently;
- recognise the role of parents in encouraging their children to behave well in school. This will require active attempts to consult with parents and communities and to find ways of involving them in developing and implementing a school's behaviour plan;
- apply the principles of the behaviour policy to all school activities on- or off-site to underline the message that 'the school is a community of people, not just a physical space';
- recognise that while it is the duty of the headteacher and the senior management team of a school to monitor the way in which the behaviour policy is working the whole staff should also be involved. 'We consider that the best way of doing this is by a regular review of the policy's effectiveness to which all staff should be invited to contribute';
- acknowledge the potential of bullying and racial harassment both to cause suffering to individual pupils and to damage school atmosphere. 'It is hard to see how a school can win the confidence of its students if it

fails to deal with behaviour which so seriously damages the quality of their lives.' Headteachers and staff are therefore exhorted to:

- 'be alert to signs of bullying and racial harassment;
- deal firmly with all such behaviour; and
- take action based on clear rules which are backed by appropriate sanctions and systems to protect and support victims.'
- encourage students to 'tell staff about serious cases of bullying and racial harassment of which they are aware'.

(DES, 1989, pp. 100, 101, 102, 103)

The following examples come from the Elton Report (DES, 1989) and provide a useful illustration of what school policy documents should contain.

Extract from a booklet for pupils

Code of conduct

The one rule for all of us in school is *Everyone will act with courtesy and consideration to others at all times.*
This means that:

1. *You always try to understand other people's point of view.*

2. *In class you make it as easy as possible for everyone to learn and for the teacher to teach.* (This means arriving on time with everything you need for that lesson, beginning and ending the lesson in a courteous and orderly way, listening carefully, following instructions, helping each other when appropriate and being quiet and sensible at all times.)

3. *You move gently and quietly about school.* (This means never running, barging or shouting, but being ready to help by opening doors, standing back to let people pass and helping to carry things.) In crowded areas *please keep to the left.*

4. *You always speak politely to everyone* (even if you feel bad tempered!) and use a low voice. (Shouting is *always* discourteous.)

5. *You are silent* whenever you are required to be.

6. *You keep the school clean and tidy* so that it is a welcoming place we can all be proud of. (This means putting all litter in bins, keeping walls and furniture clean and unmarked and taking great care of the displays, particularly of other people's work.)

7. *Out of school*, walking locally or with a school group, you always remember that the school's reputation depends on the way you behave.

(DES, 1989, p. 283)

The report also contains a very useful example of a booklet for staff outlining the principles for maintaining order in a school.

A booklet for staff

Inside information — the way to good order

THIS OUTLINE OF GOOD PRACTICE AND THE WAYS TO GOOD ORDER IS FOR YOU, PLEASE USE IT.

Acceptable standards	of behaviour, work and respect depend on the example of us all. • All have positive contributions to make.
Good order	has to be worked for: it does not simply happen. • Set high standards. • *Apply* rules firmly and fairly.
Most important	of all: • *Expect* to give and to receive respect.
Everyone	at school is here for a purpose. • *Respect* every person. • *Treat* everyone as an individual.
Relationships	are vital: relationships between everyone and at every level. *Take the initiative:* • greet and be greeted • speak and be spoken to • smile and relate • communicate.
Problems	are normal where children are learning and testing the boundaries of acceptable behaviour.
Our success	is tested not by the absence of problems but *by the way we deal with them.*
Don't react:	address the problem: • avoid confrontation • listen • establish the facts • judge only when certain • use punishments sparingly.

Removal of privilege is the most effective strategy. Teachers should, however, ensure that they explain quietly to students why the privilege is being removed and what specific rule has been broken. This explanation should avoid anger and personal criticisms, that is 'put down' statements, or threats. It is most important that students are told when and how the privilege can be restored.

Out and about the school

All informal contact contributes to standards of behaviour. *Control* that *behaviour* by taking the initiative at every opportunity. Expect to:

- start the dialogue
- greet pupils
- deal with all misbehaviour – to ignore it is to condone it!
- set high standards of speech, manner and dress
- enjoy relating to pupils.

In the classroom

Create and *sustain* a positive, supportive and secure environment. *Well prepared*, stimulating lessons generate good behaviour and earn respect.

   Expect to:
- arrive before the class and begin on time
- be prepared for the lesson
- keep everyone occupied and interested
- extend and motivate all pupils
- mark all work promptly and constructively
- set homework regularly to schedule
- encourage creative dialogue – confidence in discussion is important
- keep an attractive, clean and tidy room
- maintain interesting wall displays
- use first names.

Do all you can to avoid:

- humiliating . . . . it breeds resentment
- shouting . . . . it diminishes you
- over-reacting . . . . the problems will grow
- blanket punishments . . . . the innocent will resent them
- over-punishment . . . . keep your powder dry, never punish what
                                                                 you can't prove
- sarcasm . . . . it damages you!

Please *never* leave pupils outside rooms. The 'problem' needs a solution not complicating. *Seek help* if you need it. *And do all you can to:*

- use humour . . . . it builds bridges
- keep calm . . . . it reduces tensions
- listen . . . . it earns respect
- be positive and build relationships
- know your pupils as individuals
- carry out any threats you have to make
- be consistent.

Always apply schools rules positively.

                                                                 (DES, 1989, pp. 288–90)

Policy development process

The process of creating school behaviour policies and the way decisions are taken about policy content are crucial to the effectiveness of practice. Radford (2000) reports an initiative by a London Borough Education Authority to help schools with the development of behaviour policies which is aimed at involving all who are members of the school community. She used a model (Radford, 2000, p. 87) which provides a framework for reflection at each stage of the process of policy formulation. During Phase A of policy development staff discussed:

- Aims and priority values
- Rationale of policy
- Key values in practice.

Phase B comprised:

- Staff self-review
- Action plans
- Systems and training needs
- INSET [in-service training].

The final stage of the process, Phase C, involved:

- Monitoring
- Evaluation.

Radford also explores: 'How do head teachers or SENCOs empower their staff to participate actively in collaborative decision-making about behaviour?' (ibid., p. 86).

She identifies (ibid., p. 88) the skills senior staff need if the process is to be successful:

- create an environment in which there are non-judgemental opportunities to reflect on one's beliefs, values, attitudes and feelings about behaviour;
- draw staff into active involvement, using their ideas as part of the process;
- invite staff to take responsibility for decisions taken;
- provide opportunities to formulate ideas that will influence future planning, including changes to practical arrangements;
- inspire confidence such that staff will be prepared to reflect on their own practice.

While Radford is concerned solely with a process strategy for developing school policies, a key feature of this work is the collaborative involvement of all those who have to operate or are affected by the policy. During an In-Service (INSET) professional development day for teachers, Stella Sankey, Head of the Beeches Pupil Referral Unit, stresses the importance of a team approach and how the development of whole school behaviour policies can remove the emphasis of the student as the problem, and instead place the focus on how the staff and the school community can develop a team approach:

> Very often, when we talk about behaviour and when we think about managing behaviour, particularly in relation to school, we focus on a black spot, who is very often a child, right? And we don't see any of the periphery . . . When we talk about behaviour in school, often what we do is focus on the child and it's the child who is the real problem and that becomes our black spot, if you like.
>
> A Behaviour Management Policy has got to be part of what everyone does in, the whole school. Particularly with behaviour because it isn't a discreet area, it, it's part of everything that everyone does in the whole of the school life. So, first of all, we are talking about core values. What are your values, the ones that you share together about beliefs, about behaviour? What do you value most of all? . . . What's the biggest thing that you might value?
>
> (Sankey, in Open University, 2000)

The responses from the teachers included discussion of friendship and security. Sankey thought that the right to feel safe, and be safe, emotionally and physically was also important. As well as the right to learn to the best of one's ability, to be treated with respect and dignity at all times, the right to justice, a sense of fairness and equality of opportunity for everyone. According to Sankey, schools need to create a warm, calm, friendly, welcoming context and a behaviour recovery system that provides clear pathways for students to be responsible for changing their own behaviour. Remaining objective and calm, and reflecting on what a student's behaviour means, can result in appropriate responses to the individual's behaviour:

> Something that I've learned over time is that whatever a child makes me feel is very, very often what that child is feeling, because there's this thing, weird thing which is called transference. And what we do is we shove our feelings onto somebody else, and so, if I have a really hard time in the morning before I come out to work, then I might get in the car and really slam the door, and so I've transferred my angry feelings onto the car door . . . What the children do to us is they make us feel what they are feeling, probably most of the time. So a child who makes you feel despair is a child who is in despair.
>
> (ibid.)

Sankey suggests that it is important to remain emotionally detached in order to not be overwhelmed by the student's anxiety, anger, despair or guilt. Students need to have their positive behaviour recognised, have their concerns heard, be treated with respect and be protected from verbal abuse. Individual behaviour plans should be framed on rights and responsibilities and co-operative learning skills. Sankey's focus is therefore clearly on teacher behaviour change, and not simply on student behaviour change.

The process of drawing up a behaviour policy should include the following:

- defining key principles and drawing up a mission statement, if the school does not already have one;
- identifying and agreeing on the expected outcomes;
- clarifying rights and responsibilities (students, teachers and parents);
- determining desirable and undesirable behaviour;
- generating rules and procedures;
- establishing a hierarchy of rewards and sanctions;
- defining roles and responsibilities and providing support (staff);
- resourcing the implementation of the policy (staff development and materials);
- making provision for a regular review of policy and procedures.

Circular 8/94, *Pupil Behaviour and Discipline*, drawn up by the (then) Department for Education in England and Wales (DfE, 1994d) contains an outline of possible phases of development of schools' behaviour policies that is useful in many different national contexts:

Whole-school Behaviour Polices: Possible Phases of Development

The process of developing and implementing a whole-school behaviour policy, including rules, needs to be planned with care. The process will differ in detail from school to school. The following provides an example, covering many of the common stages:

1 Governors with head teacher consider the effectiveness of the school's current behaviour policy.
2 Governors decide to institute review and redevelopment of behaviour policy. Head teacher engages interest of staff.
3 In consultation with head teacher, governors agree on a written statement of principles for behaviour policy and timetable for developing and implementing a behaviour policy and rules based upon it.
4 Head teacher provides copies of governors' written statement of principles to staff and to parents' organisation.

However, it might be more effective and more appropriate to consult carefully with parents and community members prior to developing the written statement and to involve them in the process of constructing the statement. In this way the school would not be putting itself in the risky position of 'telling' its community what the problems and solutions to behaviour problems should be. Such an approach is unlikely to result in community ownership or support for the school's behaviour policy.

5 Head teacher convenes behaviour policy review group to report within the time allotted by the governors, agrees with them the process by which decisions will be made and appoints group leader.
6 Review group establishes programme of consultation and development work and allocates tasks.

Members of the community should be members of such a review group.

7 Review group obtains comments on existing policy. Review group decides whether the present policy reflects the principles in the governors' written statement and is satisfactory in other respects or whether it should be changed or replaced.
8 If they decide no changes are needed, they report that fact to the head teacher (if the head teacher is not a member of the group), who decides whether any further consultation is needed.
9 If changes are needed, the review group produces a draft policy statement of principles.
10 Review group consults head teacher and other staff and finalises policy statement of principles. (It will be helpful if they then also obtain the informal agreement of the governors to the statement.)
11 Review group draft school policy and rules.
12 Review group consult on school policy and rules.
13 School policy and rules finalised. Published in school brochure and other literature for implementation at a given date.
14 Monitoring and review to take place regularly.

Conclusion

In designing behaviour policies, schools should recognise that behaviour is a function of both person and context (Watkins and Wagner, 2000). A sanctions-driven discipline policy at the level of the individual student can promote a type of behaviour that schools find acceptable. However, many students will have different experiences of the use of those sanctions, according to the racialised and genderised positions often taken by those who implement the policy (Wright et al., 2000). If students perceive sanctions or policies as unfair and are unable to get staff to listen to them, then challenging and oppositional behaviours occur in which students will contest the nature of power and control in the school. Radford states that:

> Whilst it may be possible to maintain order in classrooms by the fear of graduated responses to misdemeanours, there is a need to address the more fundamental issue of how to motivate youngsters to behave in a fashion conducive to creating a supportive social community, within the school, and beyond.
>
> (2000, p. 86)

Throughout this book we have endeavoured to adopt just such a positive, focused and collaborative approach to understanding and managing behaviour. Our vision is one where schools construct safe and stimulating learning contexts in which potentially problematic behaviour will be understood and actively addressed from a variety of professional, community and cultural perspectives.

Bibliography

Alderson, P. and Arnold, S. (1999) *Civil Rights in Schools*, London, Economic and Social Research Council.

Anderson, C., Gendler, G., Riestenberg, N., Anfang, C.C., Ellison, M. and Yates, B. (1996) *Restorative Measures: Respecting Everyone's Ability to Resolve Problems*, St Paul, MN, Minnesota Department of Children, Families and Learning: Office of Community Services.

Anderson, G. (1990) *Fundamentals of Educational Research*, Basingstoke, Falmer Press.

Aponte, H.J. (1976) 'The family-school interview: an ecostructural approach', *Family Process*, 15, 303–13.

Armstrong, D. (1994) *Power and Partnership in Education: Parents, Children and Special Educational Needs*, London, Routledge.

Armstrong, D. (1995) *Power and Partnership in Education*, London, Routledge.

Armstrong, D. and Galloway, D. (1994) 'Special educational needs and problem behaviour: making policy in the classroom', in S. Riddell and S. Brown (eds) *Special Educational Needs Policy in the 90s*, London, Routledge.

Asch, S.E. (1952) *Social Psychology*, Englewood Cliffs, NJ, Prentice-Hall.

Asch, S.E. (1955) 'Opinions and social pressures', *Scientific American*, 193, 31–5.

Asch, S.E. (1958) 'Effects of group pressure upon modification and distortion of judgements', in E.E. Maccoby, T.M. Newcomb and E.L. Hartley (eds) *Readings in Social Psychology*, 3rd edn, New York, Holt, Rinehart and Winston.

Asperger, H. (1944) in S.W. Waterhouse (2000) *A Positive Approach to Autism*, London, Jessica Kingsley.

Atkinson, R.L., Atkinson, R.C., Smith, E.E. and Bem, D.J. (1993) *Introduction to Psychology*, 11th edn, Fort Worth, TX, Harcourt Brace College Publishers.

Audit Commission (1992) *Getting in on the Act: Provision for Pupils with Special Educational Needs*, London, HMSO.

Audit Commission (1996) *Misspent Youth*, London, Audit Commission.

Baer, D.M., Wolf, M.M. and Risely, T.R. (1968) 'Some current dimensions of applied behavior analysis', *Journal of Applied Behavior Analysis*, 1, 91–7.

Bagnato, S.J. and Neisworth, J.T. (1991) *Assessment for Early Intervention: Best Practices for Professionals*, London, Guilford Press.

Bagnato, S.J. and Neisworth, J.T. (1995) 'A national study of the social and treatment "invalidity" of intelligence testing for early intervention', *School Psychology Quarterly*, 9(2), 81–102.

Ball, S.J. (1990) *Foucault and Education: Disciplines and Knowledge*, London, Routledge.

Banks, S.R. (1997) 'Caregiver and professional perceptions of assessment practices and validity for American Indian/Alaskan native families', *Journal of American Indian Education*, 37(1), 16–44.

Barrow, P. (1998) *Disaffection and Inclusion: Merton's Mainstream Approach to Difficult Behaviour*, Bristol, CSIE.

Barton, L. and Tomlinson, S. (eds) (1984) *Special Education and Social Interests*, London, Croom Helm.

Bateson, G. (1972) *Steps to an Ecology of Mind*, New York, Chandler.

Bateson, G. (1979) *Mind and Nature: A Necessary Unity*, New York, Dutton.

Bateson, G., Jackson, D., Haley, J. and Weakland, J. (1956) 'Towards a theory of schizophrenia', *Behavioural Science*, 1, 251–4.

Bazemore, G. (1992) 'On mission statements and reform in juvenile justice: the case of the balanced approach', *Federal Probation*, 56, 64–70.

Beaman, A.L., Barnes, P.J., Klentz, B. and McQuirk, B. (1978) 'Increasing helping rates through information dissemination: teaching pays', *Personality and Social Psychology Bulletin*, 4, 406–11.

Beauchamp, T.L. and Childress, J.F. (1979) *Principles of Biomedical Ethics*, Oxford, Oxford University Press.

Belenky, M.F., Bond, L.A. and Weinstock, J.S. (1997) *A Tradition that Has No Name: Nurturing the Development of People, Families and Communities*, New York, Basic Books.

Belenky, M.F., Clinchy, B.M., Goldberger, N.R., and Tarule, J.M. (1997) *Women's Ways of Knowing: The Development of Self, Voice, and Mind*, New York, Basic Books.

Bell, J. (1999) *Doing Your Research Project: A Guide for First-Time Researchers in Education and Social Science*, 3rd edn, Buckingham, Open University Press.

Bennathan, M. (2000) 'Children at risk of failure in primary schools', in M. Bennathan and M. Boxall (eds) *Effective Intervention in Primary Schools: Nurture Groups*, 2nd edn, London, David Fulton, pp. 1–18.

Bennathan, M. and Boxall, M. (1996) *Effective Intervention in Primary School: Nurture Groups*, London, David Fulton.

Bennathan, M. and Boxall, M. (2000) *Effective Intervention in Primary Schools: Nurture Groups*, 2nd edn, London, David Fulton.

Bennett, R. (1992) 'Discipline in schools: the report of the Committee of Enquiry chaired by Lord Elton', in K. Wheldall (ed.) *Discipline in Schools: Psychological Perspectives on the Elton Report*, London, Routledge.

Benson, P.L. (1997) *All Kids Are Our Kids: What Communities Must Do to Raise Caring and Responsible Children and Adolescents*, San Francisco, Jossey-Bass.

Berridge, D., Brodie, I., Pitts, J., Porteous, D. and Tarling, R. (2001) *The Independent Effects of Permanent Exclusion from School on the Offending Careers of Young People*, London, Home Office.

Berryman, M. and Glynn, T. (2001) *Hei Awhina Matua: Strategies for Bicultural Partnership in Overcoming Behavioural and Learning Difficulties*, Wellington, Specialist Education Service.

Berryman, M. and Glynn, T. (2003) *Transition from Māori to English: A Community Approach*, Wellington, NZCER.

Berryman, M., Glynn, T., Walker, R., Reweti, M., O'brien, K., Boasa-Dean, T., Glynn, V., Langdon, Y. and Weiss, S. (2002) *SES Sites of Effective Special Education Practice for Māori 2001*, report to the SES Board and Executive Team, Tauranga, Poutama Pounamu Education Research and Development Centre.

Besag, V.E. (1989) *Bullies and Victims in Schools*, Buckingham, Open University Press.

Bevan-Brown , J. (2003) *The Cultural Self-Review: Providing Culturally Effective, Inclusive, Education for Māori Learners*, Wellington, NZCER.

Bevan-Brown, J. and Bevan-Brown, W. (1999) *Special Education 2000 Monitoring and Evaluation of the Policy: Kura Kaupapa Māori Report*, Report commissioned by the Ministry of Education to the Massey University College of Education, Wellington, Ministry of Education.

Bevan-Brown, J., Bourke, R., Carroll-Lind, J., Chapman, J., Cullen, J., Kearney, A., Mandia, M., Poskitt, J., Prochnow, J., Ryba, K., O'neill, J., Bevan-Brown, W., Grant, S., Morton, M. and Stringer, P. (1999) *Special Education 2000 Monitoring and Evaluation of the Policy: Phase 1 1999*, Report commissioned by the Ministry of Education to the Massey University College of Education, Wellington, Ministry of Education.

Birmingham City Council Education Department (1998) 'A three-level approach to intervention for individual behaviour difficulties', in J. Wearmouth, R.C. Richmond and T. Glynn (eds) *Addressing Pupils' Behaviour: Responses at District, School and Individual Levels*, London, Fulton

Bishop, R. (1994) 'Initiating empowering research', *New Zealand Journal of Educational Studies*, 29(1), 1–14.

Bishop, R. (1996a) 'Addressing issues of self determination and legitimation in kaupapa Māori research', in B. Webber, (ed.) *He Paepae Kōrero Research Perspectives in Māori Education*, Wellington, NZCER.

Bishop, R. (1996b) *Collaborative Research Stories: Whakawhanaungatanga*, Palmerston North, New Zealand, Dunmore Press.

Bishop, R., Berryman, M., and Richardson, C. (2001). *Te Toi Huarewa: Effective Teaching and Learning Strategies, and Effective Teaching Materials for Improving the Reading and Writing in Te Reo Māori of Students Aged Five to Nine in Māori Medium Education*, Wellington, New Final Report to the Curriculum Division of the Ministry of Education.

Bishop, R., Berryman, M., Glynn, T., Mckinley, L., Devine, N. and Richardson, C. (2001a) *The Experiences of Māori Children in the Year 9 and Year 10 Classrooms: Part 1, the Scoping Exercise*, report presented to the Research Division of the Ministry of Education, Wellington, New Zealand, Ministry of Education.

Bishop, R., Berryman, M., Richardson, C. and Tiakiwai, S. (2001b) *Te Kotahitanga: Experiences of Year 9 and 10 Māori Students in Mainstream Classrooms*, report prepared for the Ministry of Education, Wellington, New Zealand, Ministry of Education.

Bishop, R., Berryman, M., Richardson, C. and Tiakiwai, S. (2003) *Te Kotahitanga: The Experiences of Year 9 and 10 Māori Students in Mainstream Classrooms*, final report to the Ministry of Education, Wellington, New Zealand. Available online: http://www.minedu.govt.nz/goto/tekotahitanga

Bishop, R. and Glynn, T. (1993) 'Participant driven empowering Research: issues arising in a bi-cultural context', in S. Barratt, M. Gold and L. Lawn (eds) *Towards*

Excellence, Providing Effective Services for Learners with Special Needs, Dunedin, New Zealand, Inaugural Conference of the Specialist Education Service.

Bishop, R. and Glynn, T. (1999) *Culture Counts: Changing Power Relations in Education*, Palmerston North, New Zealand, Dunmore Press.

Blair, M. (2001) 'The education of Black children: why do some schools do better than others?', in R. Majors, *Educating our Black Children*, London, Routledge-Falmer.

Blair, M. (2004) 'The education of Black children: why do some schools do better than others?', in J. Wearmouth, R.C. Richmond and T. Glynn (eds) *Addressing Pupils' Behaviour: Responses at District, School and Individual Levels*, London, Fulton, pp. 67–85.

Blair, M. and Bourne, J. (1998) *Making the Difference: Teaching and Learning Strategies in Successful Multiethnic Schools*, London, DfEE.

Blair, M. and Gillborn, J. (1999) 'Face up to racism', *TES*, 5 March.

Blunkett, D. (1999a) 'Excellence for the many, not just the few: raising standards and extending opportunities in our schools', CBI President's Reception Address by the Rt. Hon. David Blunkett MP 19 July 1999, London, DfEE.

Blunkett, D. (1999b) 'Social exclusion and the politics of opportunity: a mid-term progress check', a speech by the Rt. Hon. David Blunkett MP, London, DfEE.

Blunkett, D. (2000) 'Raising aspirations for the 21st century', a speech to the North of England Education Conference, Wigan, 6 January 2000, London, DfEE.

Booth, T. (1981) 'Demystifying integration', in W. Swann (ed.) *The Practice of Special Education*, Oxford, Basil Blackwell.

Booth, T., Ainscow, M., Black-Hawkins, K., Vaughn, M. and Shaw, L. (2000) *Index for Inclusion: Developing Learning and Participation in Schools*, Bristol, CSIE.

Booth, T., Ainscow, M. and Dyson, A. (1998) 'England: inclusion and exclusion in a competitive system', in T. Booth and M. Ainscow (eds) *From Them to Us: An International Study of Inclusion in Education*, London, Routledge

Bourdieu, P. and Passeron, J.C. (1973) *Reproduction in Education*, Society and Culture, London, Sage.

Bowers, T. (1996) 'Putting back the "E" in EBD', *Emotional and Behavioural Difficulties*, 1(1), 8–13.

Bowlby, J. (1944) 'Forty-four juvenile thieves: their characters and home life', *International Journal of Psycho-Analysis*, 25, 19–52, 107–27.

Bowlby, J. (1952) 'A two-year-old goes to hospital', *Proceedings of the Royal Society of Medicine*, 46, 425–7.

Bowlby, J. (1988) *A Secure Base: Clinical Applications of Attachment Theory*, London, Routledge.

Boxall, M (2000) 'The nurture group in the primary school', in M. Bennathan and M. Boxall (eds) *Effective Intervention in Primary Schools: Nurture Groups*, 2nd edn, London, David Fulton, pp. 19–38.

Braithwaite, J. (1997) *Restorative Justice: Assessing an Immodest Theory and a Pessimistic Theory*, Canberra: Australian Institute of Criminology, Australian National University.

Breen, R. (1991) *Education, Employment and Training in the Youth Labour Market*, Dublin, Economic and Social Research Institute.

Brescia, W. and Fortune, J.C. (1989) 'Standardized testing of American Indian/ Alaskan Native students', *College Student Journal*, 23(2), 98–104.

Bridgeland, M. (1971) *Pioneer Work with Maladjusted Children*, London: Staples.

British Psychological Society (BPS) (1996) *Attention Deficit Hyperactivity Disorder (ADHD): A Psychological Response to an Evolving Concept*, Leicester, BPS.

Broadfoot, P. (1996) *Education, Assessment and Society*, Buckingham, Open University Press.

Brodie, I. (2000) 'Children's homes and school exclusion: redefining the problem', *Support for Learning*, 15(1), 25–9.

Bronfenbrenner, U. (1978) 'Is early intervention effective? Facts and principles of early intervention: a summary', in A.M. Clarke and A.D.B. Clarke (eds) *Early Experience: Myth and Evidence*, New York, The Free Press.

Bronfenbrenner, U. (1979) 'Who needs education?', *Teachers College Record*, 79(4), 773–4.

Bronfenbrenner, U., Mcclellan, P., Wethington, E., Moen, P. and Ceci, S. (1996) *The State of Americans: This Generation and the Next*, New York, The Free Press.

Brown, D. (2002) 'Preparing for inclusive education through effective teaching', unpublished PhD thesis, University of Waikato, New Zealand.

Brown, D., Moore, D., Thomson, C., Anderson, A., Walker, J., Glynn, T., Macfarlane, A., Medcalf, J. and Ysseldyke, J. (2000) 'Resource teachers of learning and behaviour: an ecological approach to special education', *Australian Journal of Special Education*, 24(1), 15–20.

Brown, D. and Thomson, C. (1988) 'How do we get there from here?', paper presented at the Conference of the New Zealand Institute of Mental Retardation (Inc): Community integration for people with intellectual handicaps 'Good News' conference, Dunedin, New Zealand.

Brown, D.F. (1992) *The Development of Strategic Classrooms in Two Secondary Schools*, Waikanae, New Zealand, Wordsmiths.

Bruner, J. (1990) *Acts of Meaning*, Cambridge, MA, Harvard University Press.

Bruner, J. (1996) *The Culture of Education*, London, Harvard University Press.

Buhler, C. (1935) *From Birth to Maturity: An Outline of the Psychological Development of the Child*, London, Kegan Paul.

Buhler, C. (1940) *The Child and his Family*, London, Kegan Paul.

Butterworth, G. and Butterworth, S. (1998) *Reforming Education: The New Zealand Experience, 1984–1996*, Palmerston North, New Zealand, Dunmore Press.

Cameron, M. and Walker, J. (1994) *The Paired Writing Handbook*, Auckland, New Zealand, Longman Paul.

Campion, J. (1985) *The Child in Context: Family Systems Theory in Educational Psychology*, London, Methuen.

Canter, L. and Canter, M. (1992) *Assertive Discipline: Positive Behaviour Management for Today's Classroom*, Santa Monica, CA, Lee Canter and Associates.

Capra, F. (1982) *The Turning Point: Science, Society and the Rising Culture*, London, Collins.

Carey, M. (1996) 'Restorative justice in community corrections', *Corrections Today*, August, 152–5.

Carpenter, S.L. and McKee Higgins, E. (1996) 'Behaviour management in inclusive classrooms', *Remedial and Special Education*, 17(4), p. 195.

Carrington, S. and Elkins, J. (2002) 'Bridging the gap between inclusive policy and inclusive culture in secondary schools', *Support for Learning*, **17**(2), 51–7.

Centre for Studies of Inclusive Education (CSIE) (2004) 'Ten reasons for inclusion', http://inclusion.uwe.ac.uk/csie/10rsns.htm

Chazan, M., Laing, A. and Davies, D. (1994) *Emotional and Behavioural Difficulties in Middle Childhood*, London, Falmer Press.

Clark, C., Dyson, A. and Millward, A. (1998) *Theorising Special Education*, London, Routledge.

Clark. C., Dyson, A., Millward, A. and Robson, S. (1999) 'Theories of inclusion, theories of schools: deconstructing and reconstructing the inclusive school', *British Educational Research Journal*, **25**(2), 157–77.

Clark, C., Dyson, A., Millward, A. and Skidmore, D. (1997) *New Directions in Special Needs*, London, Cassell.

Cline, T. (ed.) (1992) *The Assessment of Special Educational Needs*, London, Routledge.

CMRS Education Commission (1992) *Education and Poverty: Eliminating Disadvantage in the Primary School Years*, Dublin, Education Commission.

Cole, T. (1986) *Residential Special Education: Living and Learning in a Special School*, Milton Keynes, Open University Press.

Cole, T. (1989) *Apart or A Part? Integration and the Growth of British Special Education*, Milton Keynes, Open University Press.

Cole, T. (2002) 'Pupil Referral Unit Review', *National Newsletter of AWCEBD*, Autumn, pp. 7–9.

Cole, T. (2004) 'The development of provision for children and young people "with emotional and behavioural difficulties": past, present and future', in J. Wearmouth, T. Glynn, R.C. Richmond and M. Berryman (eds) *Inclusion and Behaviour Management in Schools: Issues and Challenges*, London, Fulton, pp. 17–33.

Cole, T., Daniels, H., Berridge, D., Brodie, I., Beecham, J., Knapp, M. and Macneill, V. (2003b) *Residential Schools for Pupils with Emotional and Behavioural Difficulties: Client and Organisational Characteristics*, Birmingham, Birmingham University School of Education.

Cole, T., Daniels, H. and Visser, J. (2003a) 'Patterns of provision for pupils with behavioural difficulties in England', *Oxford Review of Education*, **29**(2), 187–205.

Cole, T. and Visser, J. (1998) 'How should the effectiveness of schools for pupils with EBD be assessed?', *Emotional and Behavioural Difficulties*, 3(1), 37–43.

Cole, T., Visser, J. and Upton, G. (1998) *Effective Schooling for Pupils with Emotional and Behavioural Difficulties*, London, David Fulton.

Coleman, P. (1998) *Parent, Student and Teacher Collaboration: The Power of Three*, Thousand Oaks, CA, Corwin Press.

Commission for Racial Equality (CRE) (1998) *Education and Training in Britain*, London, CRE.

Connors, B. (2004) Contributions to Open University (2004) *E804 Managing behaviour in schools, Study Guide*, Milton Keynes, Open University.

Cooper, J.O., Heron, T.E. and Heward, W.E. (1987) *Applied Behavior Analysis*, Columbus, OH, Merrill Publishing Company.

Cooper, P. (1990) 'Respite, relationships and re-signification: the effects of residential schooling on pupils with emotional and behavioural difficulties, with particular reference to the pupils' perspective', unpublished PhD thesis, University of Birmingham.

Cooper, P. (1993) 'Learning from pupils' perspectives', *British Journal of Special Education*, **20**(4), 129–33.

Cooper, P. (1999) 'Changing perceptions of EBD: maladjustment, EBD and beyond', *Emotional and Behavioural Difficulties*, **4**(1), 3–11.

Cooper, P. (2004) 'Nurture groups: the research evidence', in J. Wearmouth, R.C. Richmond and T. Glynn (eds) *Addressing Pupils' Behaviour: Responses at District, School and Individual Levels*, London, Fulton, pp. 176–96.

Cooper, P., Arnold, R. and Boyd, E. (2001) 'The effectiveness of nurture groups: preliminary research findings', *British Journal of Special Education*, **28**(4), 160–6.

Cooper, P. and Lovey, J. (1999) 'Early intervention in emotional and behavioural difficulties: the role of nurture groups', *European Journal of Special Educational Needs Education*, **14**(2), 122–31.

Cooper, P. and Upton, G. (1991) 'Controlling the urge to control: an ecosystemic approach to behaviour in schools', *Support for Learning*, **6**(1), 22–6.

Cooper, P, Smith, C and Upton, G (1994) *Emotional and Behavioural Difficulties: Theory to Practice*, London, Routledge.

Coopersmith, S. (1967) *The Antecedents of Self-Esteem*, San Francisco, Freeman and Company.

Coopersmith, S. (1975) 'Building self-esteem in the classroom', in S. Coopersmith (ed.) *Developing Motivation in Young Children*, San Francisco, Albion Publishing Co.

Copeland, I. (1993) 'Is there a sociology of special education and integration?', *European Journal of Special Needs Education*, **8**(1), 1–13.

Corbett, J. (2001) 'Teaching approaches which support inclusive education: a connective pedagogy', *British Journal of Special Education*, **28**(2), 55–9.

Cornwall, J. (2000) 'Might is right? A discussion of the ethics and practicalities of control and restraint in education', *Emotional and Behavioural Difficulties*, **5**(4), 19–25.

Cornwall, J. (2004) 'Pressure, stress and children's behaviour at school', in J. Wearmouth, R.C. Richmond, T. Glynn and M. Berryman (eds) *Understanding Pupil Behaviour in Schools: A Diversity of Approaches*, London, Fulton, pp. 307–21.

Coulling, N. (2000) 'Definitions of successful education for the "looked after" child: a multi-agency perspective', *Support for Learning*, **15**(1), 30–5.

Council of Europe (1966) *European Convention on Human Rights (Rome, 1950) and its Five Protocols*, Strasbourg, Council of Europe.

Crooks, T. (1990) 'The Dublin inner city education project', in G. McNamara, K. Williams and D. Herron (eds) *Achievement and Aspiration: Curricular Initiatives in Irish Post-Primary Education in the 1980s*, Dublin, Drumcrondra Teachers Centre.

Cushner, K. (1998) *International Perspectives on Intercultural Education*, London, Lawrence Erlbaum.

Dahl, R. (1984) *Boy: Tales of Childhood*, New York, Penguin.

Dale, N. (1996) *Working with Families of Children with Special Needs: Partnership and Practice*, London, Routledge.

Daniels, H., Cole, T., Sellman, E., Sutton, J., Visser, J. With Bedward, J. (2003) *Study of Young People Permanently Excluded from School*, London, DfES.

Daniels, H., Norwich, B. and Anghileri, N. (1993) 'Teacher support teams: an evaluation of a school-based approach to meeting special educational needs', *Support for Learning*, 8(4) 169–73.

Daniels, H., Visser, J., Cole, T. and De Reybekill, N. (1998) *Emotional and Behavioural Difficulties in Mainstream Schools*, Research Report RR90, London, DfEE.

Davie, R. (1994) 'A consortium for children: analysis of the dialogue with policymakers leading to the 1993 Education Act and the 1994 Code of Practice', *Therapeutic Care and Education*, 3(3) 206–12.

Davies, S. (2004) 'Barriers to belonging: students' perceptions of factors which affect participation in schools', in J. Wearmouth, T. Glynn, R.C. Richmond and M. Berryman (eds) *Inclusion and Behaviour Management in Schools: Issues and Challenges*, London, Fulton, pp. 322–41.

De Shazer, S. (1982) 'Some conceptual distinctions are more useful than others', *Family Process*, **21**, 71–84.

De Shazer, S. (1985) *Keys to Solution in Brief Therapy*, New York, Norton.

Deem, R. (ed.) (1980) *Schooling for Women's Work*, London, Routledge & Kegan Paul.

Delgado-Gaitan, C. (1990) *Literacy for Empowerment: The Role of Parents in Children's Education*, London, Falmer Press.

Demko, L (2004) 'Bullying at school: the no-blame approach', in J. Wearmouth, R.C. Richmond and T. Glynn (eds) *Addressing Pupils' Behaviour: Responses at District, School and Individual Levels*, London, Fulton, pp. 160–5.

Department for Education (DfE) (1992) *Choice and Diversity: A New Framework for Schools*, White Paper, London, DfE.

Department for Education (DfE) (1994a) *Youth Cohort Study*, London, DfE.

Department for Education (DfE) (1994b) *The Education of Children with Emotional and Behavioural Difficulties*, Circular No. 9/94, London, DfE.

Department for Education (DfE) (1994c) *The Code of Practice on the Identification and Assessment of Special Educational Needs*, London, DfE.

Department for Education (DfE) (1994d) *Pupils with Problems: Pupil Behaviour and Discipline*, Circular No. 8/94, London, DfE.

Department for Education (DfE) (1994e) *Exclusions from School*, Circular No. 10/94, London, DfE.

Department for Education and Employment (DfEE) (1996) *Exclusions from Secondary Schools: Report of Her Majesty's Inspectors*, London, DfEE.

Department for Education and Employment (DfEE) (1997) *Excellence for All Children: Meeting Special Educational Needs*, Green Paper, London, DfEE.

Department for Education and Employment (DfEE) (1998a) *Section 550A of the Education Act 1996: The Use of Force to Control or Restrain Pupils*, Circular No. 10/98, London, DfEE.

Department for Education and Employment (DfEE) (1998b) *Meeting Special Educational Needs: A Programme for Action*, London, DfEE.

Department for Education and Employment (DfEE) (1998c) *Standards Fund*, Circular No. 13/98, London, DfEE.

Department for Education and Employment (DfEE) (1998d) *LEA Behaviour Support Plans*, Circular No. 1/98, London, DfEE.

Department for Education and Employment (DfEE) (1998e) *The National Literacy Strategy: Framework for Teaching*, London, DfEE.

Department for Education and Employment (DfEE) (1998f) *Supporting the Target Setting Process: Guidance for Effective Target Setting for Pupils with Special Educational Needs*, London, DfEE.

Department for Education and Employment (DfEE) (1999a) *Social Inclusion: Pupil Support*, Circular No. 10/99, London, DfEE.

Department for Education and Employment (DfEE) (1999b) *Social Inclusion: The LEA Role in Pupil Support*, Circular No. 11/99, London, DfEE.

Department for Education and Employment (DfEE) (1999c) *Sure Start: Making a Difference for Children and Families*, London, DfEE.

Department for Education and Employment (DfEE) (1999d) *Excellence in Cities*, London, DfEE.

Department for Education and Employment (DfEE) (1999e) *Meet the Challenge: Education Action Zones*, London, DfEE.

Department for Education and Employment (DfEE) (2000) *Connexions: the Best Start in Life for Every Young Person*, London, DfEE.

Department for Education and Skills (DfES) (2001a) *Special Educational Needs Code of Practice*, London, DfES.

Department for Education and Skills (DfES) (2001b) *Inclusive Schooling: Children with Special Educational Needs, Guidance on Pupil Support and Access*, London, DfES.

Department for Education and Skills (DfES) (2002a) *Statistics of Education: Permanent Exclusions from Maintained Schools in England*, Issue 09/02, London, DfES.

Department for Education and Skills (DfES) (2002b) *Guidance for Establishing and Managing LSUs*, London, DfES.

Department for Education and Skills (DfES) (2003) *Improving Behaviour and Attendance: Guidance on Exclusion from Schools and Pupil Referral Units*, London, DfES.

Department of Education (New Zealand) (1987a) *Curriculum Review*, Wellington, Department of Education.

Department of Education (New Zealand) (1987b) *Draft Review of Special Education*, Wellington, Department of Education.

Department of Education (New Zealand) (1995) *Special Education Policy Guidelines*, Wellington, Department of Education.

Department of Education, Northern Ireland (DENI) (1982) *The Improvement of Community Relations: The Contribution of Schools*, Circular No. 1982/21, Bangor, DENI.

Department of Education, Northern Ireland (DENI) (1998a) *Code of Practice for the Identification and Assessment of Special Educational Needs*, Bangor, DENI.

Department of Education, Northern Ireland (DENI) (1998b) *Provision for Pupils with Emotional and Behavioural Difficulties in Northern Ireland*, Bangor, DENI.

Department of Education, Northern Ireland (DENI) (2001) *Promoting Positive Behaviour*, Bangor, DENI.

Department of Education, Northern Ireland (DENI) (2002) *Towards a Model Policy in Schools on the Use of Reasonable Force*, Bangor, DENI.

Department of Education, Northern Ireland (DENI) (1998c) *Promoting and Sustaining Good Behaviour: A Discipline Strategy for Schools*, Bangor, DENI.

Department of Education and Science (DES) (1974a) *The Health of the School Child, 1971–2*, London, HMSO.

Department of Education and Science (DES) (1978) *Special Educational Needs: Report of the Committee of Enquiry into the Education of Handicapped Children and Young People*, The Warnock Report, London, HMSO.

Department of Education and Science (DES) (1988) *Secondary Schools: A Appraisal by HMI in England and Wales 1987*, London, HMSO.

Department of Education and Science (DES) (1989) *Discipline in Schools: Report of the Committee of Enquiry Chaired by Lord Elton*, The Elton Report, London, HMSO.

Department of Education and Science (DES) (Ireland) (1993) *Guidelines on Countering Bullying Behaviour in Primary and Post-primary Schools*, Dublin, The Stationery Office.

Department of Education and Science (DES) (Ireland) (1994) *School Attendance/ Truancy Report*, Dublin, The Stationery Office.

Department of Education and Science (DES) (Ireland) (2000) *Learning Support Guidelines*, Dublin, DES.

Department for Education and Skills (DfES) (2003) *The Report of the Special Schools Working Group*, London, DfES.

Department of Health and Social Security (DHSS) (1970) *Care and Treatment in a Planned Environment*. Advisory Council on Child Care. London, HMSO.

De Shazer, S. (1982) 'Some conceptual distinctions are more useful than others', *Family Process*, **21**, 71–84.

De Shazer, S. (1985) *Keys to Solution in Brief Therapy*, New York, Norton.

Deschenes, S., Cuban, L., and Tyack, D. (2001) 'Mismatch: Historical perspectives on schools and students who don't fit them', *Teachers College Record*, **103**, 525–47.

Dewey, J. (1933) *How We Think*, Boston, Health.

Dewey, J. (1962) *The Relation of Theory to Practice in Education*, Cedar Falls, IA, Association for Student Teaching.

Disley, B. (2004) Verbal presentation at the Northern Region GSE Māori staff Hui at Terengaparaoa Marae in Whangarei, New Zealand, May.

Dockrell, J. and Mcshane, J. (1993) *Children's Learning Difficulties: A Cognitive Approach*, Oxford, Blackwell.

Dowling, E. and Osbourne, E. (eds) (1985) *The Family and the School*, London, Routledge & Kegan Paul.

Doyle, R. (2001) 'Using a readiness scale for reintegrating pupils with social emotional and behavioural difficulties from a nurture group into their mainstream classroom – a pilot study', *British Journal of Special Education*, **28**(3), 126–32.

Drew, D. (1995) *Race, Education and Work: The Statistics of Inequality*, Aldershot, Avebury.

Dunckley, I. (1999) *Managing Extreme Behaviour in Schools*, Wellington, New Zealand, Specialist Education Services.

DuPaul, G.J. and Stoner, G. (1994) *ADHD (Attention-Deficit Hyperactivity Disorder) in the Schools: Assessment and Intervention Strategies*, New York, Guilford Press.

Dupaul, G.J. and Stoner, G. (1995) 'Advances in behavioral, medical, and educational interventions for students with Attention Deficit Hyperactivity Disorder', professional workshop conducted at the Association for Behavior Analysis Convention, Washington, DC.

Durie, M. (1994) *Whaiora: Māori Health Development*, Auckland, Oxford University Press.

Durie, M. (1998) *Te mana, te kawanatanga: The Politics of Maori Self-Determination*, Auckland, Oxford University Press.

Dwivedi, K.N. (2004) 'Addressing emotional and behavioural issues in schools through self management training: theory and practice', in J. Wearmouth, R.C. Richmond, T. Glynn and M. Berryman (eds) *Understanding Pupil Behaviour in Schools: A Diversity of Approaches*, London, Fulton, pp. 272–86.

Dwivedi, K. and Gupta, A. (2000) '"Keeping cool": anger management through group work', Support for Learning, 15(2), 76–81.

Dyson, A. (1997) 'Social and educational disadvantage: reconnecting special needs education', *British Journal of Special Education*, 24(4), 152–7.

Dyson, A. (2001) 'Special needs in the twenty-first century: where we've been and where we're going', *British Journal of Special Education*, 28(1), 24–9.

Dyson, A. and Millward, A. (2000) *Schools and Special Needs: Issues of Innovation and Inclusion*, London, Paul Chapman.

Dyson, A. and Robson, E. (1999) *School Inclusion: The Evidence*, Newcastle, University of Newcastle Press.

Eisner, E. (1993) 'Objectivity in educational research', in M. Hammersley (ed.) *Educational Research: Current Issues*, London, Paul Chapman.

Elliott, J. (1997) 'School-based curriculum development and action research in the United Kingdom', in S. Hollingsworth (ed.) *International Action Research*, London, Falmer Press.

Elliott, M. (1991) 'Bully courts', in M. Elliott (ed.) *Bullying*, London, Longman.

Epstein, J., Coates, L., Salinas, K., Sanders, M. and Simon, B. (1997) *School, Family and Community Partnerships: Your Handbook for Action*, Thousand Oaks, CA, Corwin Press.

Eraut, M. (1994) *Developing Professional Knowledge and Competence*, London, Falmer.

Esping-Anderson, G. (1990) *The Three Worlds of Welfare Capitalism*, Cambridge, Polity Press.

Ewing, N.J. and Yong, F.L. (1992) 'A comparative study of the learning style preferences among gifted African American, Mexican American and American born Chinese middle grade students', *Roper Review*, 14(3).

Fahy Bates, B.C. (1996) 'Aspects of childhood deviancy: a study of young offenders in open centres in the Republic of Ireland, Volumes 1 and 2', unpublished PhD thesis, University College Dublin.

Faircloth, S. and Tippeconnic, J.W., III (2000) 'Issues in the education of American Indian and Alaska Native students with disabilities', *Eric Digest*, **December**.

Fancy, H. (2003) Verbal presentation at the New Zealand Ministry of Education, Managers' Forum, Wellington, New Zealand, November.

Farrell, P., Critchley, C. and Mills, C. (1999) 'The educational attainments of pupils with emotional and behavioural difficulties', *British Journal of Special Education*, 26(1), 50–3.

Farrington, D.P. (1993) 'Understanding and preventing bullying', in M. Tonny and N. Morris (eds) *Crime and Justice 17*, Chicago, University of Chicago Press.

Feiman, S. (1979) 'Technique and enquiry in teacher education: a curricular case study', *Curriculum Inquiry*, 9(1), 63–79.

Field, E.M. (1999) *Bully Busting*, Lane Cove, NSW, Finch Publishing Pty.

Fine, M. and Holt, P. (1983) 'Intervening with school problems: a family systems perspective', *Psychology in the Schools*, 20(1), 59–66.

Fisher, G., Richmond, R. and Wearmouth, J. (2004) *E804 Managing behaviour in schools, Study Guide, Part 5*, Milton Keynes, Open University Press

Ford, J., Mongon, D. and Whelan, M. (1982) *Special Education and Social Control: Invisible Disasters*, London, Routledge.

Foster, H. (1995) 'Educators and non-educators perceptions of black males: a survey', *Journal of African American Men*, 1(2), 38–42.

Foucault, M. (1967) *Madness and Civilization: A History of Insanity in the Age of Reason*, London, Tavistock.

Foucault, M. (1974) *The Archaeology of Knowledge*, London, Tavistock.

Fraser, D., Moltzen, R. and Ryba, K. (2000) *Learners with special needs in Aotearoa New Zealand*, 2nd edn, Palmerston North, Dunmore Press.

Frederickson, N. (1993) 'Using soft systems methodology to re-think special needs', in A. Dyson and C. Gains (eds) *Re-thinking Special Needs in Mainstream Schools*, London, Fulton.

Freeman, M.P. (1993) *Re-writing the Self: History, Memory, Narrative*, London, Routledge.

French, J.R. and Raven, B. (1959) 'The basics of social power', in D. Cartwright (ed.) *Studies in Social Power*, Ann Arbor, MI, University of Michigan Press.

Friend, M. and Cook, L. (1996) *Interactions: Collaboration Skills for School Professionals*, 2nd edn, White Plains, NY, Longman.

Fulcher, G. (1989) *Disabling Policies: A Comparative Approach to Educational Policy and Disabilities*, London, Fulcher.

Fullan, M. (2001) *The New Meaning of Educational Change*, 3rd edn, London, RoutledgeFalmer.

Furlong, V.J. (1985) *The Deviant Pupil: Sociological Perspectives*, Milton Keynes, Open University Press.

Furlong, V.J. (1991) 'Disaffected pupils: reconstructing the sociological perspective', *British Journal of Sociology of Education*, 12(3), 293–307.

Gable, R.A. and Arllen, N. (1995) 'Use of peer confrontation to modify disruptive behaviour in inclusion classrooms', *Preventing School Failure*, 40(1), 25.

Gallimore, R. and Goldenberg, L. (1993) 'Activity settings of early literacy: home and school factors in children's early literacy', in E. Forman, N. Minick and C. Stome (eds) *Contexts for Learning: Sociocultural Dynamics in Children's Development*, New York, Oxford University Press.

Galloway, D., Armstrong, D. and Tomlinson, S. (1994) *The Assessment of Special Educational Needs: Whose Problem*, Harlow, Longman.

Gardner, R. (1987) *Who Says?: Choice and Control in Care*, London, National Children's Bureau.

Garner, P. and Gains, C. (1996) 'Models of intervention for children with emotional and behavioural difficulties, *Support for Learning*, 11(4), 141–5.

Garner, P. and Sandow, S. (1995) *Advocacy, Self Advocacy and Special Needs*, London, Fulton.

Gee, J.P. (1990) *Social Linguistics and Literacies: Ideology in Discourses*, Basingstoke, Falmer Press.

Gerber, M. (2004) 'Reforming special education: beyond inclusion', in J. Wearmouth, T. Glynn, R.C. Richmond and M. Berryman (eds) *Inclusion and Behaviour Management in Schools: Issues and Challenges*, London, Fulton, pp. 341–60.

Gersch, I. (1995) 'Involving the child', in *Schools' Special Educational Needs Policies Pack*, London, National Children's Bureau.

Gersch, I. (2001) 'Listening to Children: an initiative to increase the active involvement of children in their education by an educational psychology service', in J. Wearmouth (ed.) *Special Educational Provision in the Context of Inclusion*, London, Fulton.

Gewirtz, S., Ball, S.J. and Bowe, R. (1995) *Markets, Choice and Equity in Education*, Buckingham, Open University Press.

Giddens, A. (1998) *The Third Way: The Renewal of Social Democracy*, Cambridge, Polity Press.

Gillborn, D. (1990) *Race, Ethnicity and Education: Teaching and Learning in a Multi-ethnic School*, London, Unwin Hyman.

Gillborn, D. (2001) 'Racism, policy and the (mis)education of Black children', in R. Majors (ed.) *Educating Our Black Children: New Directions and Radical Approaches*, London, RoutledgeFalmer, pp. 13–27.

Gillborn, D. (2004) 'Racism, policy and the (mis)education of Black children', in J. Wearmouth, T. Glynn, R.C. Richmond and M. Berryman (eds) *Inclusion and Behaviour Management in Schools: Issues and Challenges*, London, Fulton, pp. 194–210.

Gillborn, D. and Gipps, C. (1996) *Recent Research on the Achievements of Ethnic Minority Pupils*, Report for the Office for Standards in Education, London, HMSO.

Gillborn, D. and Youdell, D. (1998) 'Raising standards and deepening inequality: league tables and selection in multi-ethnic secondary schools', paper presented at the annual meeting of the American Educational Research Association, San Diego, 13–17 April.

Gillborn, D. and Youdell, D. (2000) *Rationing Education: Policy, Practice, Reform and Equity*, Buckingham, Open University Press.

Gipps, C., Gross, J. and Goldstein, H. (1987) *Warnock's Eighteen Per Cent*, Lewes, Falmer Press.

Glynn, T. (1982) 'Antecedent control of behaviour in educational contexts', *Educational Psychology*, 2, 215–29.

Glynn, T. (1985) 'Contexts for independent learning', *Educational Psychology*, 5(1), 5–15.

Glynn, T. (1987) 'Effective learning contexts for exceptional children', in D. Mitchell and N. Singh (eds), *Exceptional Children in New Zealand*, Palmerston North, Dunmore Press, pp. 158–67.

Glynn, T. (1995) 'Pause, prompt, praise: reading tutoring procedures for home and school partnership', in S. Wolfendale and K. Topping (eds) *Family Involvement in Literacy*, London, Cassell.

Glynn, T. (1998a) *A Collaborative Approach to Teacher Development: New Initiatives in Special Education*, paper presented at the Australian Teacher Education Association Annual Conference, July, Melbourne.

Glynn, T. (1998b) 'Bicultural challenges for educational professionals in Aotearoa, inaugural lecture, University of Waikato', *Waikato Journal of Education*, 4, 3–16.

Glynn, T., Berryman, M., Atvars, K. and Harawira, W. (1997) *Hei Āwhina Mātua: A Home and School Behavioural Programme*, final report to the Ministry of Education, Wellington, Ministry of Education.

Glynn, T., Berryman, M., Bidois, P., Atvars, K. and Duffull, T. (1997) 'Involving children in research: the Hei Awhina Matua Project', *Childrens Issues*, 1(1), 17–22.

Glynn, T., Berryman, M., Bidois, P., Furlong, M., Walker, R., Thatcher, J. and Atvars, K. (1996) 'Bilingual gains for tutors and tutees in a Māori language immersion programme', in *He Paepae Kōrero Research Perspectives in Māori Education*, Wellington, New Zealand Council for Education Research.

Glynn, T., Berryman, M. and Glynn, V. (2000a) *The Rotorua Home and School Literacy Project*, Final report to the Rotorua Energy Charitable Trust and the Research and Statistics Division, Wellington, New Zealand, Ministry of Education.

Glynn, T., Berryman, M. and Glynn, V. (2000b) 'Reading and writing gains for Māori students in mainstream schools: effective partnerships in the Rotorua home and school literacy project', paper presented at the 18th World Congress on Reading, Auckland, New Zealand.

Glynn, T., Berryman, M., Walker, R., Reweti, M. and O'Brien, K. (2001) 'Partnerships with indigenous people: modifying the cultural mainstream', keynote address at the Partnerships in Educational Psychology Conference, Brisbane, Australia.

Glynn, T. and Bishop, R. (1995) 'Cultural issues in educational research: a New Zealand perspective', *He Pūkengo Kōrero*, 1(1), 37–43.

Glynn, T., Fairweather, R. and Donald, S. (1992) 'Involving parents in improving children's learning at school: policy issues for behavioural research', *Behaviour Change*, 9(3), 178–85.

Glynn, T. and Macfarlane, A. (1999) 'Māori and bicultural positions within the training programme for Resource Teachers (Learning and Behaviour)', paper presented at the Learning and Behaviour: Future Directions, Waipuna Conference Centre, Auckland.

Glynn, T. and Mcnaughton, S. (2002) 'Trust your own observations: assessment of reader and tutor behaviour in learning to read in English and Māori', *International Journal of Disability, Development and Education*, 49(2), 163–73.

Glynn, T., Mcnaughton, S., Robinson, V. and Quinn, M. (1979) *Remedial Reading at Home: Helping You to Help Your Child*, Wellington, NZCER.

Glynn, T., Moore, D., Gold, M., and Sheldon, L. (1992) *Support Teams for Regular Education*, Wellington, Research and Statistics Division, Ministry of Education.

Golding, W. (1954) *Lord of the Flies*, London, Faber and Faber.

Goleman, D. (2000) 'Leadership that gets results', *Harvard Business Review*, **March–April**, pp. 78–90.

Goodwin, W.L. and Goodwin, L.D. (1996) *Understanding Quantitative and Qualitative Research in Early Childhood Education*, New York, Teachers College Press.

Gottfredson, D.C., Gottfredson, G.D. and Skroban, S. (1993) 'Can prevention work where it is needed most?', *Evaluation Review*, 22(3), 315–40.

Grant, D. and Brooks, K. (2000) 'School exclusion of black pupils: an LEA response', *Support for Learning*, 15(1), 19–23.

Grant, L. and Evans A. (1994) *Principles of Applied Behavior Analysis*, New York, HarperCollins College Publishers.

Gray, B. (1984) *Helping Children to Become Language Learners in the Classroom*, Professional Services Branch of Northern Territory Department of Education, August 1984.

Gray, P., Miller, A. and Noakes, J. (1996) *Challenging Behaviour in Schools*, London, Routledge.

Greenhalgh, P. (1994) *Emotional Growth and Learning*, London, Routledge

Greeno, J.G. (1998) 'The situativity of knowing, learning and research', *American Psychologist*, **53**(1), 5–17.

Greenwood, C.R., Delquadri, J., Stanley, S.O., Terry, B. and Hall, R.V. (1985) 'Assessment of eco-behavioural interaction in school settings', *Behavioral Assessment*, **7**, 331–47.

Gross, J. (1996) 'The weight of the evidence: parental advocacy and resource allocation to children with statements of special educational need', *Support for Learning*, **11**(1), 3–8.

Habel, J., Bloom, L.A., Ray, M.S. and Bacon, E. (1999) 'Consumer reports: what students with behavior disorders say about school', *Remedial and Special Education*, **20**(2), 93–105.

Hallam, S. (1996) *Grouping Pupils by Ability: Selection, Streaming, Banding and Setting*, London, Institute of Education.

Hanko, G. (1985) *Special Needs in Ordinary Classrooms: An Approach to Teacher Support and Pupil Care in Primary and Secondary Schools*, Oxford, Basil Blackwell.

Hanko, G. (1993) 'The right to teach: but what are "Lee Canter's Children" learning?', *British Journal of Special Education*, **20**(2), 71.

Hanko, G. (1994) 'Discouraged children: when praise does not help', *British Journal of Special Education*, **21**(4), 166–8.

Hanko, G. (1995) *Special Needs in Ordinary Classrooms: From Staff Support to Staff Development*, London, David Fulton.

Hargreaves, D. and Hopkins, D. (1991) *The Empowered School: The Management and Practice of Development Planning*, London, Cassell.

Hargreaves, D.H. (1972) *Interpersonal Relations and Education*, London, Routledge & Kegan Paul.

Hargreaves, D.H. (1975) *Interpersonal relations and education*, 2nd edn, London, Routledge.

Hargreaves, D.H. (1982) *The Challenge for the Comprehensive School: Culture, Curriculum and Community*, London, Routledge.

Harlen, W. and James, M. (1997) 'Assessment and learning: differences and relationships between formative and summative assessment', *Assessment in Education*, **4**(3), 365–79.

Harlow, H.F. and Harlow, H.K. (1972) 'The affectional systems', in A. Schrier *et al.*, *Behaviour of Non-human Primates*, New York, Academic Press.

Harrington, C.B. and Merry, S.E. (1988) 'Ideological production: the making of community mediation', *Law and Society Review*, **22**, 709–35.

Harris, N., Eden, K. with Blair, A. (2000) *Challenges to School Exclusion*, London, RoutledgeFalmer.

Harris, S. (1976) 'Rational-emotive education and the human development program: a guidance study', *Elementary School Guidance and Counselling*, **10**, 113–22.

Harris-Hendriks, J. and Figueroa, J. (1995) *Black in White: The Caribbean Child in the UK Home*, London, Pitman.

Hart, S. (1995) 'Differentiation by task or differentiation by outcome?' in National Children's Bureau, *Schools' Special Educational Needs Policies Pack*, London, NCB.

Hastings, N. (1992) 'Questions of motivation', *Support for Learning*, 7(3), 135–7.

Heaton, P. (1996) *Parents in Need*, London, Whurr.

Helm, S. (2000) 'It's lawless out there', *The Guardian*, 29 November.

Hinshaw, S. (1994) *Attention Deficit Disorders and Hyperactivity in Children*, Thousand Oak, CA, Sage.

Hirschorn, L. (1998) *The Workplace Within: Psychodynamics of Organisational Life*, Cambridge, MA, MIT Press.

Hitchcock, G. and Hughes, D. (1995) *Research and the Teacher: A Qualitative Introduction to School-Based Research*, 2nd edn, London, Routledge.

Hobby, R. and Smith, F. (2002) *A National Development Agenda: What Does It Feel Like to Learn in Our Schools?*, London, The Hay Group.

Hoffman, L. (1981) *Foundations of Family Therapy*, New York, Basic Books.

Holmes, J. (1993) *John Bowlby and Attachment Theory*, London, Routledge.

Holowenko, H. and Pashute, K. (2000) 'ADHD in schools: a survey of prevalence and coherence across a local UK population', *Educational Psychology in Practice*, 16(2), 181–91.

Hopkins, B. (2004) 'Restorative justice in schools', in J. Wearmouth, Robin C. Richmond and Ted Glynn, *Addressing Pupils' Behaviour Responses at District, School and Individual Levels*, London, David Fulton.

Howard, P. (1999) 'Accepting diversity: refocusing interventions over EDB', in J. Visser and S. Rayner (eds), *Emotional and Behavioural Difficulties: A Reader*, Queensland, Lichfield.

Huberman, A.M. and Miles, M.B. (1994) 'Data management and analysis methods', in N.K. Denzin and Y.S. Lincoln (eds), *A Handbook of Qualitative Research*, Thousand Oaks, CA, Sage.

Hyland, J. (1993) *Yesterday's Answers: Development and Decline of Schools for Young Offenders*, London, Whiting and Birch/Social Care Association.

Ideus, K. (1995) 'Cultural foundations of ADHD: a sociological analysis' in P. Cooper and K. Ideus (eds), *Attention Deficit/Hyperactivity Disorder: Educational, Medical and Cultural Issues*, Maidstone, AWCEBD.

Inner London Education Authority (ILEA) (1985) *Educational Opportunities for All?*, Report of the Fish Committee, London, ILEA.

Ireland (1937) *Bunreacht na hEireann, Constitution of Ireland*, Dublin, The Stationery Office.

Ireland (1992) *Education for a Changing World*, Green Paper, Dublin, The Stationery Office.

Ireland (1993) *National Development Plan, 1994–1999*, Dublin, The Stationery Office.

Ireland (1999) *National Development Plan, 2000–2006*, Dublin, The Stationery Office.

Ireland (2000) *Learning Support Guidelines*, Dublin: Department of Education

Irish National Teachers Organization (INTO) (1994) *Poverty and Educational Disadvantage: Breaking the Cycle*, Dublin, INTO.

Irvine, J. (1990) *Black Students and School Failure*, New York, Praeger.

Jerram, H., Glynn, T. and Tuck, B. (1989) 'Responding to the message: providing a social context for children learning to write', *Educational Psychology*, 8, 31–40.

Johnson, D.W. and Johnson, R.T. (1989) 'Cooperative learning and mainstreaming' in R. Gaylord-Ross (ed.), *Integration Strategies for Students with Handicaps*, Baltimore, MD, Paul H. Brooks.

Johnson, P. (2002) 'Blunkett delay on detaining child criminals', *The Daily Telegraph*, 17 April.

Jordan, R. (1999) *Autistic Spectrum Disorders: An Introductory Handbook for Practitioners*, London, David Fulton.

Jourard, S.M. (1963) *Personal Adjustment: An Approach Through the Study of Healthy Personality*, New York, Macmillan.

Judd, J. (1999) 'Young, gifted, black – and a living reproach to our racist school system', *The Independent*, 11 March.

Jung, C.G. (1971) 'Psychological types', *Collected Works*, London, Routledge & Kegan Paul.

Kanner, L. (1943) 'Autistic disturbances of affective contact', *Nervous Child*, 2, 217–50.

Kant, E. (1952) *La religion dans les limites de la simple raison, 1793.* Trans. J. Gibelin. 2nd edn, Paris, Librairie Philosophique J. Vrin.

Karetu, T. (1990a) 'The clue to identity', *New Zealand Geographic*, 5, 112–17.

Karetu, T. (1990b) *The Dance of the Noble People*, Auckland, New Zealand, Auckland Publishers.

Kauffman, J. (1997) *Characteristics of Emotional and Behavioural Disorders of Children and Youth*, Columbus, OH, Merrill.

Kellaghan, T., Weir, S., OhUallacháin, S. and Morgan, M. (1995) *Educational Disadvantage in Ireland*, Dublin, Department of Education.

Kendrick, A. (1995) 'The integration of child care services in Scotland', *Children and Youth Services Review*, 17, 5–16, 619–35.

King, A. and Chantler, Z. (2002) 'The Western Primary School "Quiet Room" project', *British Journal of Special Education*, 29(4), 183–8.

Kitchener, K.S. (1984) 'Intuition, critical evaluation and ethical principles: the foundation for ethical decisions in counselling psychology', *Counselling Psychologist*, 12, 43–55.

Kolb, D.A. (1993) 'The process of experiential learning' in M. Thorpe, R. Edwards and A. Hanson (eds) *Culture and Processes of Adult Learning*, London, Routledge/Open University Press.

Korthagen, F.A.G. (1985) 'Reflective teaching and pre-service teacher education in the Netherlands', *Journal of Teacher Education*, 36(5), 11–15.

Ladson-Billings, G. (1995) 'Towards a theory of culturally relevant pedagogy', *American Educational Research Journal*, 32(3), 465–91.

Lange, D. (1988) *Tomorrow's Schools: The Reform of Education Administration in New Zealand Schools*, Wellington, New Zealand Government Printer.

Laslett, R. (1983) *Changing Perceptions of Maladjusted Children, 1945–1981*, London, AWMC.

Lather, P. (1991) *Getting Smart: Feminist Research and Pedagogy within the Postmodern*, London, Routledge.

Lauder, H. and Thrupp, M. (2004) 'Research on compositional effects: a theoretical as well as an empirical problem', paper presented at the symposium on 'Compositional Effects', AERA, San Diego.

Lave, J. and Wenger, E. (1991) *Situated Learning: Legitimate Peripheral Participation*, Cambridge, Cambridge University Press.

Lave, J. and Wenger, E. (1999) 'Learning and pedagogy in communities of practice', in J. Leach and B. Moon (eds), *Learners and Pedagogy*, London, Paul Chapman.

LaVigna, G.W. and Donnellan, A.M. (1986) *Alternatives to Punishment: Solving Behavior Problems with Non-Aversive Strategies*, New York, Irvington Publishers, Inc.

Leadbetter, J. and Leadbetter, P. (1993) *Special Children: Meeting the Challenge in the Primary School*, London, Cassell.

Lennox, D. (1991) *See Me After School*, London, David Fulton.

Leonard, D. (1990) 'The vocational preparation and training programme', in G. McNamara, K. Williams and D. Herron (eds), *Achievement and Aspiration: Curricular Initiatives in Irish Post-Primary Education in the 1980s*, Dublin, Drumcrondra Teachers Centre.

Levine, M. (1999) 'Rethinking bystander non-intervention: social categorization and the evidence of witnesses at the James Bulger murder trial', *Human Relations*, 52(9), 1133–55.

Lewin, K. (1935) *A Dynamic Theory of Personality*, New York, McGraw-Hill.

Lewin, K. (1936) *Principles of Topological Psychology*, New York, McGraw-Hill.

Lewin, K. (1946) 'Behavior and development as a function of the whole situation', in L. Carmichael (ed.) *Manual of Child Psychology*, New York, Wiley.

Lewis, A. (1995) *Special Needs Provision in Mainstream Primary Schools*, London, Trentham Books.

Lewis, A. (2002) 'Accessing, through research interviews, the views of children with difficulties in learning', *Support for Learning*, 17(3), 110–16.

Lindsay, G. (2004) 'Inclusive education: a critical perspective', in J. Wearmouth, T. Glynn, R.C. Richmond and M. Berryman (eds) *Inclusion and Behaviour Management in Schools: Issues and Challenges*, London, Fulton, pp. 265–85.

Literacy Task Force (1997) *The Implementation of the National Literacy Strategy*, London, DfEE.

Lloyd, G. (1997) 'Can the law support children's rights in school in Scotland and prevent the development of a climate of blame?', *Pastoral Care*, 15, 13–16.

Lloyd, G. (2000) 'Excellence for all children – false promises! The failure of current policy for inclusive education and implications for schooling in the 21st century', *International Journal of Inclusive Education*, 4(2), 133–51.

Lorenz, K. (1952) *King Solomon's Ring*, London, Methuen.

Lorenz, K. (1969) *On Aggression*, London, Methuen.

Mac an Ghaill, M. (1988) *Young, Gifted and Black*, Milton Keynes, Open University Press.

McCall, C. (2004) 'A whole-school approach to behaviour change at Tennyson High School, 1998–2003', in J. Wearmouth, R.C. Richmond and T. Glynn (eds) *Addressing Pupils' Behaviour: Responses at District, School and Individual Levels*, London, Fulton.

McDermott, R.P. (1999) 'On becoming labelled – the story of Adam', in P. Murphy (ed.) *Learners, Learning and Assessment*, London, Paul Chapman.

McDonnell, A. (1995) 'The ethos of Catholic voluntary secondary schools', vols 1 and 2, unpublished PhD thesis, University College Dublin.

Macfarlane, A. (1997) 'The Hikairo rationale: teaching students with emotional and behavioural difficulties; A bicultural approach', *Waikato Journal of Education*, 3, 135–68.

Macfarlane, A. (1998) 'The Hikairo Rationale teaching students with EBD', in J. Wearmouth, R.C. Richmond and T. Glynn (eds) *Addressing Pupils' Behaviour: Responses at District, School and Individual Levels*, London, Fulton, pp. 86–103.

Macfarlane, A. (2000a) 'Māori perspectives on development', in L. Bird and W. Drewery (eds) *Human Development in Aotearoa: A Journey through Life*, Auckland, McGraw-Hill Book Company.

Macfarlane, A. (2000b) 'The value of Māori ecologies in special education', in D. Fraser, R. Moltzen and K. Ryba (eds) *Learners with Special Needs in Aotearoa New Zealand*, 2nd edn, Palmerston North, New Zealand, Dunmore Press.

Macfarlane, A. (2000c) 'Listening to culture: Māori principles and practices applied to support classroom management, *SET Research Information for Teachers*, vol. 2, Wellington, New Zealand, pp. 23–8.

McKernan, J. (1996) *Curriculum Action Research*, London, Kogan Page.

McKinley, S. and Else, A. (2002) *Māori Parents and Education: Ko nga Matua Māori me te Matauranga*, Wellington, NZCER.

McLean, A. (2004) Audio interview in *E804 Managing behaviour in Schools*, Milton Keynes, Open University.

MacLeod, F. (2001) 'Towards inclusion – our shared responsibility for disaffected pupils', *British Journal of Special Education*, **28**(4), 191–4.

McLeod, J. (1998) *An Introduction to Counselling*, 2nd edn, Buckingham, Open University Press.

McNamara, G., Williams, K., Herron, D. (eds) (1990) *Achievement and Aspiration: Curricular Initiatives in Irish Post-Primary Education in the 1980s*, Dublin, Drumcondra Teachers Centre.

McNaughton, S. and Glynn, T. (1998) 'Effective collaboration: what teachers need to know about communities', paper presented at the New Zealand Council for Teacher Education, Hamilton, New Zealand.

McNiff, J. (1993) *Teaching as Learning*, London, Routledge.

McNiff, J., Lomax, P. and Whitehead, J. (1996) *You and Your Action Research Project*, London, Routledge/Hyde.

Macpherson, W. (1999) *The Stephen Lawrence Inquiry: Report of an Inquiry by Sir William Macpherson of Cluny*, Cm 426-I, London, The Stationery Office.

Mahrer, A. (1989) *The Integration of Psychotherapies: A Guide for Practicing Therapists*, New York, Human Sciences Press.

Maines, B. and Robinson, G. (1991) *Stamp Out Bullying*, Bristol, Lame Duck.

Majors, R. (2001) 'Understanding the current educational status of black children', in R. Majors (ed.) *Educating Our Black Children: New Directions and Approaches*, London, RoutledgeFalmer.

Majors, R. and Billson J.M. (1992) *Cool Pose: The Dilemmas of Black Manhood in America*, New York, Lexington Books.

Majors, R., Gillborn, D. and Sewell, T. (1998) 'The exclusion of black children: implications for a racialised perspective', *Multicultural Teacher*, **16**(3), 35–7.

Margerison, A. and Rayner, S. (1999) 'Troubling targets and school needs: assessing behaviour in the classroom context', *Support for Learning*, **14**(2), 87–92.

Maslow, A. (1968) *Toward a Psychology of Being*, New York, Van Nostrand Reinhold.

Mayhew, J. *et al.*, (1996) 'Preparing special educators to work with culturally and linguistically diverse exceptional learners: a rural case study', in D. Montgomery (ed.) *Rural Goals 2000: Building Programs that Work*, Oklahoma City, American Council on Rural Special Education.

Maykut, P. and Morehouse, R. (1994) *Beginning Qualitative Research: A Philosophic and Practical Guide*, London, Falmer Press.

Medcalf, J. (1992) *Peer Tutoring Programme for Written Language: Helping Your Friend to Write*, Hastings, Psychological Service.

Mehan, H. (1996) 'The politics of representation', in S. Chaiklin and J. Lave (eds) *Understanding Practice: Perspectives on Activity and Context*, Cambridge, Cambridge University Press.

Meichenbaum, D. and Turk, D. (1976) 'The cognitive-behavioural management of anxiety, anger and pain', in P.O. Davidson (ed.) *The Behavioural Management of Anxiety, Anger and Pain*, New York, Brunner/Mazel.

Merrett, F. (1985) *Encouragement Works Better than Punishment*, Birmingham, Positive Products.

Milgram, S. (1963) 'Behavioural study of obedience', *Journal of Abnormal and Social Psychology*, 67, 371–8.

Milgram, S. (1974) *Obedience to Authority: An Experimental View*, New York, Harper and Row.

Mill, J.S. (1868) *Considerations on Representative Government*, London, Longmans, Green.

Miller, C., Lacey, P. and Layton, L. (2003) 'Including children with special educational needs in the Literacy hour: a continuing challenge', *British Journal of Special Education*, 30(1), 13–20.

Millham, S., Bullock, R. and Cherrett, P. (1975) *After Grace – Teeth*, London, Chaucer.

Ministry of Education (1955) *Report on the Committee on Maladjusted Children* (The Underwood Report) London, HMSO.

Ministry of Education (MoE) (1997) *Special Education 2000*, Wellington, New Zealand, Ministry of Education.

Ministry of Education (MoE) (1998a) *Special Education 2000 Update*, Wellington, New Zealand, Ministry of Education.

Ministry of Education (MoE) (1998b) *The IEP Guidelines. Planning for Students with Special Educational Needs*, Wellington, New Zealand, Ministry of Education.

Ministry of Education (MoE) (2001a) *Educational Statistics for July 1, 2001*, Wellington, New Zealand, Ministry of Education.

Ministry of Education (MoE) (2001b) *National Administration Guidelines*, Wellington, New Zealand, Ministry of Education.

Ministry of Education (MoE) (2003a) *Statement of Intent 2003–2008*, Wellington, New Zealand, Ministry of Education.

Ministry of Education (2003b) *Nga haeata màtauranga: Annual Report on Māori Education 2001/2002 and Direction for 2003*, Wellington, The Ministry of Education, Group Māori.

Minuchin, S. (1974) *Families and Family Therapy*, Cambridge, MA, Harvard University Press.

Mitchell, D. (1999) 'Special education in New Zealand: a decade of change', *New Zealand Journal of Educational Studies*, 34(1), 199–210.

Mittler, P. (2000) *Working towards Inclusive Education: Social Contexts*, London, Fulton.

Molnar, A. and Lindquist, B. (1989) *Changing Problem Behaviour in Schools*, San Francisco, Jossey-Bass.

Moore, D. (2004) 'Behaviour in context: functional assessment of disruptive behaviour in classrooms', in J. Wearmouth, R.C. Richmond and T. Glynn (eds) *Addressing Pupils' Behaviour: Responses at District, School and Individual Levels*, London, Fulton, pp. 287–309.

Moore, D., anderson, A., Timperley, H., Glynn, T., McFarlane, A., Brown, D. and Thomson, C. (1999) *Caught between Stories: Special Education in New Zealand*, Wellington, NZCER.

Moore, D., Glynn, T. and Gold, M. (1993) 'Support teams in New Zealand schools: a national survey of establishment and practice', *International Journal of Disability, Development and Education*, 40(3), 193–204.

Moore, D.W. and Sheldon, L.L. (1989) 'What are support teams and what have they to do with classroom teachers?', paper presented at National Support Teams Conference.

Morgan, M. (2000) 'Levels of literacy in Ireland: the educational system and the general population', in D. Bates, C. Galvin, D. Swan and K. Williams (eds) *The Teaching and Usage of English in Contemporary Ireland*, Dublin, University College Dublin.

Mosley, J. (1996) *Quality Circle Time in the Primary Classroom: Your Essential Guide to Enhancing Self-Esteem, Self-Discipline and Positive Relationships*, Cambridge, LDA.

Mosley, J. (1998) *The Whole School Quality Circle Time Model*, Trowbridge, All Round Success.

Mosley, J. (undated) *Quality Circle Time: The Heart of the Curriculum*, Trowbridge, Jenny Mosley Consultancies.

Mosley, J. and Tew, M. (1999) *Quality Circle Time in the Secondary School: A Handbook of Good Practice*, London, David Fulton.

Munn, P., Cullen, M.A., Johnstone, M. and Lloyd, G. (2004) 'Exclusion from school: a view from Scotland of policy and practice', in J. Wearmouth, T. Glynn, R.C. Richmond and M. Berryman (eds) *Inclusion and Behaviour Management in Schools: Issues and Challenges*, London, Fulton, pp. 68–88.

Murphy, T. (1998) 'A preliminary evaluation of the early start intervention programme for pre-school children in disadvantaged areas in the Republic of Ireland', unpublished MEd thesis, University College Dublin.

National Assembly for Wales (NAW) (1998) *The Use of Reasonable Force to Control or Restrain Pupils*, Circular No. 37/98, http://www.wales.gov.uk/subieducation training/content/circulars/3798/3798-3.htm (accessed 19 March 2004).

National Assembly for Wales (NAW) (2001) *Pupil Support and Social Exclusion*, Circular No. 3/99, Cardiff, NAW.

National Autistic Society (2004) web site http://www.nas.org.uk/nas/jsp/polopoly. jps?d=211 (accessed 19 January 2004).

National Council of Churches (1996) *Restoring Justice*, Louisville, KY, Presbyterian Media Services.

National Education Convention Secretariat (1994) *Report on the National Education Convention*, Dublin.

Neisworth, J.T. and Bagnato, S.I. (1992) 'The case against intelligence testing in early intervention', *Topics in Early Childhood Special Education*, 12(1), 1–20.

Nind, M. and Kellett, M. (2002) 'Responding to individuals with severe learning difficulties and stereotyped behaviour: challenges for an inclusive era', *European Journal of Special Needs Education*, 17(3), 265–82.

Nisbett, R.E., Caputo, C., Legant, P. and Marcek, J. (1973) 'Behaviour as seen by the actor and as seen by the observer', *Journal of Personality and Social Psychology*, 27, 157–64.

Norwich, B. (1996) *Special Needs Education: Inclusive Education or Just Education for All?*, London, Institute of Education at London University.

Norwich, B. (1999) 'The connotation of special education labels for professionals in the field', *British Journal of Special Education*, 26(4), 179–83.

Norwich, B., Cooper, P. and Maras, P. (2002) 'Attentional and activity difficulties: findings from a national study', *Support for Learning*, 17(4), 182–6.

Nugent, W.R. and Paddock, J.B. (1995) 'The effect of victim-offender mediation on severity of reoffense', *Mediation Quarterly*, 12, 353–67.

Oakley, A. (2002) 'Social science and evidence-based everything: the case of education', *Educational Review*, 54(3), 277–86.

O'Connor, T. and Colwell, J. (2002) 'The effectiveness and rational of the "nurture group" approach to helping children with emotional and behavioural difficulties who remain within mainstream education', *British Journal of Special Education*, 29(2), 96–100.

Office for Standards in Education (OFSTED) (1996) *Exclusions from Secondary Schools 1995/6*, London, OFSTED.

Office for Standards in Education (OFSTED) (1997) *The SEN Code of Practice: Two Years on*, London, OFSTED.

Office for Standards in Education (OFSTED) (1999a) *Raising the Attainment of Minority Ethnic Pupils: School and LEA's Response*, London, OFSTED.

Office for Standards in Education (OFSTED) (1999b) *Principles into Practice: Effective Education for Pupils with Emotional and Behavioural Difficulties*, London, OFSTED.

Office for Standards in Education (OFSTED) (1999c) *Handbook for Inspecting Special Schools and Pupil Referral Units with Guidance on Self-Evaluation*, London, The Stationery Office.

Office for Standards in Education (OFSTED) (1999d) *Handbook for Inspecting Primary and Nursery Schools with Guidance on Self-Evaluation*, London, The Stationery Office.

Office for Standards in Education (OFSTED) (2000) *Strategies to Promote Educational Inclusion: Improving City Schools*, London, OFSTED.

Office for Standards in Education (OFSTED) (2001) *Improving Attendance and Behaviour in Secondary Schools*, London, OFSTED.

Ogbu, J.U. (1997) 'Understanding the school performance of urban blacks: some essential background knowledge' in H. Walberg, O. Reyes and R. Weissburg (eds) *Children and Youth: Interdisciplinary Perspectives*, London, Sage.

Ogilvie, V. (1957) *The English Public School*, London, Batsford.

Olweus, D. (1973) *Hackkycklingar och översittare: Forskning om skolmobbning* [Whipping boys and bullies: research on school bullying], Stockholm: Almqvist & Wiksell.

Olweus, D. (1978) *Aggression in the Schools: Bullies and Whipping Boys*, Washington, DC, Hemisphere.

Olweus, D. (1993) *Bullying at School*, Cambridge, MA, Blackwell.

Olweus, D. (1999) 'Sweden', in P.K. Smith, Y. Morita, J. Junger-Tas, D. Olweus, R. Catalano and P.T. Slee (eds) *The Nature of School Bullying: A Cross-National Perspective*, London, Routledge.

Open University (2001a) *Study Guide, E831 Professional Development for Social Educational Needs Co-ordinators*, Milton Keynes, Open University.

Open University (2001b) Video Programme 5, *E831 Professional Development for Social Educational Needs Co-ordinators*, Milton Keynes, Open University.

Open University (2002) *Study Guide, E801 Difficulties in Literacy Development*, Milton Keynes, Open University.

Open University (2003) *Study Guide, E829 Developing Inclusive Curricula: equality and diversity in education*, Milton Keynes, Open University.

Open University (2004) *Study Guide, E804 Managing Behaviour in Schools*, Milton Keynes, Open University.

Osborne, J. (2004) 'Academic disidentification: unravelling underachievement among Black boys', in J. Wearmouth, R.C. Richmond, T. Glynn and M. Berryman (eds) *Understanding Pupil Behaviour in Schools: A Diversity of Approaches*, London, Fulton, pp. 51–66.

Ostler, C. (1991) *Dyslexia: A Parents' Survival Guide*, Godalming, Ammonite Books

Paige-Smith, A. unpublished manuscript.

Palmer, C., Redfern, R. and Smith, K. (1994) 'The four P's of policy', *British Journal of Special Education*, **21**(1), 4–6.

Parsons, C. (1999) 'School inclusion and school improvement', *Support for Learning*, **14**(4), 179–83.

Parsons, C. and Howlett, K. (2000) *Investigating the Re-integration of Permanently Excluded Pupils in England*, Cambridge, Include.

Peck, S. (1978) 'Child–child discourse in second language acquisition', in E. Hatch (ed.) *Second Language Acquisition: A Book of Readings*, London, Sage, pp. 383–400.

Peeters, T. and Gilberg C. (1999) in Roth, I. (2002) 'The autistic spectrum: from theory to practice', in N. Brace and H. Westcott (eds) *Applying Psychology*, Milton Keynes, Open University, pp. 243–315.

Pere, R. (1994) *Ako: Concepts and Learning in the Maori Tradition*, Wellington, Te Kohanga Reo.

Peters, R.S. (1966) *Ethics and Education*, London, Allen and Unwin.

Peters, R.S. (ed.) (1967) *The Concept of Education*, London, Routledge & Kegan Paul.

Pikas, A. (1989) 'The common concern method for the treatment of mobbing', in E. Roland and E. Munthe (eds), *Bullying: An International Perspective*, London, Fulton.

Pitchford, M. (2004) 'An introduction to multi-element planning for primary aged children', in J. Wearmouth, R.C. Richmond and T. Glynn (eds) *Addressing Pupils' Behaviour: Responses at District, School and Individual Levels*, London, Fulton, pp. 310–27.

Poulou, M. and Norwich, B. (2002) 'Cognitive, emotional and behavioural responses to students with emotional and behavioural difficulties: a model of decision-making', *British Educational Research Journal*, **28**(1), 111–38.

Power, T. and Bartholomew, K. (1985) 'Getting uncaught in the middle: a case study in family-school system consultation', *School Psychology Review*, 14(2), 222–9.

Pranis, K. (1996) 'A hometown approach to crime', *State Government News*, 14–16, 29.

Prendergast, M., Taylor, E., Rapaport, J.L., Bartko, J., Donnelly, M., Kametkin, A., Ahearn, M.B., Dunn, G. and Weiselburg, H.M. (1998) 'The diagnosis of childhood hyperactivity, a US–UK cross national study of DSMIII and ICD9', *Journal of Child Psychology and Psychiatry*, 29, 289–300.

Pugh, G. (1987) 'Portage in perspective: parental involvement in pre-school programmes', in R. Hedderty and K. Jennings (eds) *Extending and Developing Portage*, Windsor, NFER-Nelson.

Punch, M. (1994) 'Politics and ethics in qualitative research', in N.K. Denzin and Y.S. Lincoln (eds) *A Handbook of Qualitative Research*, Thousand Oaks, CA, Sage.

Qualifications and Curriculum Authority (QCA) (2001) *Supporting School Improvement: Emotional and Behavioural Development*, London, QCA.

Quest Rapuara (1992) *Cultural Identity: Whakamana Tangata: A Resource for Educators*, Wellington, New Zealand, Quest Rapuara.

Quicke, J. (1996) 'The reflective practitioner and teacher education: an answer to critics', *Teachers and Teaching: Theory and Practice*, 2(1), 11–22.

Radford, J. (2000) 'Values into practice: developing whole school behaviour policies', *Support for Learning*, 15(2), 86–9.

Rampton, A. (1981) *West Indian Children in Our Schools*, Cmnd 8273, London, HMSO.

Randall, P.E. (1991) *The Prevention of School Based Bullying*, Hull, University of Hull.

Rapport, M.D., Denney, C., DuPaul, G.J. and Gardner, M.J. (1994) 'Attention deficit disorder and methylphenidate: normalization rates, clinical effectiveness and response prediction in 76 children', *Journal of the American Academy of Child's Adolescent Psychiatry*, 32, 333–42.

Ravenette, A.T. (1984) 'The recycling of maladjustment', *AEP Journal*, 6(3), 18–27.

Ravitch, D. (1999) 'Physicians leave education researchers for dead', *Sydney Morning Herald*, 22 February.

Renwick, F. and Spalding, B. (2002) '"A Quiet Place" project: an evaluation of early therapeutic intervention within mainstream schools', *British Journal of Special Education*, 29(3), 144–9.

Restorative Practices Development Team (2003) *Restorative Practices for Schools*, Hamilton, NZ, University of Waikato.

Rex, J. and Tomlinson, S. (1979) *Colonial Immigrants in a British City: A City Analysis*, London, Routledge & Kegan Paul.

Richards, I.C. (1999) 'Inclusive schools for pupils with emotional and behaviour difficulties', *Support for Learning*, 14(3), 99–103.

Richardson, R. (1990) 'The evolution of reflective teaching and teacher education', in R.T. Clift, W.R. Houston and M.C. Pugach (eds) *Encouraging Reflective Practice in Teacher Education*, New York, Teachers' College Press.

Riddell, S. (2000) 'Special educational needs and competing policy frameworks in England and Scotland', *Journal of Educational Policy*, 15(6), 621–35.

Riddick, B. (1996) *Living with Dyslexia*, London and New York, Routledge.

Rigby, K. (1997) 'What children tell us about bullying in schools', *Children Australia*, **22**(2), 28–34.

Rigby, K. (2002) *New Perspectives on Bullying*, London, Jessica Kingsley.

Ritzer, G. (1980) *Sociology: A Multiple Paradigm Science*, rev. edn, Boston, Allyn and Bacon.

Rivers, I. (2000) 'Social exclusion, absenteeism and sexual minority youth', *Support for Learning*, **15**(1), 13–18.

Robinson, G. and Maines, B. (1994) 'Who manages pupil behaviour? Assertive discipline: a blunt instrument for a fine task', *Pastoral Care in Education*, **12**(3), 30–5.

Rogers, B. (1994) 'Teaching positive behaviour in behaviourally disordered students in primary schools', *Support for Learning*, **9**(4), 166–70.

Rogers, C.R. (1942) *Counseling and Psychotherapy*, Boston, Houghton Mifflin.

Rogers, C.R. (1957) 'The necessary and sufficient conditions of therapeutic personality change', *Journal of Consulting Psychology*, **21**, 95–103.

Rogers, W. (1991) *You Know the Fair Rule*, Harlow, Longman.

Rogers, W. (1994a) *The Language of Discipline*, Plymouth, Northcote House.

Rogers, W. (1994b) *Behaviour Recovery: A Whole School Approach for Behaviourally Disordered Children*, Melbourne, Australian Council for Educational Research.

Rogers, W. (2002) *Classroom Behaviour*, London, Paul Chapman.

Rogoff, B. (1990) *Apprenticeship in Thinking*, Oxford, Oxford University Press.

Rose, R. (2002) 'Teaching as a "research-based profession": encouraging practitioner research in special education', *British Journal of Special Education*, **29**(1), 44–8.

Rosenthal, R. and Jacobson, L. (1968) *Pygmalion in the Classroom*, New York, Holt, Rinehart and Winston.

Rothman, D. (1971) *The Discovery of the Asylum: Social Order and Disorder in the New Republic*, Boston, Little Brown.

Rouse, M. and Florian, L. (1997) 'Inclusive education in the market place', *International Journal of Inclusive Education*, **1**(4), 323–36.

Rowe, D. (1994) *Time on our Side*, London, HarperCollins.

Royal Tangaere, A. (1997) *Learning Māori Together: Kōhanga Reo and Home*, Wellington, New Zealand, NZCER.

Rudd, J. (1972) *National School Terminal Leavers*, Dublin, Gemaine (Mimeo).

Russell, P. (1997) 'Parents as partners: some early impressions of the impact of the Code of Practice', in S. Wolfendale (ed.) *Working with Parents after the Code of Practice*, London, Fulton.

Rutter, M. *et al.* (1979) *Fifteen Thousand Hours: Secondary Schools and their Effects on Children*, London, Open Books.

Ryan, A. (1996) 'Teachers, travellers and education: a sociological perspective', unpublished MEd thesis, University College Dublin.

Ryba, K. and Annan, J. (2000) 'Students with intellectual disabilities', 2nd edn, in D. Fraser, R. Moltzen and K. Ryba (eds) *Learners with Special Needs in Aotearoa New Zealand*, Palmerston North, New Zealand, Dunmore Press.

Salmon, P. (1998a) *Psychology for Teachers: An Alternative Approach*, London, Hutchinson.

Salmon, P. (1998b) *Life at School*, London, Constable.

Sanders, D. and Hendry, L. (1997) *New Perspectives on Disaffection*, London, Cassell.

Sankey, S. (2000) Video programme 5 in *E831 Professional Development for Special Educational Needs Co-ordinators*, Milton Keynes, Open University.

Schachar, R. (1991) 'Childhood hyperactivity', *Journal of Child Psychology and Psychiatry*, **32**, 155–92.

Schön, D. (1983) *The Reflective Practitioner: How Professionals Think in Action*, New York, Basic Books.

Schön, D. (1987) *Educating the Reflective Practitioner*, London, Jossey-Bass.

Schweigert, F.J. (1999) 'Moral behaviour in victim offender conferencing', *Criminal Justice Ethics*, **Summer/Fall**, 29–40.

Scottish Executive (1999) *Social Justice: A Scotland Where Everyone Matters*, Edinburgh, Scottish Executive.

Scottish Executive (2001) *Better Behaviour – Better Learning: Report of the Discipline Task Group*, Edinburgh, Scottish Executive.

Scottish Executive Education Department (SEED) (2001) *Assessing our Children's Educational Needs: The Way Forward?*, Edinburgh, SEED.

Seligman, A.B. (1995/1996) 'The changing precontractual frame of modern society', *The Responsive Community*, **6**, 28–40.

Selvini, M. (1988) *The Work of Mara Selvini-Palazzoli*, New York, Aroson.

Selvini-Palazzoli, M. *et al.* (1973) *Paradox and Counterparadox*, New York, Aronson.

Sewell, T. (1997) *Black Masculinities and Schooling: How Black Boys Survive Modern Schooling*, Stoke on Trent, Trentham Books.

Shapiro, S. and Cole, L. (1994) *Behaviour Change in the Classroom: Self-Management Interventions*, New York, Guilford Press.

Sharron, H. (1995) 'Behaviour drugs – headteachers speak out', *Special Children*, **April**, 10–13.

Sheehy, K. (2004) 'Approaches to autism', in J. Wearmouth, R.C. Richmond and T. Glynn (eds) *Addressing Pupils' Behaviour: Responses at District, School and Individual Levels*, London, Fulton, pp. 338–56.

Silverman, D. (2000) *Doing Qualitative Research: A Practical Handbook*, London, Sage.

Simmons, K. (1996) 'In defence of entitlement', *Support for Learning*, **11**(3), 105–8.

Skinner, B.F. (1938) *The Behaviour of Organisms*, New York, Appleton Century Crofts.

Skinner, B.F. (1953) *Science and Human Behaviour*, New York, Macmillan.

Slavin, R.E. (1987) *Co-operative Learning – Student Teams: What Research Says to the Teacher*, Washington, DC, National Educational Association.

Slee, P.T. (1995) 'Peer victimization and its relationship to depression among Australian primary school students', *Personality and Individual Differences*, **18**(1), 57–62.

Smith, C. (2004) 'Confrontation in the classroom', in J. Wearmouth, R.C. Richmond and T. Glynn (eds) *Addressing Pupils' Behaviour: Responses at District, School and Individual Levels*, London, Fulton, pp. 248–66.

Smith, C.J. and Laslett, R. (1993) *Effective Classroom Management: A Teacher's Guide*, 2nd edn, London, Routledge.

Smith, G. (1990) 'Taha Māori: Pakeha capture', in J. Codd, R. Harker and R. Nash (eds) *Political Issues in New Zealand Education*, Palmerston North, Dunmore Press, pp. 183–97.

Smith, G. (1995) 'Whakaoho whanau: new formations of whanau as an innovative intervention into Māori cultural and educational crisis', *He Pukenga Korero: A Journal of Māori Studies*, **1**(1), 18–35.

Smith, P.K. and Sharp, S. (eds) (1994) *School Bullying: Insights and Perspectives*, London, Routledge.

Social Exclusion Unit (SEU) (1998a) *Truancy and School Exclusion*, London, The Stationery Office.

Social Exclusion Unit (SEU) (1998b) *Bringing Britain Together: A National Strategy for Urban Renewal*, London, SEU.

Social Exclusion Unit (SEU) (2003) 'What is the SEU?' http://www.socialexclusion unit.gov.uk/what_is_SEU.htm (accessed 27 May 2003).

Spalding, B. (2000) 'The contribution of "A Quiet Place" to early intervention strategies for children with emotional and behavioural difficulties in mainstream schools', *British Journal of Special Education*, **27**(3), 129–34.

Special Education Services (undated) *Eliminating Violence – Managing Anger – Processes and Strategies for Peaceful Relationships and Safe Schools, Teachers' Resource Handbook*, Business Development Unit, Special Education Service, Manukau North.

Sproson, B. (2003) 'Solution or smokescreen? The use of further education colleges in making Key Stage 4 provision for difficult to manage (D2M) students', *Support for Learning*, **18**(1), 18–23.

Sproson, B. (2004) 'Behaviour support from an external agency to mainstream schools: policy and practice', in J. Wearmouth, T. Glynn, R.C. Richmond and M. Berryman (eds) *Inclusion and Behaviour Management in Schools: Issues and Challenges*, London, Fulton, pp. 89–100.

Steele, C. (1992) 'A threat in the air: how stereotypes shape intellectual identity and performance', *American Psychologist*, **52**, pp. 613–29.

Sulzer-Azaroff, B. and Meyer, G.R. (1977) *Applying Behavior Analysis Procedures with Children and Youth*, New York, Harcourt Brace College Publishers.

Sutton, J., Smith, P.K. and Swettenham, J. (1999) 'Social cognition and bullying: social inadequacy or skilled manipulation', *British Journal of Developmental Psychology*, **17**, 435–50.

Swan, T.D. (1978) *Reading Standards in Irish Schools*, Dublin, The Educational Company.

Swann, Lord (1985) *Education for All. Final report of the Committee of Enquiry into the Education of Children from Ethnic Minority Groups*, Cmnd 9453, London, HMSO.

Swanson, J.M., McBurnett, K., Wigal, T., and Pfiffner, L.J. *et al.* (1993) 'Effect of stimulant medication on children with attention deficit disorder: a "review of reviews"', *Exceptional Children*, **60**(2), 154–62.

Swinson, J. and Cording, M. (2002) 'Assertive discipline in a school for pupils emotional and behavioural difficulties', *British Journal of Special Education*, **29**(2), 72–5.

Tattum, D.P. and Lane, D.A. (eds) (1989) *Bullying in Schools*, London, Trentham Books.

Taylor, E. (1994) 'Syndrome of attention deficit and overactivity', in M. Rutter, E. Taylor and L. Hersov (eds) *Child and Adolescent Psychiatry: Modern Approaches*, 3rd edn, Oxford, Blackwell Scientific Publications.

TEACCH (1998) 'Treatment and education of autistic and related communication handicapped children', http://www.unc.edu/depts/teacch/teacch.htm (accessed 9 December 2003).

Teacher Training Agency (TTA) (1999) *National Special Educational Needs Specialist Standards*, London, TTA.

Teacher Training Agency (TTA) (2002a) *National Special Educational Needs Standards: Identifying Your Training Needs*, London, TTA.

Teacher Training Agency (TTA) (2002B) *Qualifying to Teach: Handbook of Guidance*, London, TTA.

Tellier-Robinson, D. (1999) 'The experiences of Portuguese-speaking families with special needs children as related by their mothers: an ethnographic interview', paper presented at the annual meeting of the National Association for Bilingual Education, Denver, Colorado.

Tett, L., Munn, P., Blair, A., Kay, H., Martin, I., Martin, J. and Ranson, S. (2001) 'Collaboration between schools and community education agencies in tackling social exclusion', *Research Papers in Education*, 16(1), 3–21.

Tew, M. (1998) 'Circle time: a much neglected resource in secondary schools', *Pastoral Care*, **Sept.**, 18–27.

Thomas, G. and Loxley, A. (2001) *Deconstructing Special Education and Constructing Inclusion*, Buckingham, Open University Press.

Thomas, J.D. and Glynn, E. (1976) *Mangere Guidance Unit: Evaluation of Behavioural Programmes*, Final report to the Director General of Education, Auckland, New Zealand, Auckland University.

Thomson, C., Brown, D., Jones, E. and Manins, E. (2000) 'The development of resource teachers in New Zealand. A quarter century of paradigm change', in F. Livingstone (ed.) *New Zealand Annual Review of Education*, vol. 10, 79–98, Wellington, School of Education, Victoria University, pp. 79–98.

Thomson, C., Brown, D., Jones, L., Walker, J., Moore, D.W., Anderson, A., Davies, T., Medcalf, J. and Glynn, T. (2001) 'Resource teachers learning and behaviour: collaborative problem solving to support inclusion', paper presented at the International Conference on Special Education 2001: Interaction and Collaboration, Antalya, Turkey.

Thomson, C., Brown, D., Jones, L., Walker, J., Moore, D., Anderson, A., Davies, T., Medcalf, J., and Glynn, T. (2003) 'Resource teachers learning and behaviour: collaborative problem solving to support inclusion', *Journal of Positive Behavioral Interventions*, 5(2), 101–11.

Thousand, J., Rosenberg, R.L., Bishop, K.D., and Villa, R.A. (1997) 'The evolution of secondary inclusion', *Remedial and Special Education*, 18(5), 270–84.

Thrupp, M., Lauder, H. and Robinson, T. (2002) 'School composition and peer effects', *International Journal of Educational Research*, 37(5), 438–504.

Timutimu-Thorpe, H. (1994) 'Ngā tangi a te whānau: raising a child who has a disability', in K. Ballard (ed.) *Disability, Family, Whānau and Society*, Palmerston North, New Zealand, The Dunmore Press.

Tod, J., Castles, F. and Blamires, M. (1998) *Implementing Effective Practice*, London, Fulton.

Tom, A. R. (1985) 'Inquiring into inquiry-oriented teacher education', *Journal of Teacher Education*, 36(5), 35–44.

Tomlinson, S. (1981) *Educational Subnormality: A Study in Decision-Making*, London, Routledge.

Tomlinson, S. (1982) *A Sociology of Special Education*, London, Routledge.

Tomlinson, S. (1985) 'The expansion of special education', *Oxford Review of Education*, 11(2), 157–65.

Tomlinson, S (1988) 'Why Johnny can't read: critical theory and special education', *European Journal of Special Needs Education*, 3(1), 45–58.

Tomlinson, S. (2001) 'Sociological perspectives on special and inclusive education', *Support for Learning*, 16(4), 191–2.

Toothill, R. and Spalding, B. (2000) 'How effective can reintegration be for children with emotional and behavioural difficulties?', *Support for Learning*, 15(3), 111–12.

Travell, C. (1999) 'Emotional and behavioural difficulties: perspectives on perspectives', in J. Visser and S. Rayner (eds) *Emotional and Behavioural Difficulties: A Reader*, Staffordshire, QEd.

Troyna, B. and Hatcher, R. (1992) *Racism in Children's Lives: A Study of Mainly White Primary Schools*, London, Routledge.

Umbreit, M.S. and Coates, R.B. (1992) 'Victim–Offender Mediation: An Analysis of Programs in Four States of the U.S., St Paul, MN, Minnesota Citizens Council on Crime and Justice.

United Nations Education Service Children's Organisation (UNESCO) (1994) *The UNESCO Salamanca Statement and Framework for Action on Special Needs Education*, Paris, UNESCO.

Upton, G. and Cooper, P. (1990) 'A new perspective on behaviour problems in schools: the ecosystemic approach', *Maladjustment and Therapeutic Education*, 8(1), 3–18.

Visser, J. (2001) 'Aspects of physical provision for pupils with emotional and behavioural difficulties', *Support for Learning*, 16(2), 64–8.

Visser, J., Cole, T. and Daniels, H. (2002) 'Inclusion for the difficult to include', *Support for Learning*, 17(1), 23–6.

Visser, J. and Stokes, S. (2003) 'Is education ready for the inclusion of pupils with emotional and behavioural difficulties: a rights perspective?', *Educational Review*, 55(1), 65–75.

von Bertalanffy, L. (1950) 'An outline of general systems theory', *British Journal for the Philosophy of Science*, 1, 139–64.

von Bertalanffy, L. (1968) *General Systems Theory*, New York, Brazillier.

Vulliamy, G. and Webb, R. (eds) (1992) Teacher Research and *Special Educational Needs*, London, David Fulton.

Wade, b. and Moore, m. (1993) *Experiencing Special Education: What Young People with Special Needs Can Tell Us*, Buckingham, Open University Press.

Watkins, C. and Wagner, P. (1995) 'School behaviour and special educational needs – what's the link?' in National Children's Bureau, *Discussion Papers 1:, Schools' Special Educational Needs Policies Pack*, London, NCB.

Watkins, C. and Wagner, P. (2000) *Improving School Behaviour*, London, Paul Chapman.

Watson, J. (2001) 'Social constructivism in the classroom', *Support for Learning*, 16(3), 140–7.

Watt, D., Sheriffe, G. and Majors, R. (1999) 'Mentoring black male pupils', unpublished manuscript, Manchester, City College.

Watzlawick, P., Weakland, J. and Fisch, R. (1974) *Change: Principles of Problem Formation and Resolution*, New York, Norton.

Wayson, W.W., de Voss, G.G., Kaeser, S.G., Lasley, T. and Pinnel, G.S. (1982) *Handbook for Developing Schools with Good Discipline*, Bloomington, IN, Phi Delta Kappa.

Wearmouth, J. (1999) 'Another one flew over: '"maladjusted" Jack's perception of his label', *British Journal of Special Education*, 26(1), 15–23.

Wearmouth, J. (2000) *Special Educational Provision: Meeting the Challenges in Schools*, London, Hodder.

Wearmouth, J. (2002) 'Exploring the "Problem Space" in special educational provision in mainstream schools', unpublished PhD dissertation, The Open University.

Wearmouth, J. (2003) 'Interviewing disaffected students with "Talking Stones"', paper given at BERA Annual Conference, Edinburgh, September.

Wearmouth, J. (2004a) 'Issues in addressing children's difficulties in literacy development through family-school partnerships', *Curriculum Journal*, 15(1), 5–18.

Wearmouth, J. (2004b) '"Talking Stones", an interview technique for disaffected young people', *Journal of Pastoral Care in Education*, 22(2), 7–13.

Wearmouth, J. and Reid, G. (2002) 'Issues for assessment and planning of teaching and learning', in G. Reid and J. Wearmouth (eds) *Dyslexia and Literacy: Theory and Practice*, Chichester, Wiley.

Wedell, K. (2000) Audio interview in Open University, *E831 Professional Development for Special Educational Needs Coordinators*, Milton Keynes, Open University.

Wenger, E. (1999) *Communities of Practice: Learning, Meaning and Identity*, Cambridge, Cambridge University Press.

Westera, J. and Moore, D. (1995) 'Reciprocal teaching of reading comprehension in a New Zealand high school', *Psychology in Schools*, 81, 283–93.

Wexler, P. (1987) *Social Analysis of Education: After the New Sociology*, London, Routledge & Kegan Paul.

Wheldall, K. (1982) 'A positive approach to classroom discipline', in K. Wheldall and R. Riding (eds) *Psychological Aspects of Learning and Teaching*, London, Croom Helm.

Wheldall, K. and Glynn, T. (1989) *Effective Classroom Learning*, Oxford, Blackwell.

Wheldall, K., Merrett, F. and Glynn, T. (eds) (1986) *Behaviour Analysis in Educational Psychology*, London, Croom Helm, in association with Positive Products.

White, J. and Cones, J. (1999) *Black Man Emerging*, New York, Routledge.

Wilde, J. (1994) 'The effects of the let's get rational board game on rational thinking, depression and self-acceptance in adolescents', *Journal of Rational-Emotive and Cognitive-Behaviour Therapy*, 12, 189–96.

Wilde, J. (1995) *Anger Management in Schools: Alternatives to Student Violence*, Lancaster, PA, Technomic Publishing Co.

Wilde, J. (2001) 'Interventions for children with anger problems', *Journal of Rational–Emotive and Cognitive Behaviour Therapy*, 19(3), 191–7.

Wilkie, M. (1999) *So What's so Special about Special Education for Māori?*, New Zealand Council for Educational Research, Wellington, Ministry of Education.

Williams, H. and Birmingham City Council Education Department (1998) *Behaviour in Schools: Framework for Intervention*, Birmingham, Birmingham City Council Education Department.

Wilson, M. (1985) 'Teaching as therapy?', *Journal of Educational Therapy*, **1**(1), 75–86.

Wilson, M. (1996) 'Asking questions', in R.J. Sapsford and V. Jupp (eds) *Data Collection and Analysis*, London, Sage/The Open University.

Wilson, M. and Evans, M. (1980) *Education of Disturbed Pupils*, London, Methuen.

Wing, L. and Gould, J. (1979) 'Severe impairments of social interaction and associated abnormalities in children: epidemiology and classification', *Journal of Autism and Developmental Disorders*, **9**, 11–29.

Winnicott, D. W. (1984) *The Maturational Process and the Facilitating Environment*, London, Hogarth.

Wong-Fillmore, L. (1991) 'When learning a second language means losing the first', *Early Childhood Research Quarterly*, **6**, 323–46.

Woolpert, S. (1991) 'Victim-offender reconciliation programs', in K.G. Duffy, J.W. Grosch and P.V. Olczak (eds) *Community Mediation: A Handbook for Practitioners and Researchers*, New York, Guilford Press.

World Health Organization (WHO) (1990) *International Classification of Diseases*, 10th edn, Geneva, WHO.

Wrench, J. and Hassan, E. (1996) *Ambition and Marginalisation: A Qualitative Study of Underachieving Young Men of Afro-Caribbean Origin*, London, DfEE.

Wright, C., Weekes D. and McGlaughlin, A. (2000) *Race, Class and Gender in Exclusion from School*, London, Falmer Press.

Wright, C., Weekes, D. and McGlaughlin, A. (2004) 'Future prospects – towards inclusive education for all', in J. Wearmouth, T. Glynn, R.C. Richmond and M. Berryman (eds) *Inclusion and Behaviour Management in Schools: Issues and Challenges*, London, Fulton, pp. 211–24.

Yapp, N. (1991) *My Problem Child: Practical Strategies for Understanding, Helping and Coping with Your Problem Child*, Harmondsworth, Penguin.

Ysseldyke, J. and Christenson, S. (1987) 'Evaluating students' instructional environments', *Remedial and Special Education*, **8**(3), 17–24.

Ysseldyke, J. and Christenson, S. (1993) *The Instructional Environment System-II: A System to Identify a Student's Instructional Needs*, J. Leutheuser, published and distributed by Sopris West, USA.

Ysseldyke, J. and Thurlow, M. (1994) 'What results should be measured to decide whether instruction is working for students with disabilities?' in J. Ysseldyke and M. Thurlow (eds) *Educational Outcomes for Students with Disabilities*, Minneapolis, MN, The Haworth Press.

Zimbardo, P.G. (1970) 'The human choice: individuation, reason and order versus deindividuation, impulse and chaos', in W.J. Arnold and D. Levine (eds) *Nebraska Symposium on Motivation*, **16**, Lincoln, NE, University of Nebraska Press.

Index